BLACK PANTHER

MARVEL KNIGHTS

STAN LEE PRESENTS: **BLACK PANTHER**

THE CLIENT

CHRISTOPHER PRIEST *story*

MARK TEXEIRA AND VINCE EVANS *art*

JOE QUESADA *storytelling*

ALITHA MARTINEZ *background assists*

BRIAN HABERLIN AND AVALON COLOR *colors*
RS AND COMICRAFT'S *letters*
SIOBHA HANNA AND WES ABBOTT
JOE QUESADA, JIMMY PALMIOTTI, *original series editors*
AND NANCI DAKESIAN

MATTY RYAN
book design

MIKHAIL BORTNIK
assistant editor

BEN ABERNATHY
collections editor

BERNADETTE THOMAS
manufacturing manager

BOB GREENBERGER
director: editorial operations

JOE QUESADA
editor in chief

BLACK PANTHER®: THE CLIENT. Contains material originally published in magazine form as BLACK PANTHER Vol. 2. #'s 1-5. Published by MARVEL COMICS. Bill Jemas, President; Frank Fochetta, Senior Vice President, Publishing; Joe Quesada, Editor-in-Chief; Stan Lee, Chairman Emeritus. OFFICE OF PUBLICATION: 387 PARK AVENUE SOUTH, NEW YORK, N.Y. 10016. Copyright © 1998, 1999 and 2001 Marvel Characters, Inc. All rights reserved. No similarity between any of the names, characters, persons, and/or institutions in this magazine with those of any living or dead person or institution is intended, and any such similarity which may exist is purely coincidental. This periodical may not be sold except by authorized dealers and is sold subject to the condition that it shall not be sold or distributed with any part of its cover or markings removed, nor in a mutilated condition. BLACK PANTHER (including all prominent characters featured in this issue and the distinctive likenesses thereof) is a registered trademark of MARVEL CHARACTERS, INC. No part of this book may be printed or reproduced in any manner without the written permission of the publisher. Printed in Canada. First Printing, June, 2001. ISBN: 0-7851-0789-4. GST #R127032852. MARVEL COMICS is a division of MARVEL ENTERPRISES, INC. Peter Cuneo, Chief Executive Officer; Avi Arad, Chief Creative Officer. 10 9 8 7 6 5 4 3 2 1

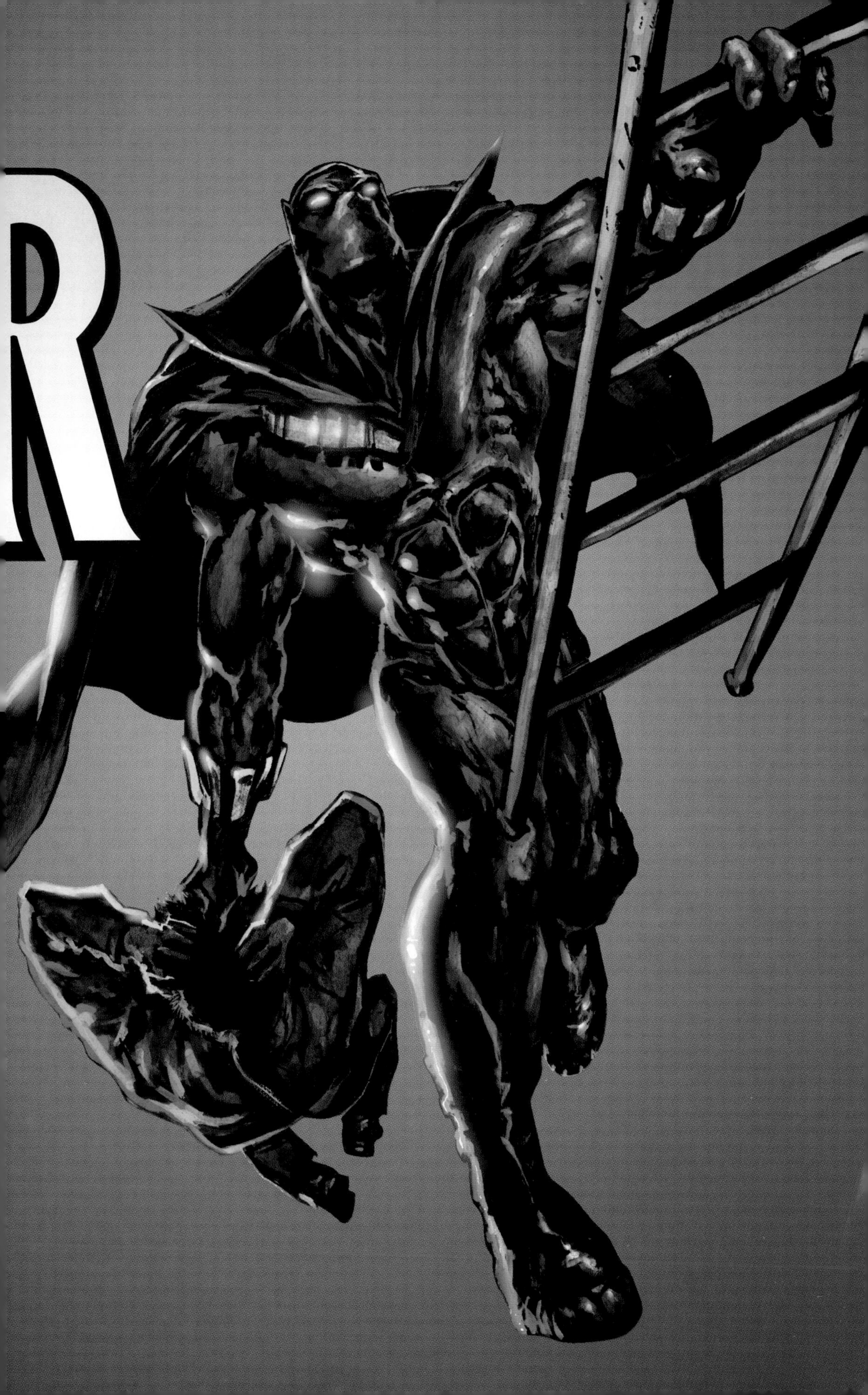

CHRISTOP

THE STORY THUS FAR:

I was so excited. Artist Joe Quesada and I had been missing each other's phone calls for a week, but I knew he wanted to talk to me about his new MARVEL KNIGHTS imprint. This was it, I thought: I was finally gonna get my dream shot. I was finally gonna get a chance to write DAREDEVIL.

I was a little horrified when the words "Black" and "Panther" came out of Joe's mouth. I mean, Black Panther? Who reads Black Panther? Black Panther?! The guy with no powers? The guy in the back of the Avengers class photo, whose main job was to point and cry out, "Look— A BIG, SCALY MONSTER! THOR— GO GET HIM!!" That guy?!

No, PANTHER was not the move. Panther was, by most any objective standards, dull. He had no powers. He had no witty speech pattern, bub. His supporting cast were a bunch of soul brothers in diapers with bones through their noses. King T'Challa is, by necessity, a man of secrecy and cunning, which is difficult to illustrate if he has thought balloons over his head telling the reader everything he's thinking. Or, worse, if he's narrating his own story and blathering on and on and on. Hard to convey cunning from a motormouth.

Also, Panther was a black super hero, and the most basic economic lesson this business can teach you is minorities and female super heroes do not sell (but, kudos to Marvel for trying to do both with the black female version of CAPTAIN MARVEL).

But Joe and his partner, inker Jimmy Palmiotti, were adamant: the book can work, they insisted. If we have a fresh approach, perhaps along the lines of Eddie Murphy's *Coming To America*, where the crown prince of an African nation comes to America in search of a bride. Given that kind of energy, taking Wakanda and the Panther seriously, and concentrating on how people react to him -- that approach might have a chance in the market. Get him out of the jungle. Bring him to Brooklyn. Make him a night creature, a fearsome African warrior, a manner of black man most blacks in Brooklyn have never seen.

Nah. I was still unconvinced. "Look, guys, we're talking about a king. A black king of not just an African nation but a powerful nation with advanced technology capable of posing a threat to U.S. national security. A king who is prone to occasionally leaping out of windows dressed in a kitty cat outfit. If this guy, and his nation, actually existed, there's just no way the U.S. State Department would let this guy wander around unescorted, and the CIA would be constantly trying to figure out what's going on in Wakanda. There'd be all manner of global and domestic and racial politics involved."

For me to flesh out Joe and Jimmy's PANTHER premise, I'd need to go to the wells of snarkdom, for the snarkiest snark I was capable of. Social politics as interpreted by Richard Belzer or Dennis Miller. And Marvel hasn't been the home of true snark since they sent Steve Gerber and his duck packing. I was trying to chase Joe and Jimmy away, but this stuff just excited them.

Again and again, I whined, there's no way Marvel would let me write this. It's a violation of the Fantasy Land Nice-Nice Accords, signed by both DC and Marvel, that says the U.S. government is always good all the time, everyone accepts Panther, and the Avengers hold hands and sing and what have you. Mainstream comics were demented places where heroes actually referred to themselves as "heroes," and villains as "villains." These were places run by people who have run comic book companies far, far, far too long and have completely lost touch with popular culture or with what young people today are actually about. I have had my hand slapped more times than I can count for simply pointing out the absurdity of what we do -- of these colorful men and women who fly around wearing their underwear on the outside of their clothes.

I believe Chris Claremont was the first writer I experienced who made sense out of all of this for me when he humanized the deadly Magneto. Claremont's brilliant writing had some of his heroes acting in completely unheroic ways, and presented many of his villains as conflicted, desperate souls who never, ever, referred to themselves as "villains," and certainly never thought of Xavier and his ilk as "heroes."

Frank Miller and others followed suit, bringing more dimension and plurality to the Marvel Universe (while, for the most part, DC continues fairly entrenched in a kind of white-washed estrangement from the real world, nearly all their heroes being beloved, respected and trusted by the average citizen, to whom flying men and women are a mundane and accepted practice).

The PANTHER book Joe and Jimmy were asking me to produce could not possibly exist in such a world. It would have to exist on the fringes of that world, with our book regularly hacking chunks out of it. This was fine with the guys, and they both encouraged me towards my darker side; the wittier and more gleeful the discourse, the more they enjoyed it and the harder they fought for it.

The problem with race and popular media is, in most every "black" movie or "black" music CD you'll see or hear, there is some hostility directed towards whites. Now, were I a white male, I certainly wouldn't want to spend eight bucks to go see a film where white males are portrayed as stupid and are the butt of every joke, or where I am made to feel guilty about things I had nothing to do with, or prejudices I don't actually have.

That's my pet peeve with a lot of black film and black comedians: it's all White People Bashing, fueled by our race's legacy of anger and resentment by centuries-old unreparative wrongs. But, this

ER PRIEST

hostility polarizes rather than unites. There is no healing in it, and it limits our opportunities.

I feel the most profound statement I can make about race is to make Panther so cool he transcends the racial divide here in America. Rather than try and force the readers to identify with a black character, I accepted the fact a great many readers would not be able to overcome the race thing, and withdrew Panther from the reader entirely.

Borrowing a page from my mentor, legendary comics writer Denny O'Neil, I reinterpreted T'Challa in the mold of Denny's brilliant Ras Al Ghul, a villain from Batman's glory days. Nobody, not even Batman, ever knew, for sure, what Ras was thinking, what his true motives or true plans were. He was the world's greatest poker face, and only the legendary Darknight Detective had the power to challenge him. Ras was, like O'Neil himself, cool. And his coolness transcended race, gender, and even Ras' advanced age.

That was the energy I wanted for Panther. Rather than get into his head with an enforced intimacy that worked against his stealth, we withdrew altogether, pushing him to the shadows and, to some complaint, making him almost a guest star in his own book. Only, in any reasonable analysis of the series, Panther clearly drives the book. Even if he has only a handful of lines per issue, he is the dominating force.

So, how do we do a book about a black king of a black nation who comes to a black neighborhood and not have it be a "black" book? Moreover, how do we deal with reader apathy and resistance to the return of one of Marvel's least appreciated and dullest characters? Do we turn Panther into WolverPanther? Do we kill him off and replace him with some kid with a crab on his face? Cut off his hand and replace it with a hook?

The answer came to me while watching the brilliant Matthew Perry perform a scene in the NBC hit sitcom Friends. "Gum would be perfection," a line only Friends fans would know, made me howl with laughter for days. Perry's character, an investment banker named Chandler Bing, was actually quite competent at his job. Respected and successful, Bing nevertheless was the horrified fish out of water when caught up in the machinery of his friends' complex personal lives. This was a role Perry freely adapted for the largely ignored but very funny film Fools Rush In, where he plays a brilliant corporate developer who is nonetheless The White Boob around Salma Hayek's Latino community.

I asked Joe and Jimmy, "What if we put that guy-Chandler Bing-into the series? He could be the motormouth, he could give voice to the skeptical readers and validate their doubts and fears about the series. And, best of all, he could amplify the Panther's mystery and overall enigma as his monologues would be, at best, a guess about Panther's whereabouts and motives.

The guys loved the idea, and we started hammering away at the details. This character's name was, literally, Chandler for the first couple of weeks, until I settled on an Alex P. Keaton vibe in Everett K. Ross. Most fans assumed him to be a one-off of Michael J. Fox, and Fox could certainly bring him to life, but I was writing Chandler, not Alex. I had Ross appear in KA-ZAR #17 as a warm-up of sorts, a run-through with the quick-witted, sardonic half-pint, who effortlessly got Ka-Zar off on an attempted murder charge.

With Ross in place, the book began to take shape. Ross became the key to making the book work. He was the voice of the average Marvel reader, who no doubt wondered why Marvel was bothering with another Panther series.

Ross's monologues began to steal the show, offsetting the mysterious night creature, the man of few words whom Ross was attached to. The monologues were often outrageous, with Ross interpreting the Marvel Universe through his Everyman's eyes rather than through the eyes of someone who's been reading comics all his life. It was a new voice, one seemingly hostile towards the Marvel Universe (and, by extension, its fans), but actually, the intent is more to be a social observer and deconstructionist.

Rather than ignore or run from the looming shadow of skepticism and low expectation, Joe and Jimmy and I turned that stuff into kindling for the fire; the secret skepticism of most every Marvel reader became grist for our humor mill, as Ross blurted out what many fans were likely thinking, but never dared to so much as commit to paper or post on a newsgroup: questions of race and values and our own insecurity about being super-hero fans well into adulthood. Ross giddily makes salad of all of the anxiety of the adult super-hero fan, kicking over many a sacred cow in the process.

Panther's ethnicity is certainly a component of the series, but it is not the central theme. We neither ignore it nor build our stories around it. One of Joe and Jimmy's earliest battles with Marvel was to get the Politically Correct handcuffs off and allow us to poke fun at race (in issue #1 Ross assumed Panther's going to 'hang out at Avengers Mansion and order up some ribs').

That was the scene that would tell us whether Marvel was prepared to allow us to do this book. And, once J&J convinced the powers-that-be to leave us alone, it opened up a floodgate of possibilities for outrageous adventure and a gleeful evisceration of some of the most cherished tenets of the Marvel Universe. Jimmy and Joe were regularly summoned to the principal's office and kept after school for our Don Imus/David Letterman snark-fest (calling the Avengers "Gaudily Dressed Fascists," and wondering, "Who appointed them to 'avenge' me?! I don't need any 'avenging'!").

Which is how the book achieved its small cult following. The core die-hard PANTHER fans regularly tune in not so much for the super-hero battles or the villain of the month as to see what Ross will say about it.

To the great surprise of most industry experts, and even to myself, BLACK PANTHER is, at this writing, still going strong. Still attracting new fans and pursuing new adventures. We're thrilled and grateful to everyone who's been along for the ride. To old friends and new: to Joe, Jimmy and Nanci, to Chris Claremont who fought the good fight, to Bob Harras who often beat up Chris for us, to our pal Ruben who brought us back into the family, the great Tom Brevoort who took us to the next level, our new pal Michael Marts, to Bill Jemas for being in our corner when it really counted, the wonderful Alitha Martinez without whom we'd have NEVER shipped on time, to colorist Brian Haberlin, letterers Siobhan Hanna and Richard Starkings (who spent many an hour with me on the phone designing the look of Panther's graphics), and the fabulous Mark Texeira— thanks, everyone, for this ground-breaking comic. And for those who are meeting the Panther, Ross and the gang for the first time— enjoy!

CHRISTOPHER PRIEST
JUNE, 2001

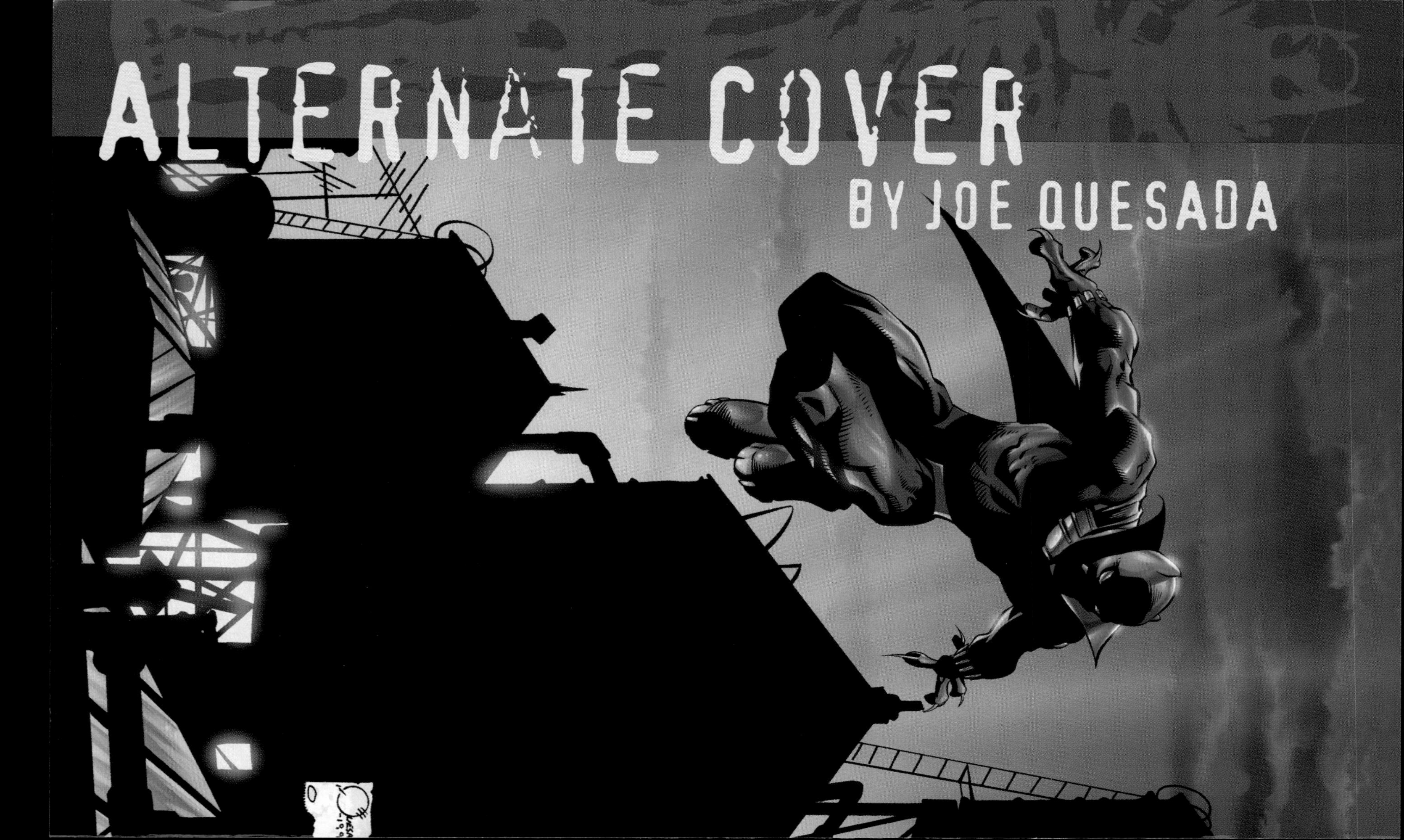
ALTERNATE COVER
BY JOE QUESADA

CHAPTER 1

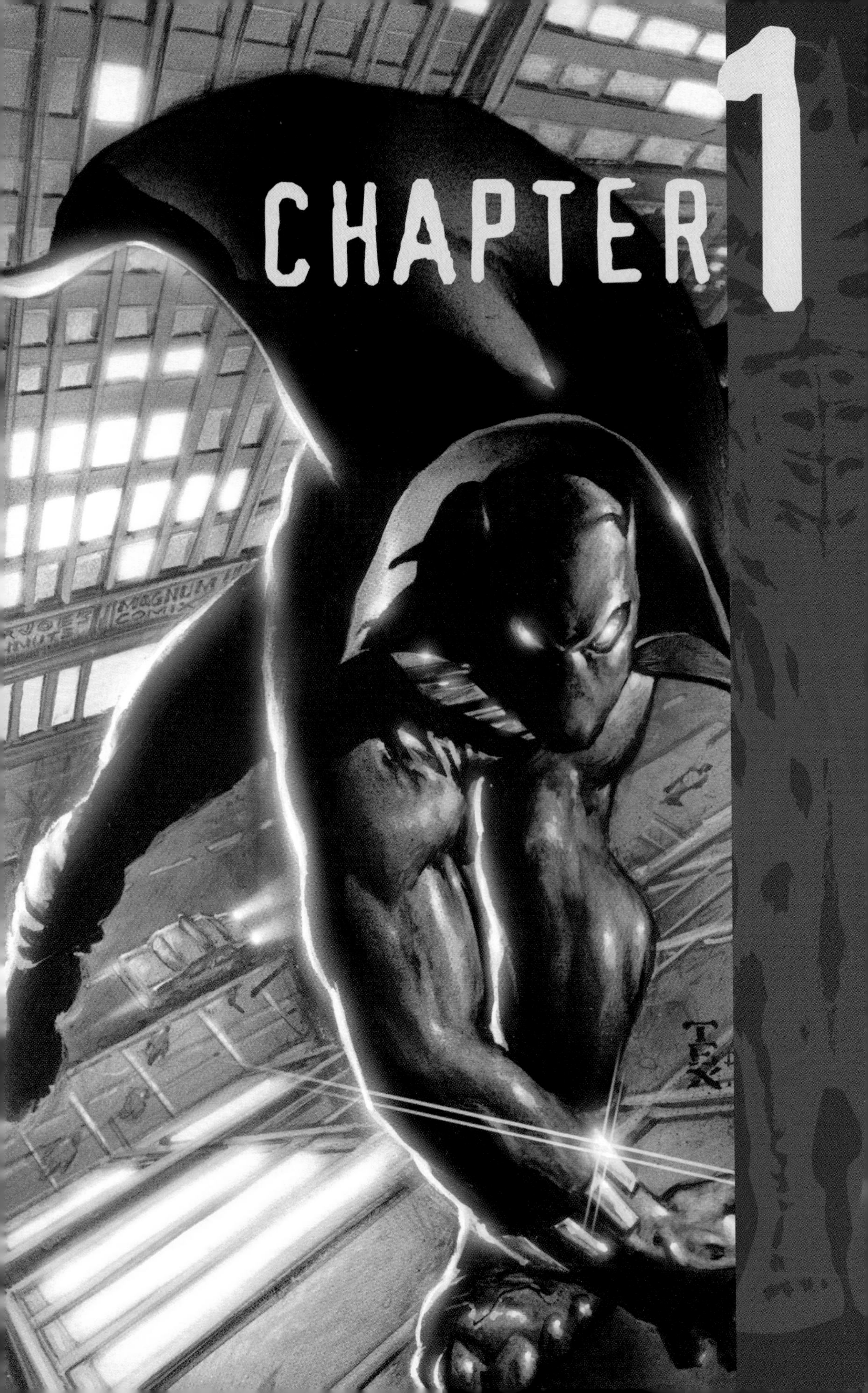
MAGNUM COMIX

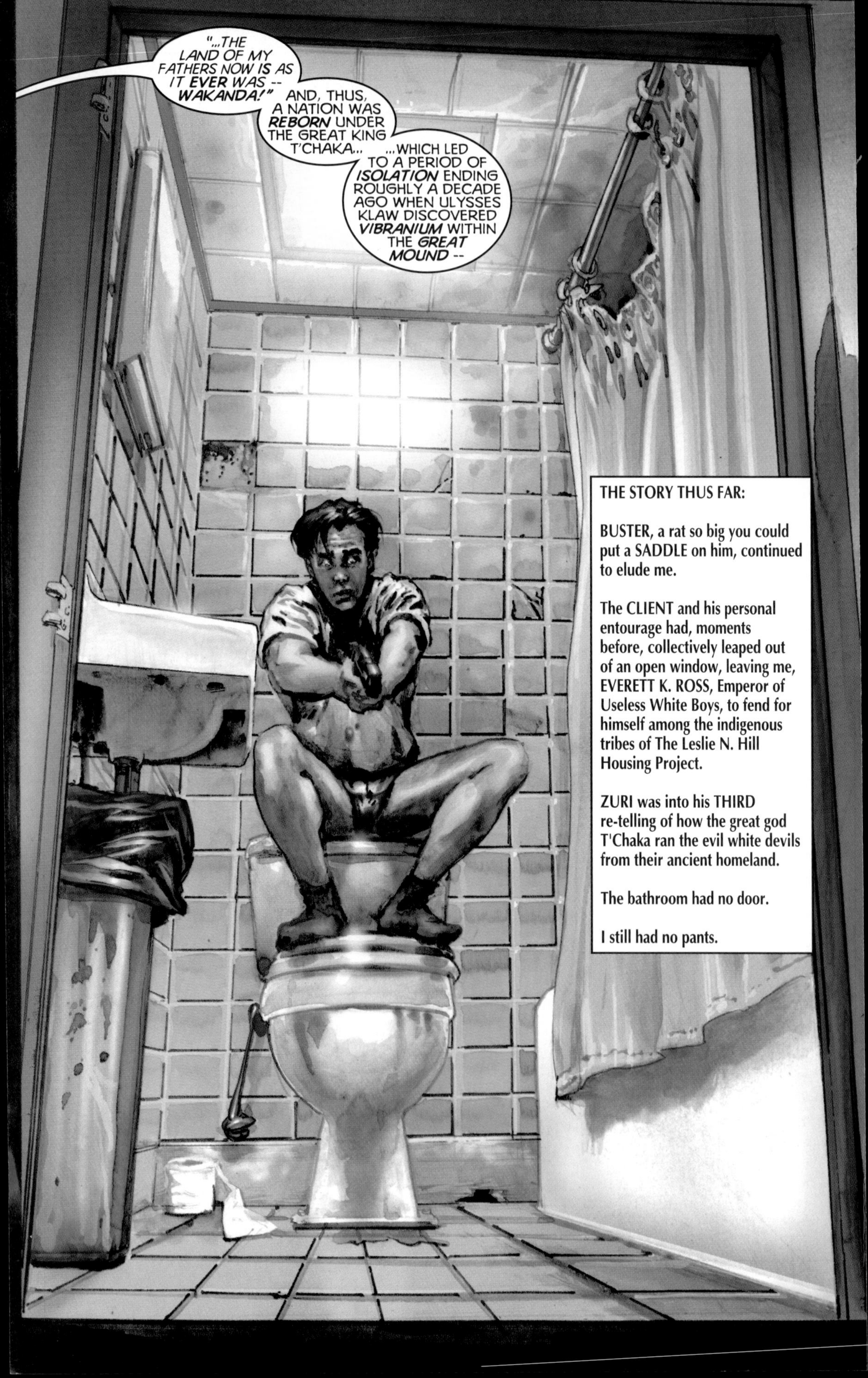
"...THE LAND OF MY FATHERS NOW IS AS IT EVER WAS -- WAKANDA!"
AND, THUS, A NATION WAS REBORN UNDER THE GREAT KING T'CHAKA...
...WHICH LED TO A PERIOD OF ISOLATION ENDING ROUGHLY A DECADE AGO WHEN ULYSSES KLAW DISCOVERED VIBRANIUM WITHIN THE GREAT MOUND --
THE STORY THUS FAR:
BUSTER, a rat so big you could put a SADDLE on him, continued to elude me.
The CLIENT and his personal entourage had, moments before, collectively leaped out of an open window, leaving me, EVERETT K. ROSS, Emperor of Useless White Boys, to fend for himself among the indigenous tribes of The Leslie N. Hill Housing Project.
ZURI was into his THIRD re-telling of how the great god T'Chaka ran the evil white devils from their ancient homeland.
The bathroom had no door.
I still had no pants.

CAT MAN DO

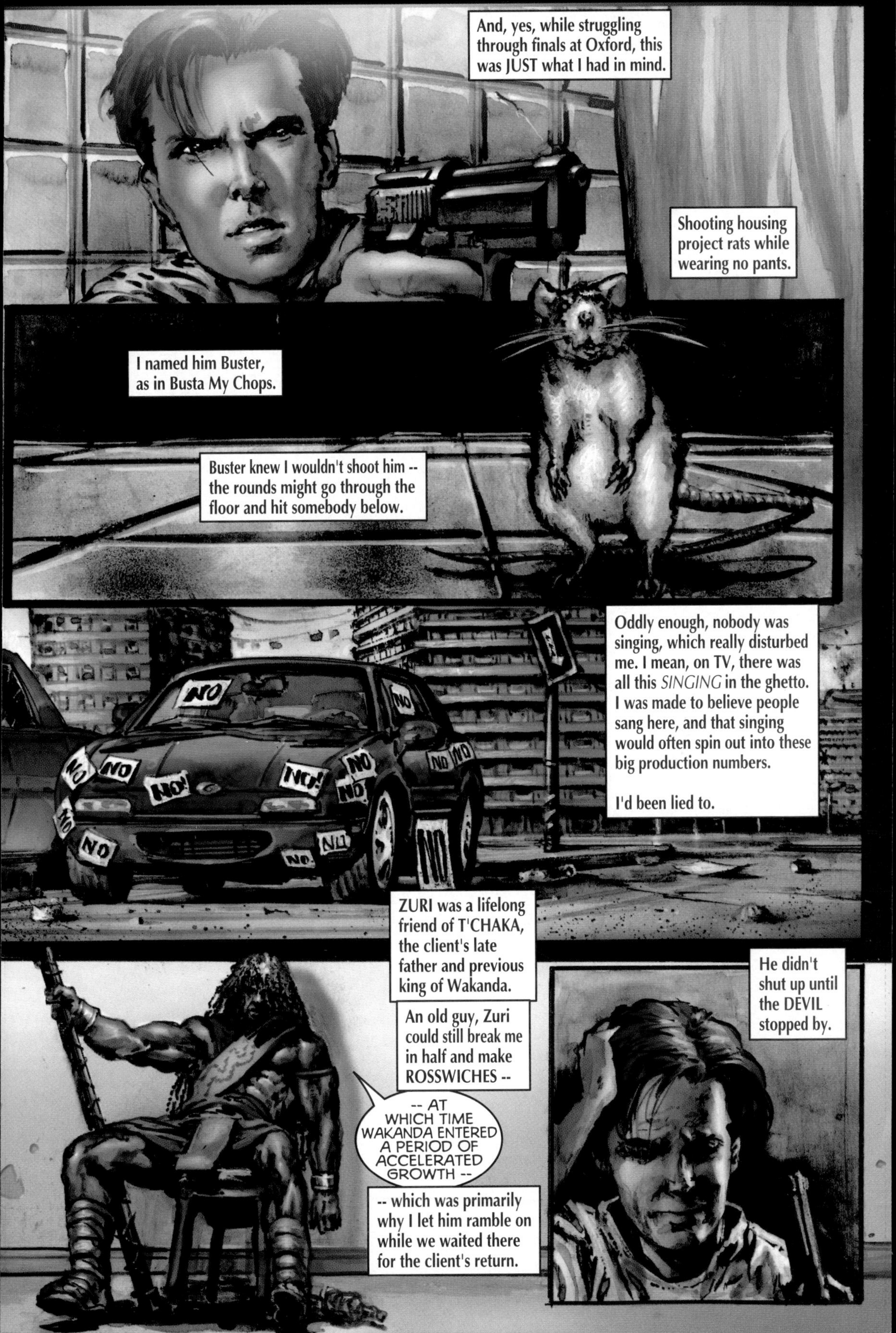

And, yes, while struggling through finals at Oxford, this was JUST what I had in mind.
Shooting housing project rats while wearing no pants.
I named him Buster, as in Busta My Chops.
Buster knew I wouldn't shoot him -- the rounds might go through the floor and hit somebody below.
NO
NO
NO
NO!
NO
NO!
Oddly enough, nobody was singing, which really disturbed me. I mean, on TV, there was all this *SINGING* in the ghetto. I was made to believe people sang here, and that singing would often spin out into these big production numbers.
I'd been lied to.
ZURI was a lifelong friend of T'CHAKA, the client's late father and previous king of Wakanda.
An old guy, Zuri could still break me in half and make ROSSWICHES --
-- AT WHICH TIME WAKANDA ENTERED A PERIOD OF ACCELERATED GROWTH --
-- which was primarily why I let him ramble on while we waited there for the client's return.
He didn't shut up until the DEVIL stopped by.

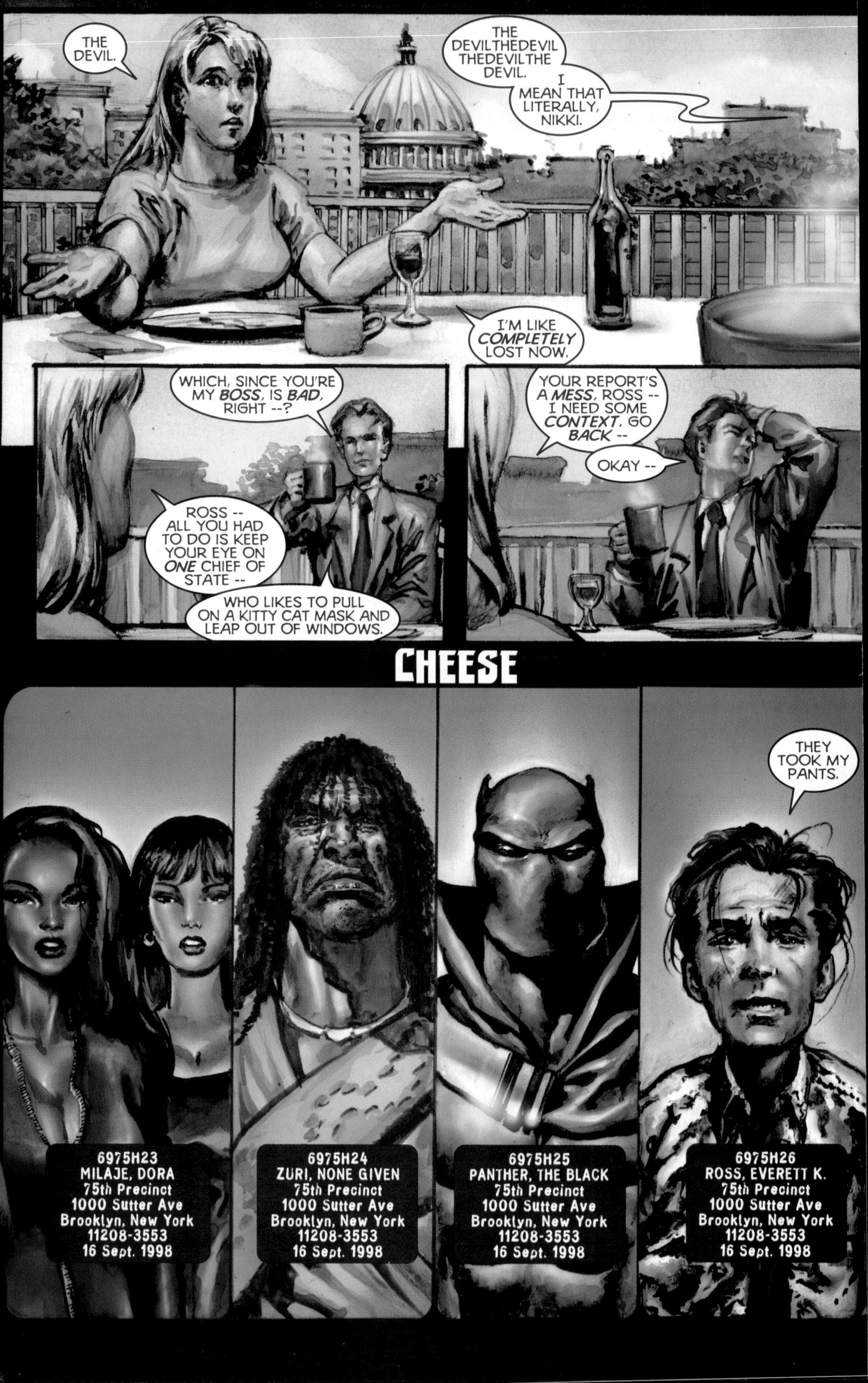
THE DEVIL.
THE DEVILTHEDEVIL THEDEVILTHE DEVIL.
I MEAN THAT LITERALLY, NIKKI.
I'M LIKE COMPLETELY LOST NOW.
WHICH, SINCE YOU'RE MY BOSS, IS BAD, RIGHT --?
ROSS -- ALL YOU HAD TO DO IS KEEP YOUR EYE ON ONE CHIEF OF STATE --
WHO LIKES TO PULL ON A KITTY CAT MASK AND LEAP OUT OF WINDOWS.
YOUR REPORT'S A MESS, ROSS -- I NEED SOME CONTEXT. GO BACK --
OKAY --
CHEESE
THEY TOOK MY PANTS.
6975H23 MILAJE, DORA 75th Precinct 1000 Sutter Ave Brooklyn, New York 11208-3553 16 Sept. 1998
6975H24 ZURI, NONE GIVEN 75th Precinct 1000 Sutter Ave Brooklyn, New York 11208-3553 16 Sept. 1998
6975H25 PANTHER, THE BLACK 75th Precinct 1000 Sutter Ave Brooklyn, New York 11208-3553 16 Sept. 1998
6975H26 ROSS, EVERETT K. 75th Precinct 1000 Sutter Ave Brooklyn, New York 11208-3553 16 Sept. 1998

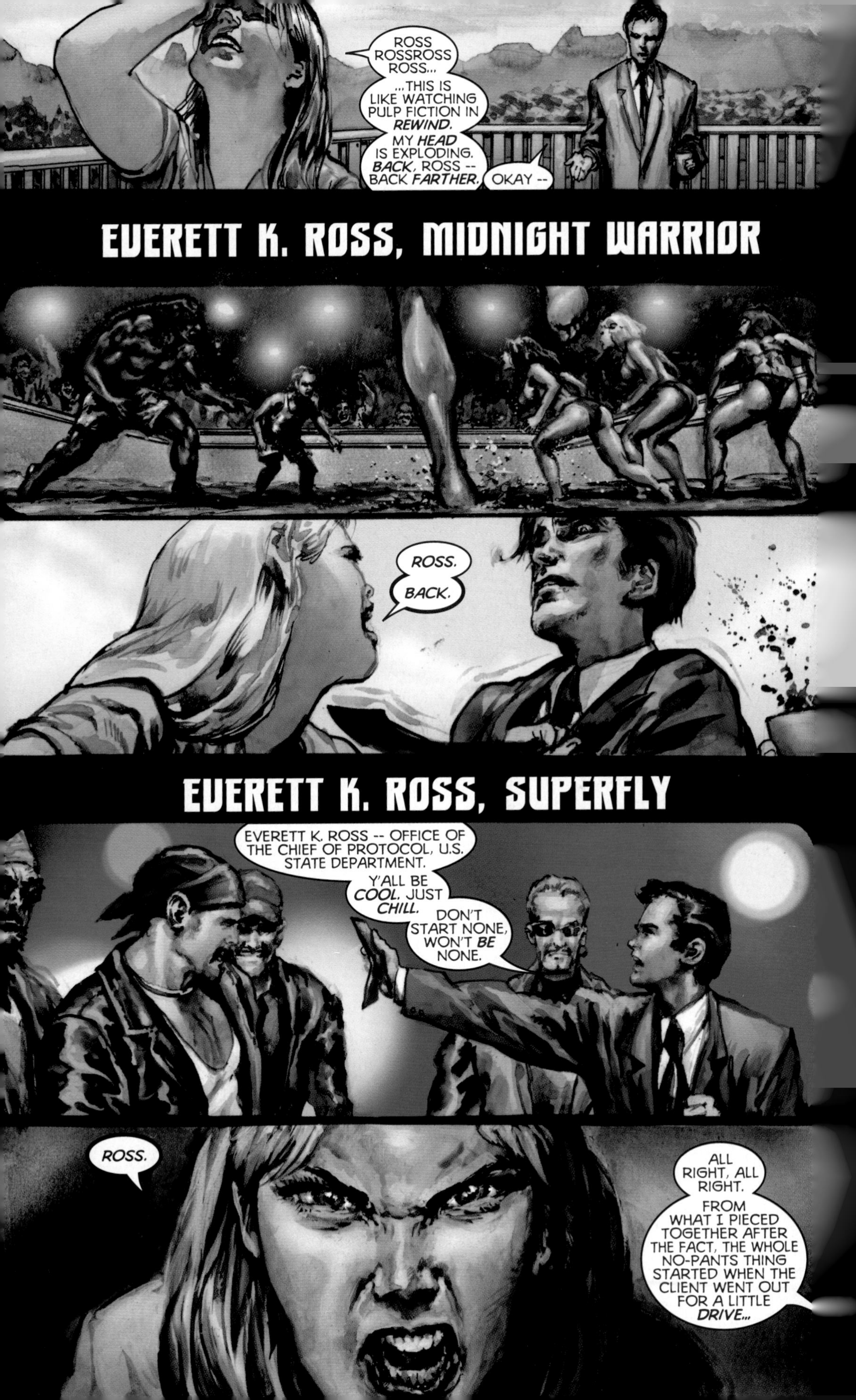
ROSS ROSSROSS ROSS...
...THIS IS LIKE WATCHING PULP FICTION IN REWIND.
MY HEAD IS EXPLODING. BACK, ROSS -- BACK FARTHER.
OKAY --
EVERETT K. ROSS, MIDNIGHT WARRIOR
ROSS.
BACK.
EVERETT K. ROSS, SUPERFLY
EVERETT K. ROSS -- OFFICE OF THE CHIEF OF PROTOCOL, U.S. STATE DEPARTMENT.
Y'ALL BE COOL. JUST CHILL.
DON'T START NONE, WON'T BE NONE.
ROSS.
ALL RIGHT, ALL RIGHT.
FROM WHAT I PIECED TOGETHER AFTER THE FACT, THE WHOLE NO-PANTS THING STARTED WHEN THE CLIENT WENT OUT FOR A LITTLE DRIVE...

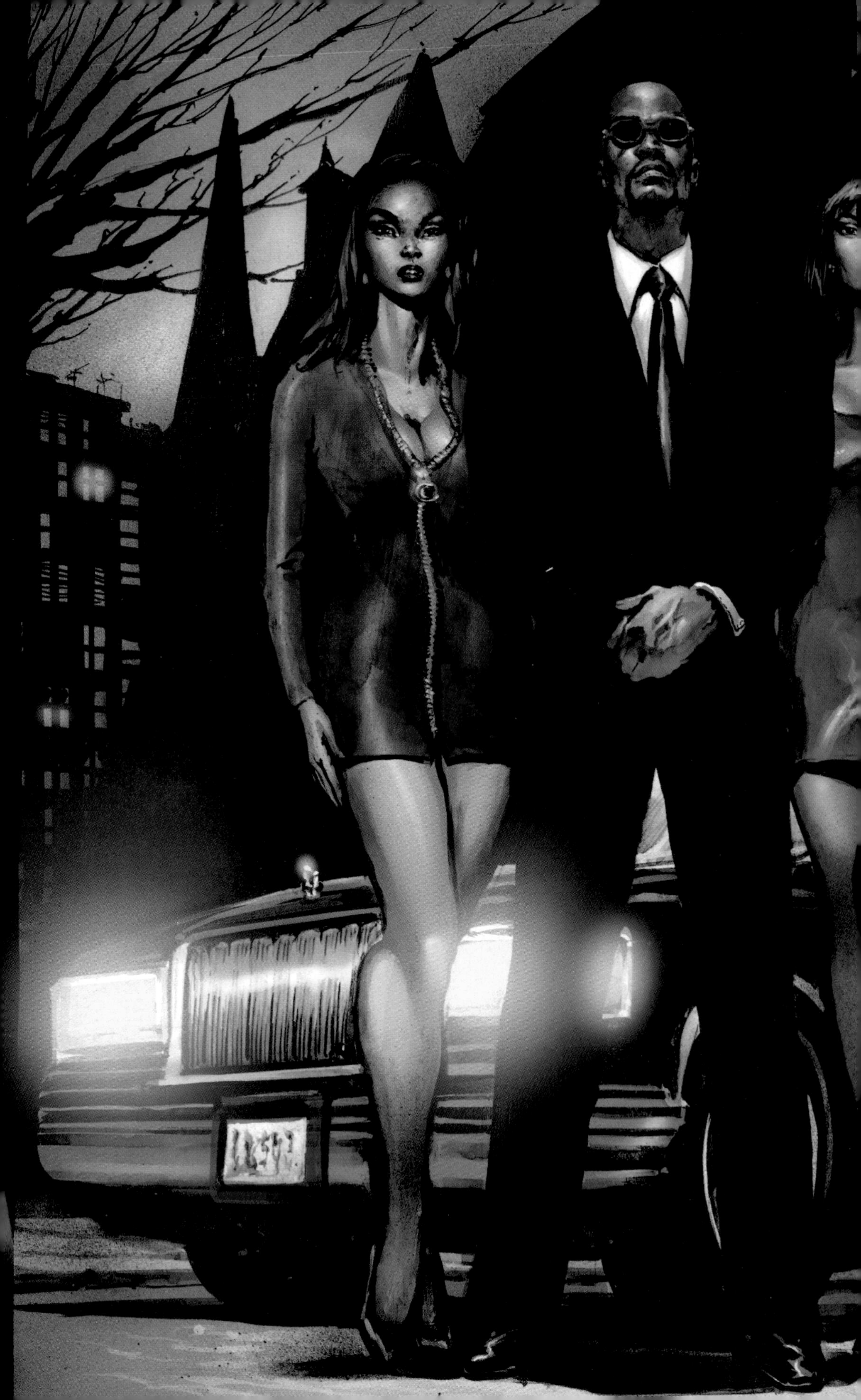

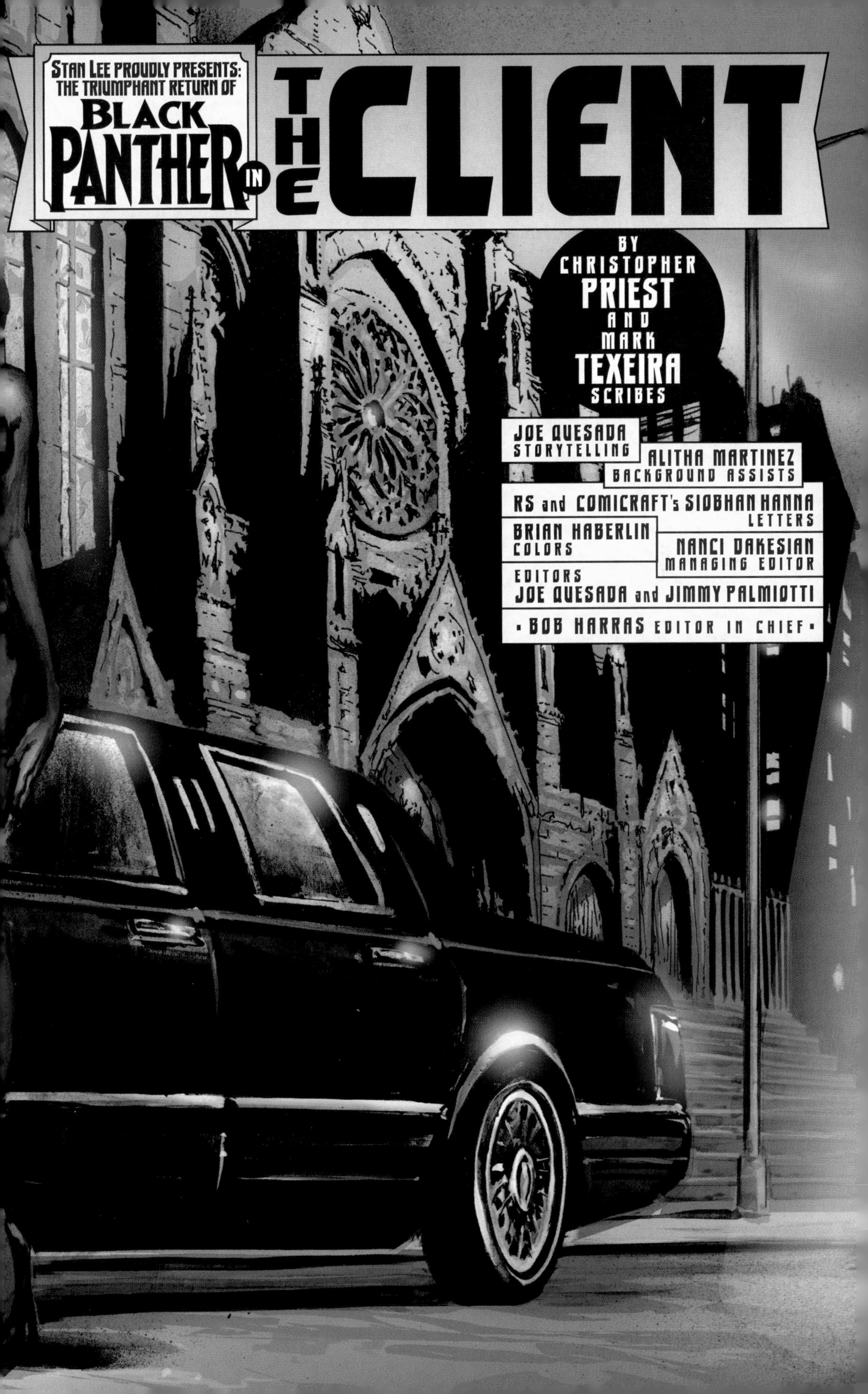
STAN LEE PROUDLY PRESENTS:
THE TRIUMPHANT RETURN OF
BLACK PANTHER IN
THE CLIENT
BY CHRISTOPHER PRIEST AND MARK TEXEIRA SCRIBES
JOE QUESADA STORYTELLING
ALITHA MARTINEZ BACKGROUND ASSISTS
RS and COMICRAFT's SIOBHAN HANNA LETTERS
BRIAN HABERLIN COLORS
NANCI DAKESIAN MANAGING EDITOR
EDITORS JOE QUESADA and JIMMY PALMIOTTI
BOB HARRAS EDITOR IN CHIEF

ME, MY AND MINE

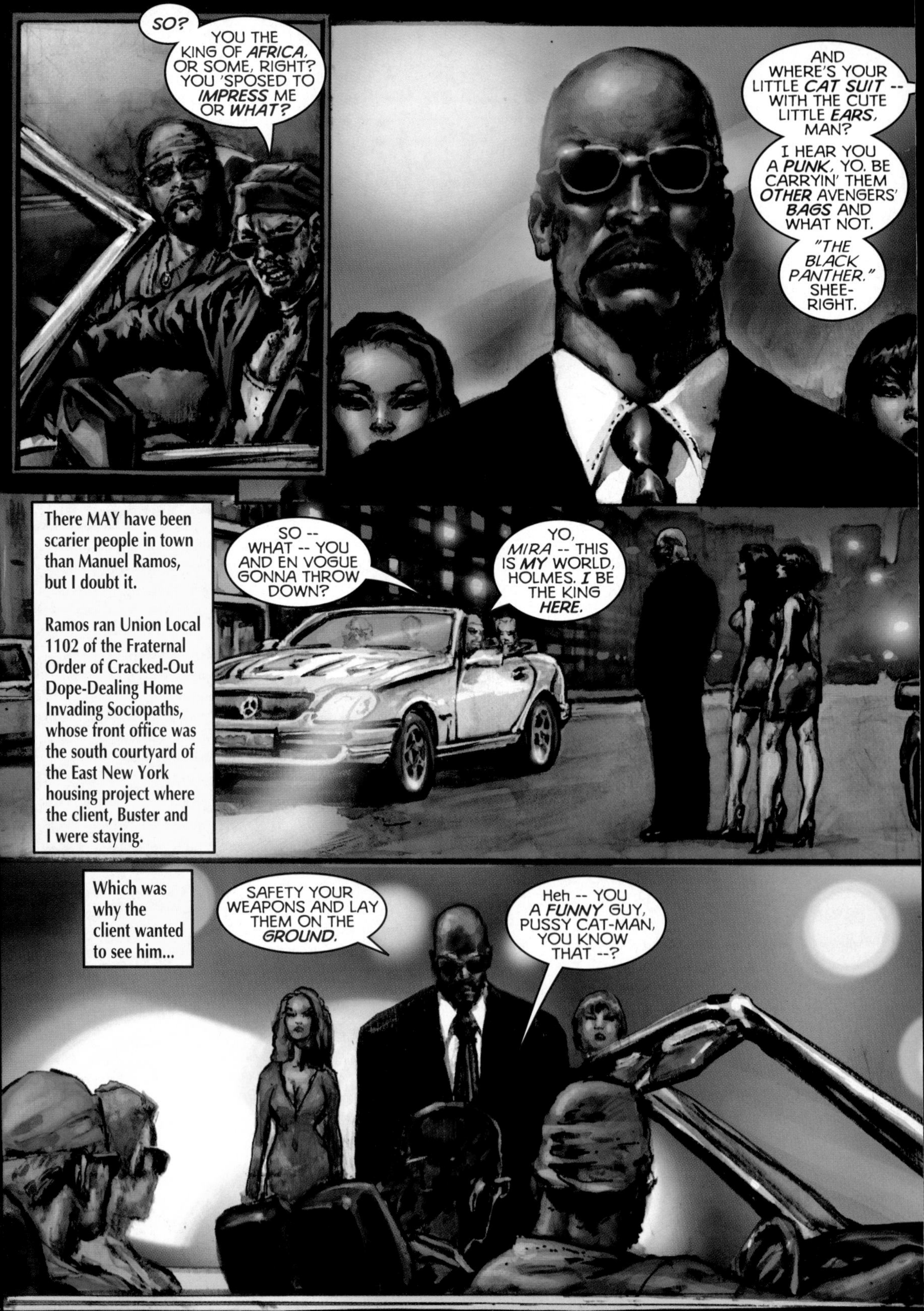
SO?
YOU THE KING OF *AFRICA*, OR SOME, RIGHT? YOU 'SPOSED TO *IMPRESS* ME OR *WHAT?*
AND WHERE'S YOUR LITTLE *CAT SUIT* -- WITH THE CUTE LITTLE *EARS*, MAN?
I HEAR YOU A *PUNK*, YO. BE CARRYIN' THEM *OTHER* AVENGERS' *BAGS* AND WHAT NOT.
"THE BLACK PANTHER." SHEE-RIGHT.
There MAY have been scarier people in town than Manuel Ramos, but I doubt it.
Ramos ran Union Local 1102 of the Fraternal Order of Cracked-Out Dope-Dealing Home Invading Sociopaths, whose front office was the south courtyard of the East New York housing project where the client, Buster and I were staying.
SO -- WHAT -- YOU AND EN VOGUE GONNA THROW DOWN?
YO, *MIRA* -- THIS IS *MY* WORLD, HOLMES. *I* BE THE KING *HERE.*
Which was why the client wanted to see him...
SAFETY YOUR WEAPONS AND LAY THEM ON THE *GROUND.*
Heh -- YOU A *FUNNY* GUY, PUSSY CAT-MAN, YOU KNOW THAT --?

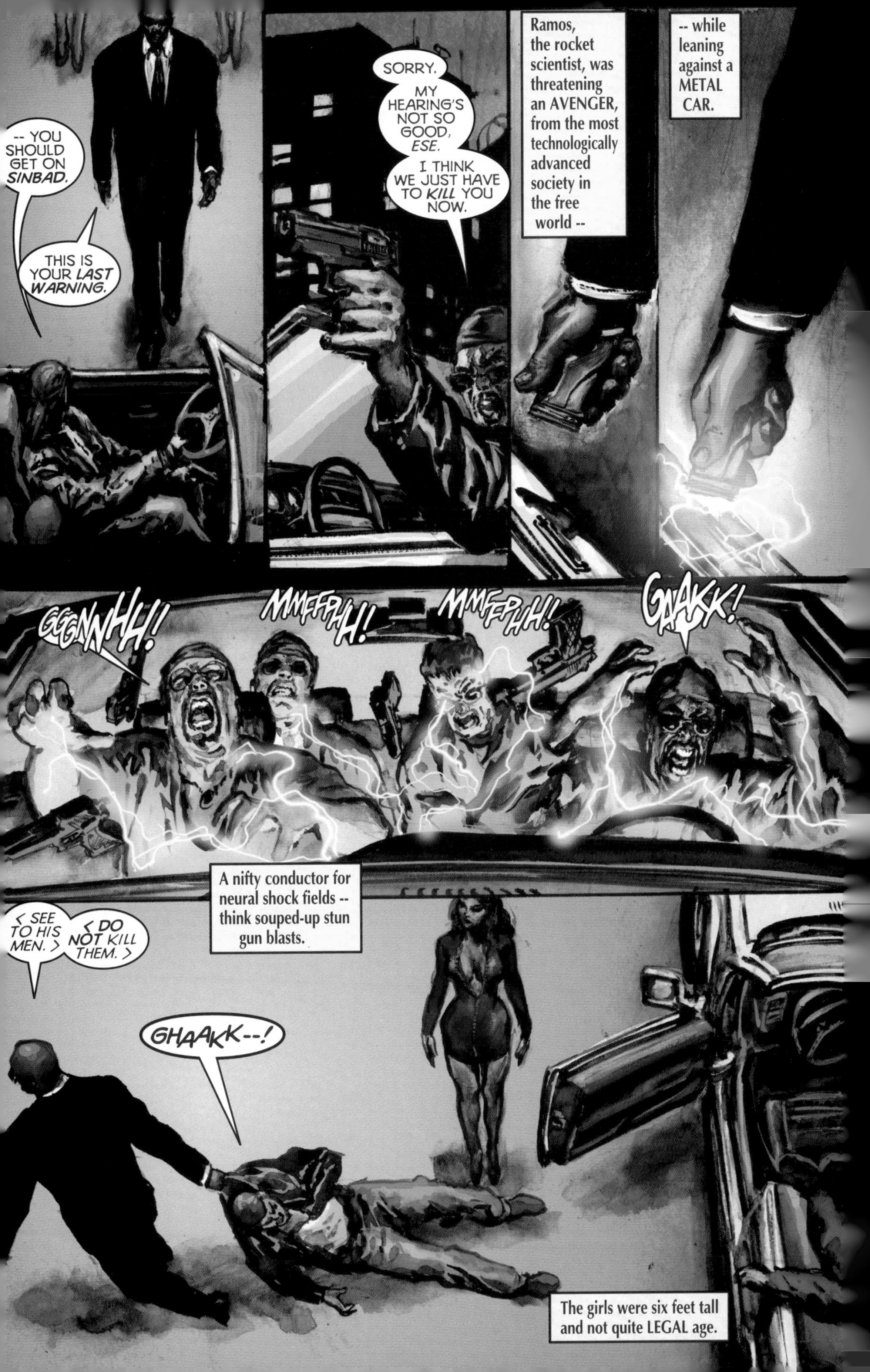
-- YOU SHOULD GET ON SINBAD.
THIS IS YOUR LAST WARNING.
SORRY.
MY HEARING'S NOT SO GOOD, ESE.
I THINK WE JUST HAVE TO KILL YOU NOW.
Ramos, the rocket scientist, was threatening an AVENGER, from the most technologically advanced society in the free world --
-- while leaning against a METAL CAR.
GGGNNHH!
MMFFPHH!
MMFFPHH!
GAAKK!
A nifty conductor for neural shock fields -- think souped-up stun gun blasts.
< SEE TO HIS MEN. >
< DO NOT KILL THEM. >
GHAAKK--!
The girls were six feet tall and not quite LEGAL age.

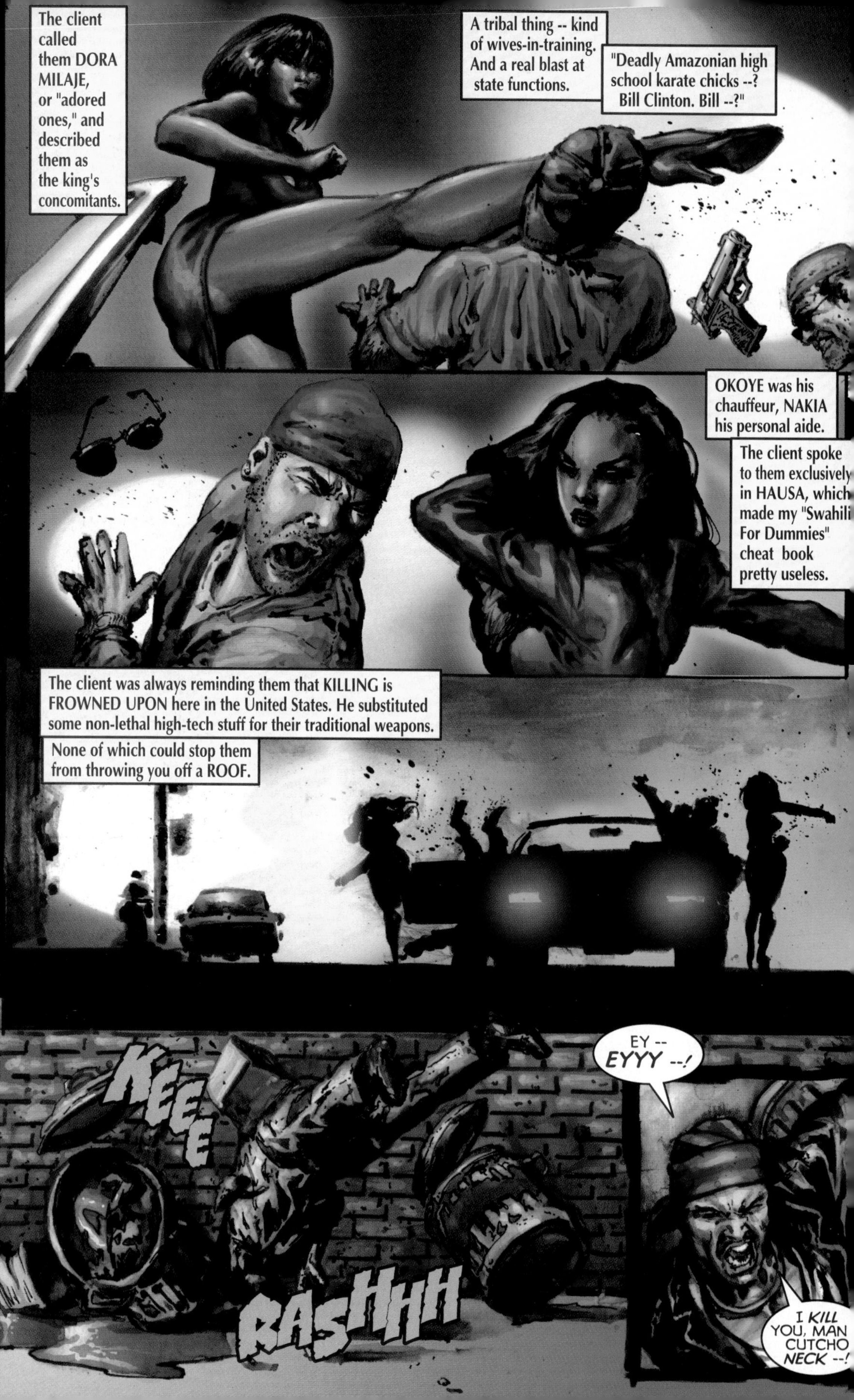
The client called them DORA MILAJE, or "adored ones," and described them as the king's concomitants.
A tribal thing -- kind of wives-in-training. And a real blast at state functions.
"Deadly Amazonian high school karate chicks --? Bill Clinton. Bill --?"
OKOYE was his chauffeur, NAKIA his personal aide.
The client spoke to them exclusively in HAUSA, which made my "Swahili For Dummies" cheat book pretty useless.
The client was always reminding them that KILLING is FROWNED UPON here in the United States. He substituted some non-lethal high-tech stuff for their traditional weapons.
None of which could stop them from throwing you off a ROOF.
KEEE
RASHHH
EY -- EYYY --!
I KILL YOU, MAN CUTCHO NECK --!

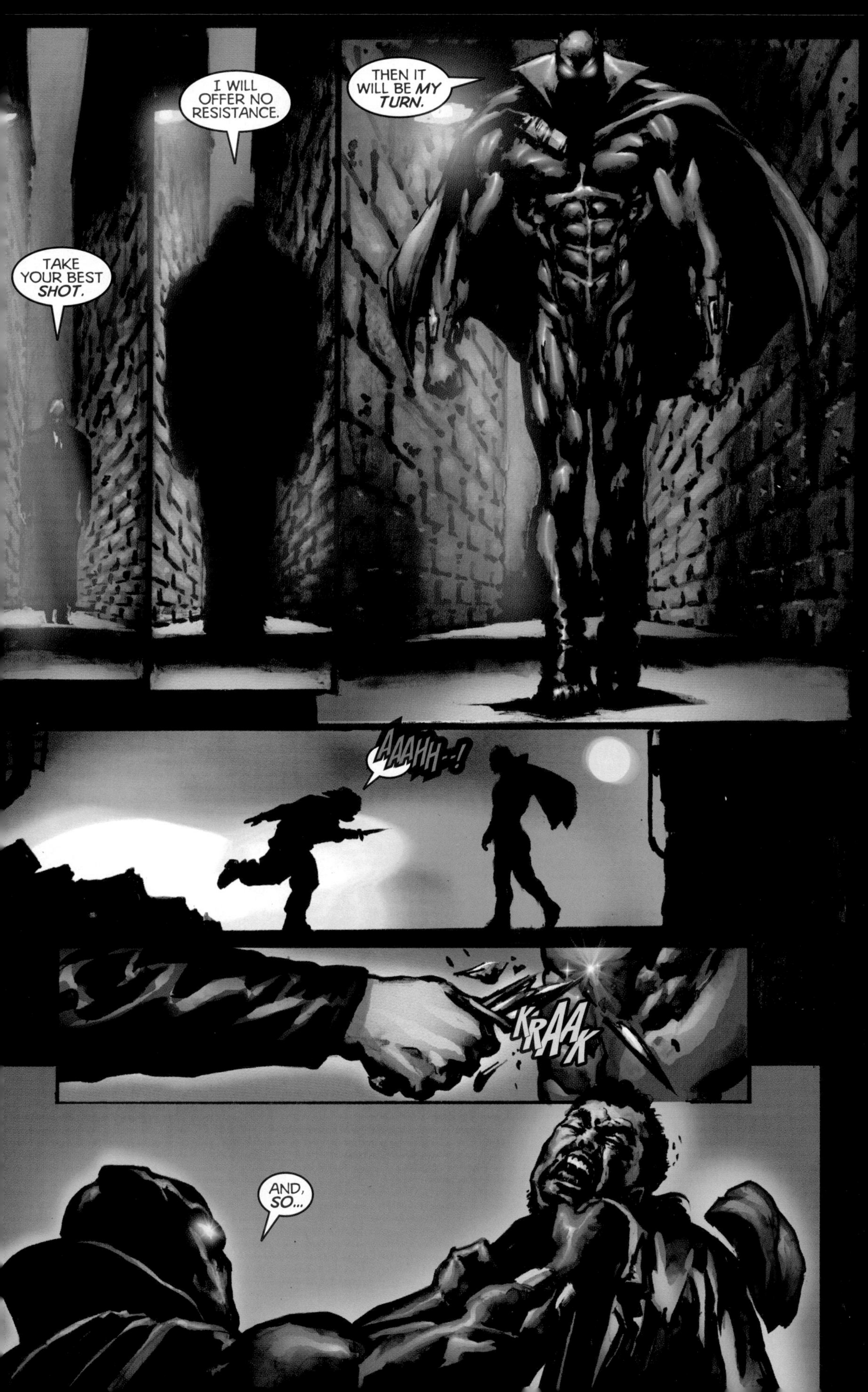
TAKE YOUR BEST SHOT.
I WILL OFFER NO RESISTANCE.
THEN IT WILL BE MY TURN.
AAAHH--!
KRAAK
AND, SO...

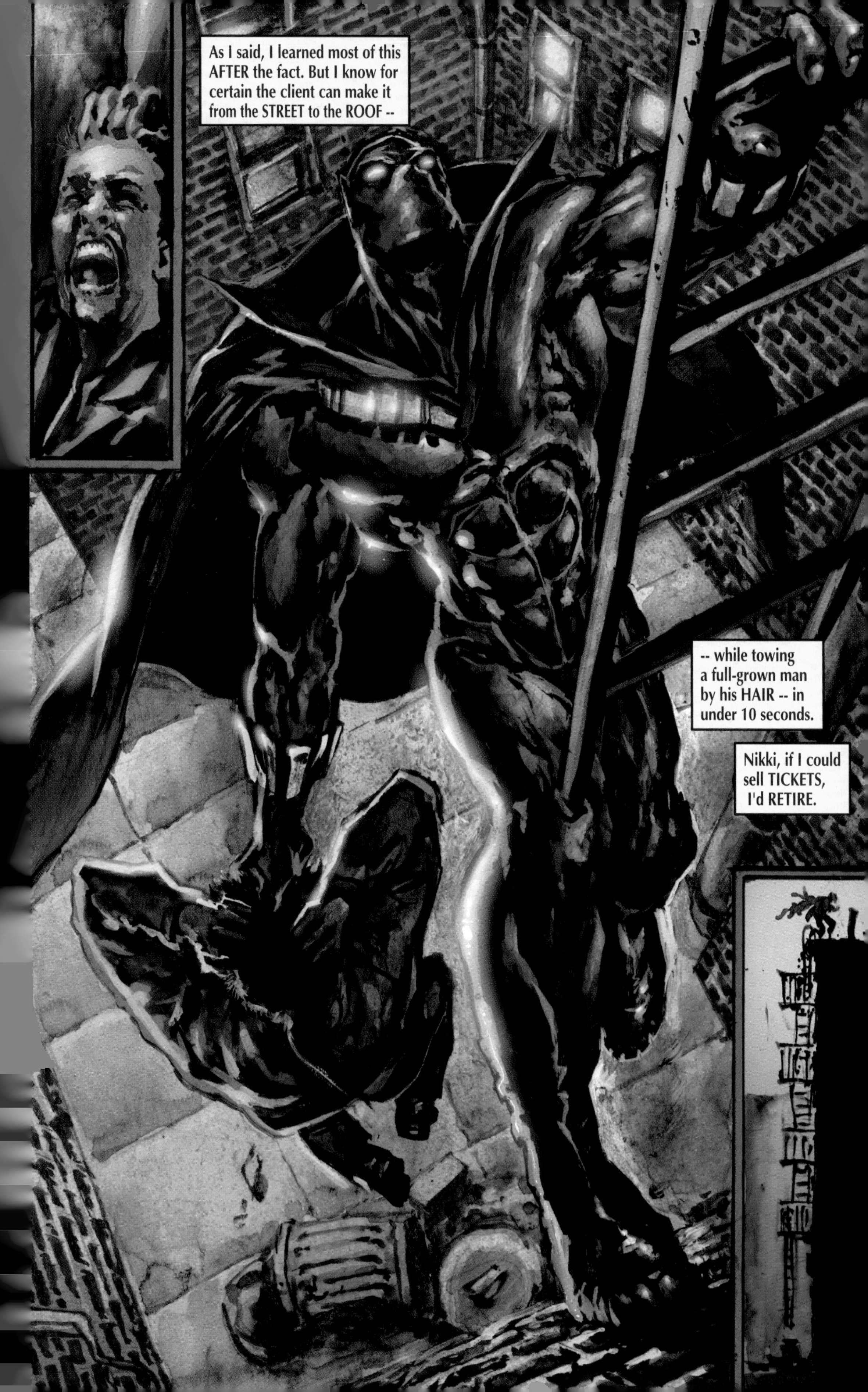
As I said, I learned most of this AFTER the fact. But I know for certain the client can make it from the STREET to the ROOF --
-- while towing a full-grown man by his HAIR -- in under 10 seconds.
Nikki, if I could sell TICKETS, I'd RETIRE.

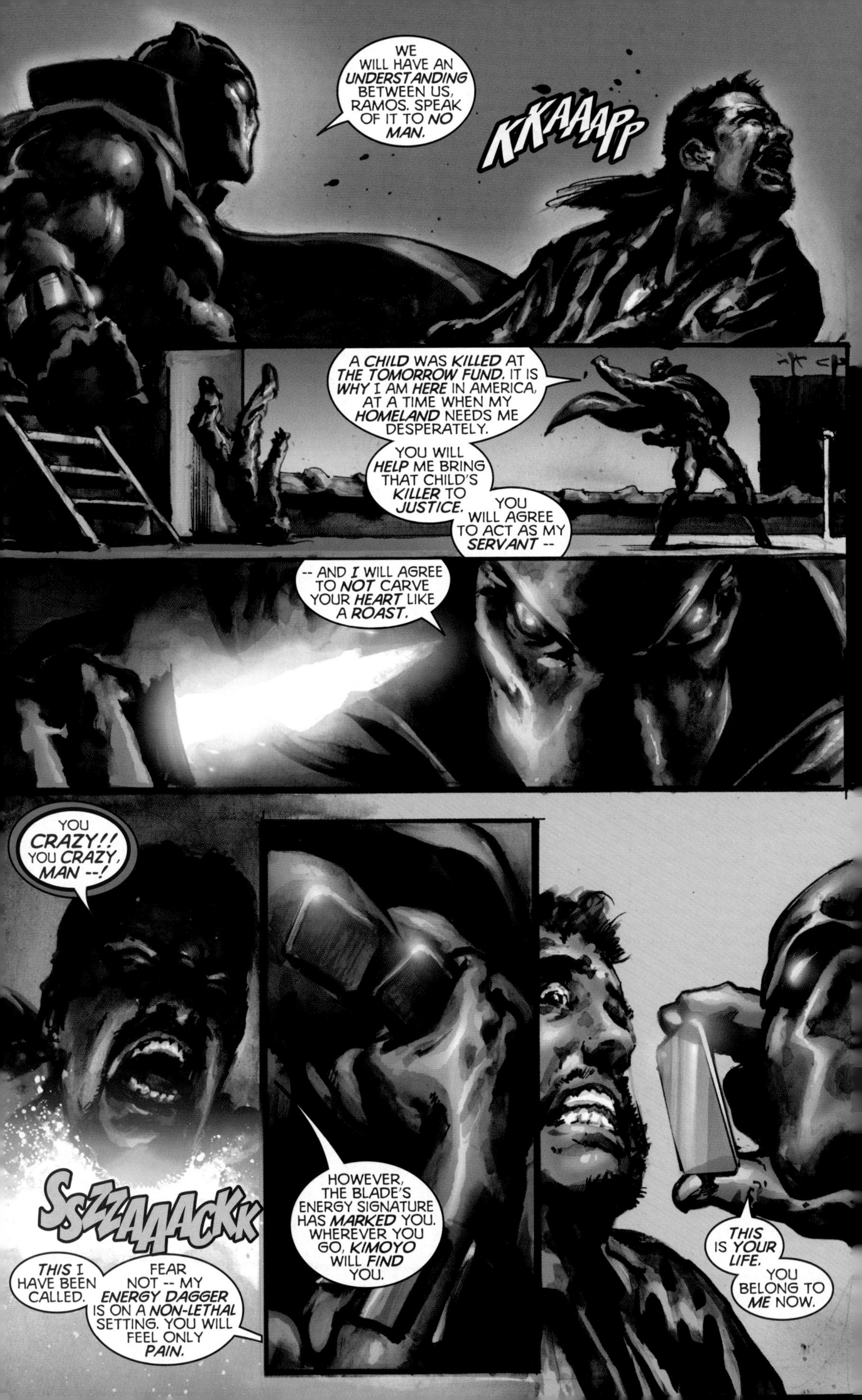
WE WILL HAVE AN UNDERSTANDING BETWEEN US, RAMOS. SPEAK OF IT TO NO MAN.
KKAAAPP
A CHILD WAS KILLED AT THE TOMORROW FUND. IT IS WHY I AM HERE IN AMERICA, AT A TIME WHEN MY HOMELAND NEEDS ME DESPERATELY.
YOU WILL HELP ME BRING THAT CHILD'S KILLER TO JUSTICE.
YOU WILL AGREE TO ACT AS MY SERVANT --
-- AND I WILL AGREE TO NOT CARVE YOUR HEART LIKE A ROAST.
YOU CRAZY!! YOU CRAZY, MAN --!
SSZZAAAACKK
THIS I HAVE BEEN CALLED.
FEAR NOT -- MY ENERGY DAGGER IS ON A NON-LETHAL SETTING. YOU WILL FEEL ONLY PAIN.
HOWEVER, THE BLADE'S ENERGY SIGNATURE HAS MARKED YOU. WHEREVER YOU GO, KIMOYO WILL FIND YOU.
THIS IS YOUR LIFE.
YOU BELONG TO ME NOW.

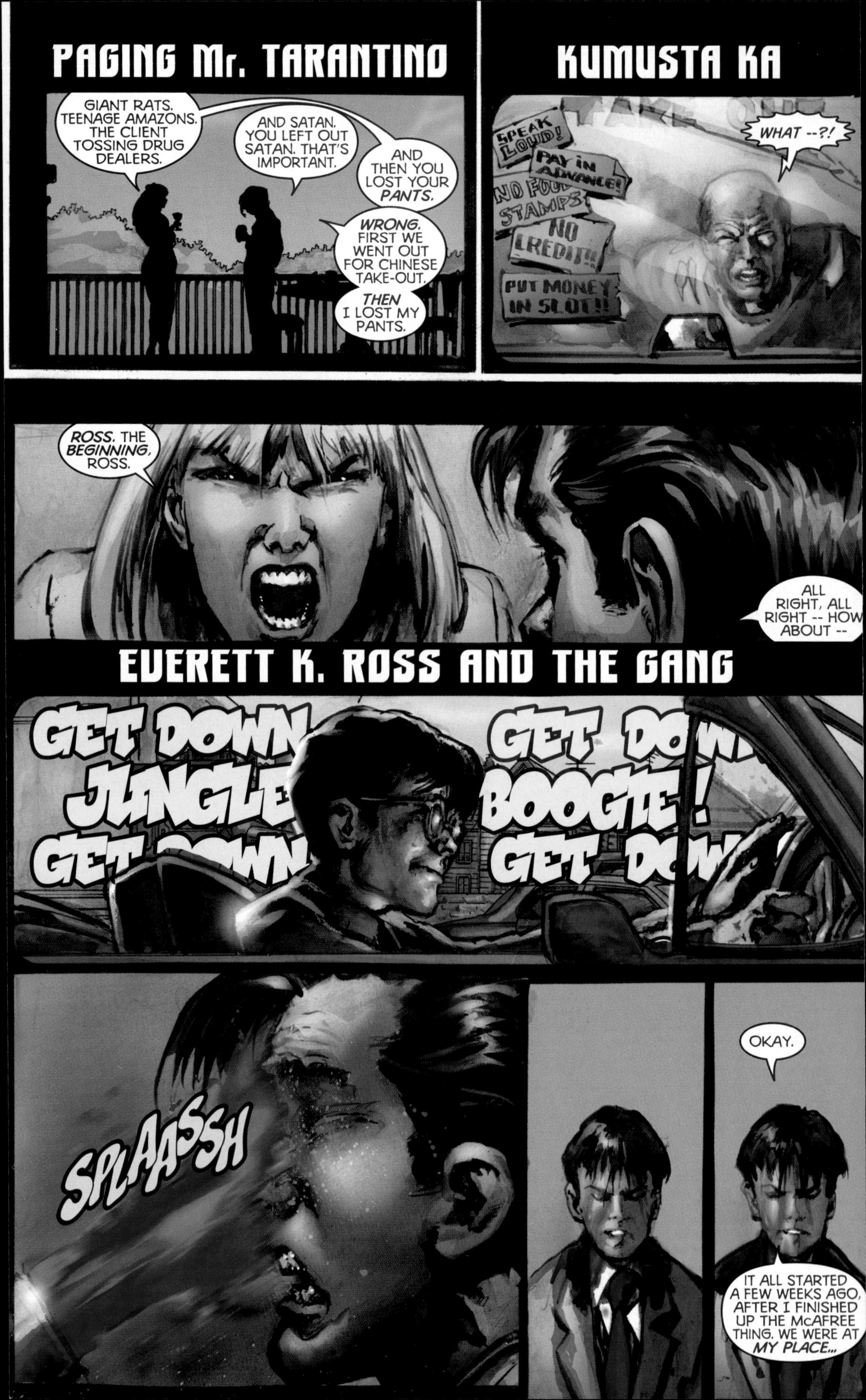
PAGING Mr. TARANTINO
GIANT RATS. TEENAGE AMAZONS. THE CLIENT TOSSING DRUG DEALERS.
AND SATAN. YOU LEFT OUT SATAN. THAT'S IMPORTANT.
AND THEN YOU LOST YOUR PANTS.
WRONG. FIRST WE WENT OUT FOR CHINESE TAKE-OUT.
THEN I LOST MY PANTS.
KUMUSTA KA
SPEAK LOUD!
PAY IN ADVANCE!
STAMPS
NO CREDIT!!
PUT MONEY IN SLOT!!
WHAT --?!
ROSS. THE BEGINNING, ROSS.
ALL RIGHT, ALL RIGHT -- HOW ABOUT --
EVERETT K. ROSS AND THE GANG
JUNGLE
BOOGIE!
SPLAASSH
OKAY.
IT ALL STARTED A FEW WEEKS AGO, AFTER I FINISHED UP THE McAFREE THING. WE WERE AT MY PLACE...

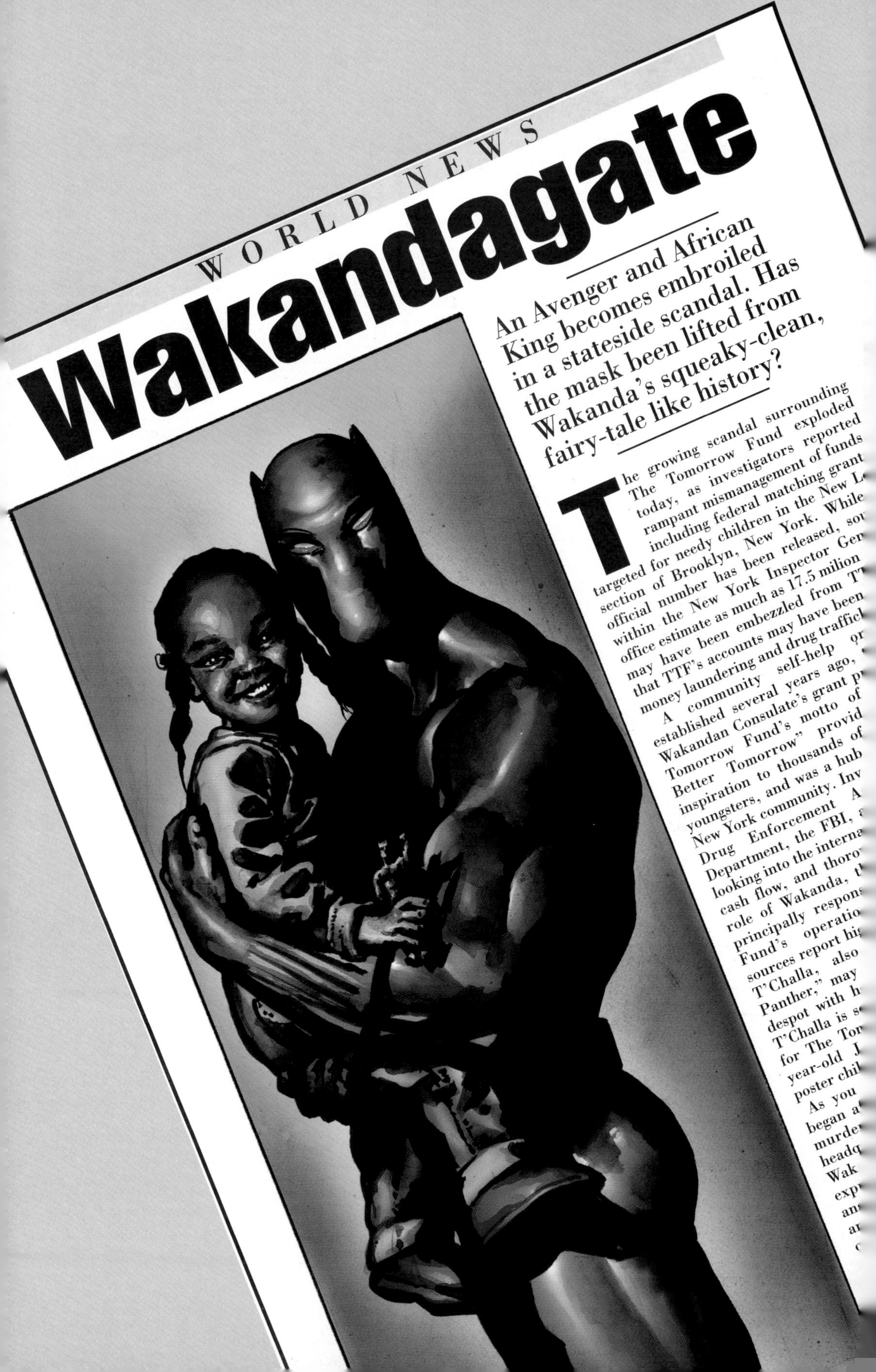

WORLD NEWS

Wakandagate

An Avenger and African King becomes embroiled in a stateside scandal. Has the mask been lifted from Wakanda's squeaky-clean, fairy-tale like history?

The growing scandal surrounding
The Tomorrow Fund exploded
today, as investigators reported
rampant mismanagement of funds
including federal matching grant
including children in the New L
targeted for needy Brooklyn, New York. While
section of Brooklyn has been released, so
official number has been released, so
within the New York Inspector Gen
office estimate as much as 17.5 milion
may have been embezzled from T
that TTF's accounts may have been
money laundering and drug traffick
A community self-help or
established several years ago,
Wakandan Consulate's grant p
Tomorrow Fund's motto of
Better Tomorrow" provid
inspiration to thousands of
youngsters, and was a hub
New York community. Inv
Drug Enforcement A
Department, the FBI, a
looking into the interna
cash flow, and thoro
role of Wakanda, t
principally respons
Fund's operatio
sources report his
T'Challa, also
Panther," may
despot with h
T'Challa is s
for The Tor
year-old J
poster chil
As you
began a
murde
headq
Wak
exp
an
ar

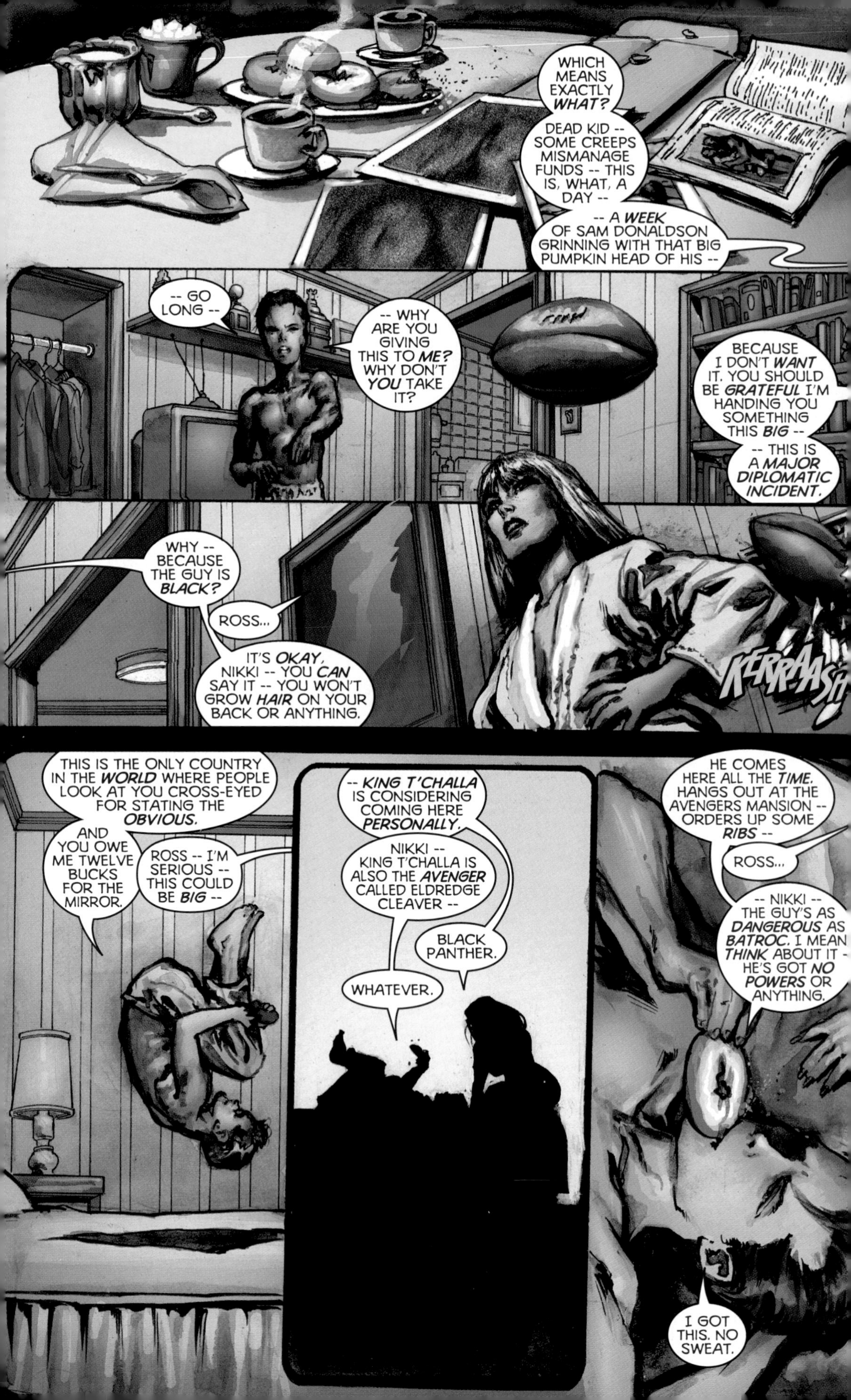
WHICH MEANS EXACTLY WHAT?
DEAD KID -- SOME CREEPS MISMANAGE FUNDS -- THIS IS, WHAT, A DAY --
-- A WEEK OF SAM DONALDSON GRINNING WITH THAT BIG PUMPKIN HEAD OF HIS --
-- GO LONG --
-- WHY ARE YOU GIVING THIS TO ME? WHY DON'T YOU TAKE IT?
BECAUSE I DON'T WANT IT. YOU SHOULD BE GRATEFUL I'M HANDING YOU SOMETHING THIS BIG --
-- THIS IS A MAJOR DIPLOMATIC INCIDENT.
WHY -- BECAUSE THE GUY IS BLACK?
ROSS...
IT'S OKAY, NIKKI -- YOU CAN SAY IT -- YOU WON'T GROW HAIR ON YOUR BACK OR ANYTHING.
KERRAAASH
THIS IS THE ONLY COUNTRY IN THE WORLD WHERE PEOPLE LOOK AT YOU CROSS-EYED FOR STATING THE OBVIOUS.
AND YOU OWE ME TWELVE BUCKS FOR THE MIRROR.
ROSS -- I'M SERIOUS -- THIS COULD BE BIG --
-- KING T'CHALLA IS CONSIDERING COMING HERE PERSONALLY.
NIKKI -- KING T'CHALLA IS ALSO THE AVENGER CALLED ELDREDGE CLEAVER --
BLACK PANTHER.
WHATEVER.
HE COMES HERE ALL THE TIME. HANGS OUT AT THE AVENGERS MANSION -- ORDERS UP SOME RIBS --
ROSS...
-- NIKKI -- THE GUY'S AS DANGEROUS AS BATROC. I MEAN THINK ABOUT IT -- HE'S GOT NO POWERS OR ANYTHING.
I GOT THIS. NO SWEAT.

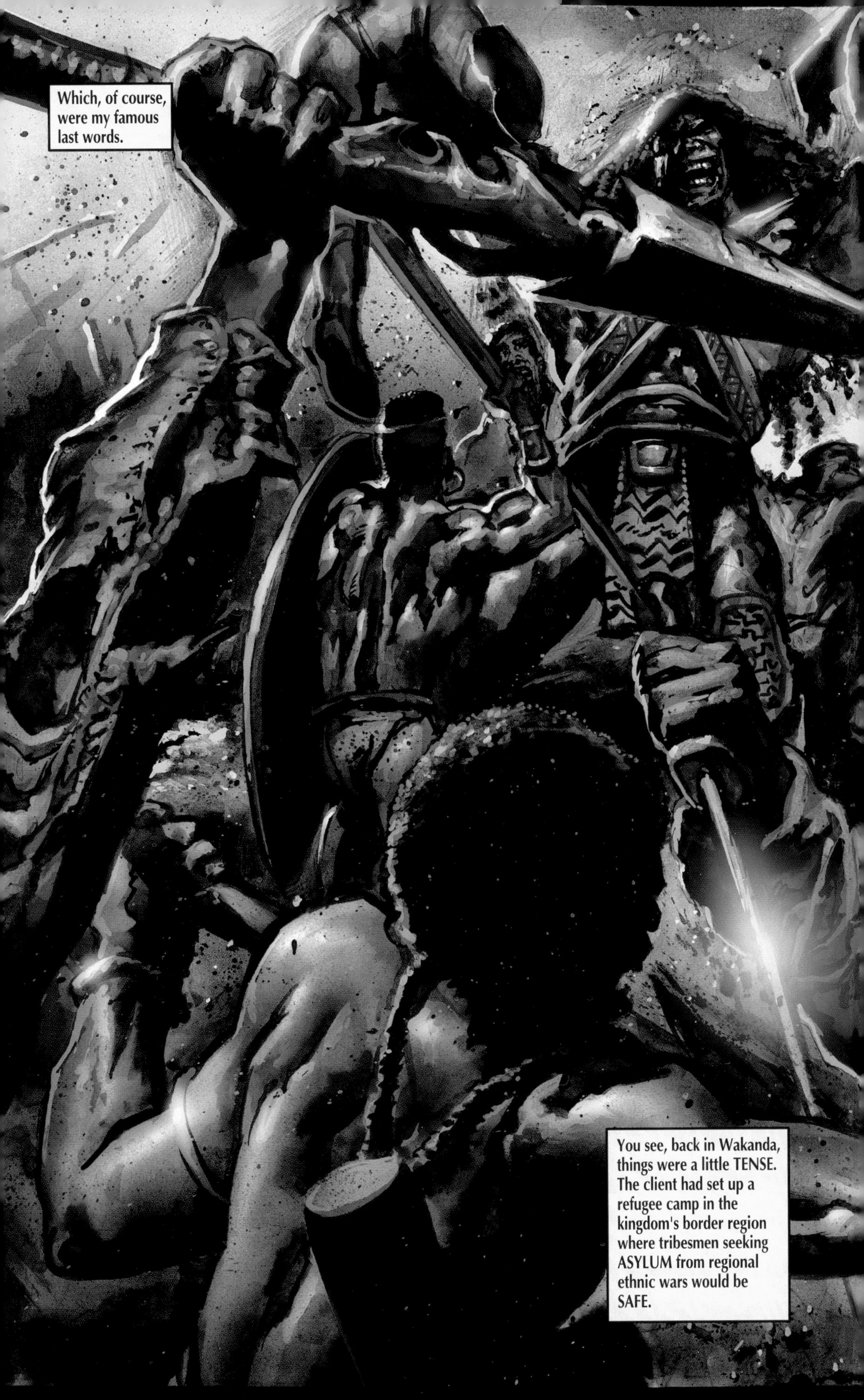
Which, of course, were my famous last words.
You see, back in Wakanda, things were a little TENSE. The client had set up a refugee camp in the kingdom's border region where tribesmen seeking ASYLUM from regional ethnic wars would be SAFE.

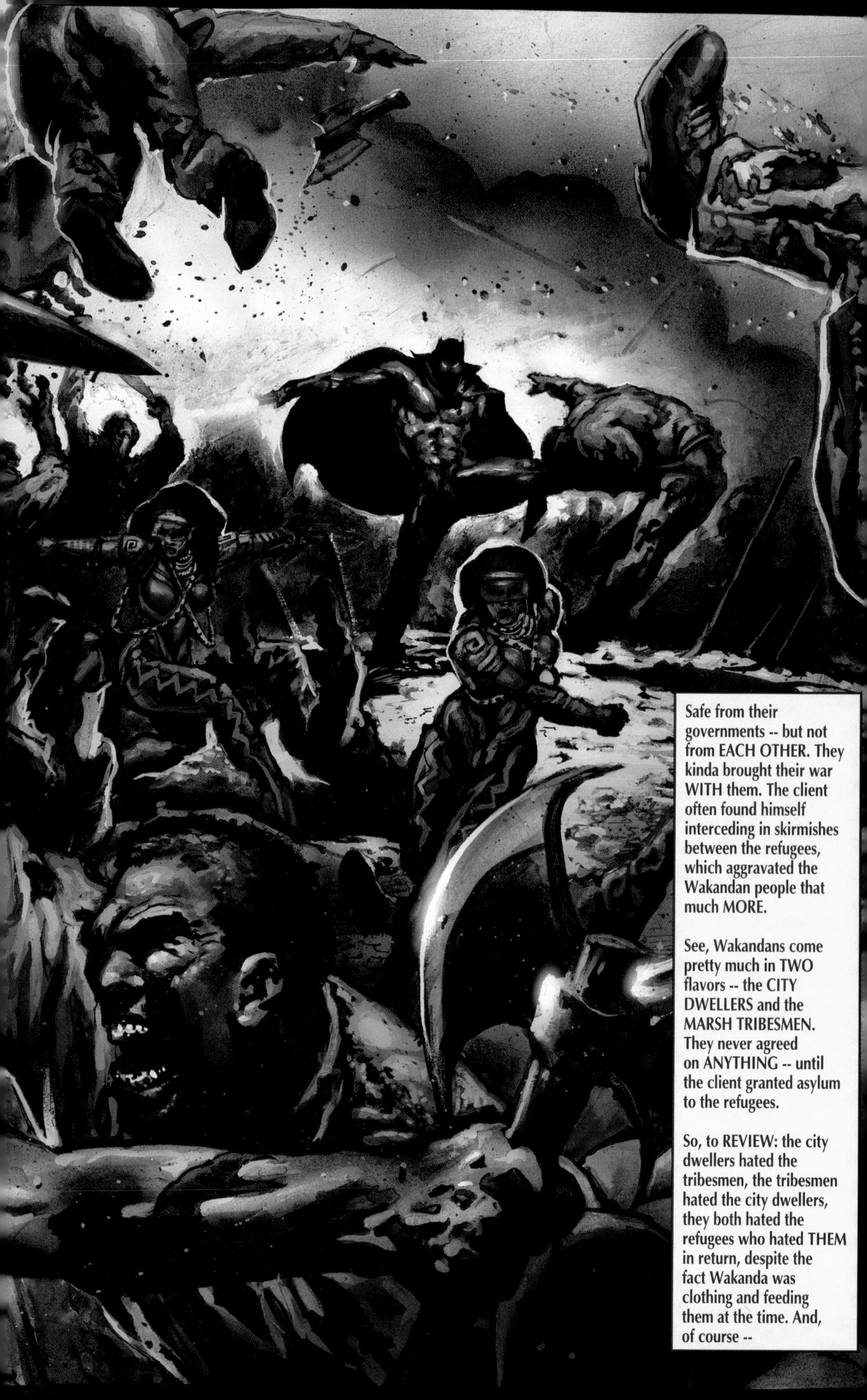
Safe from their governments -- but not from EACH OTHER. They kinda brought their war WITH them. The client often found himself interceding in skirmishes between the refugees, which aggravated the Wakandan people that much MORE.
See, Wakandans come pretty much in TWO flavors -- the CITY DWELLERS and the MARSH TRIBESMEN. They never agreed on ANYTHING -- until the client granted asylum to the refugees.
So, to REVIEW: the city dwellers hated the tribesmen, the tribesmen hated the city dwellers, they both hated the refugees who hated THEM in return, despite the fact Wakanda was clothing and feeding them at the time. And, of course --

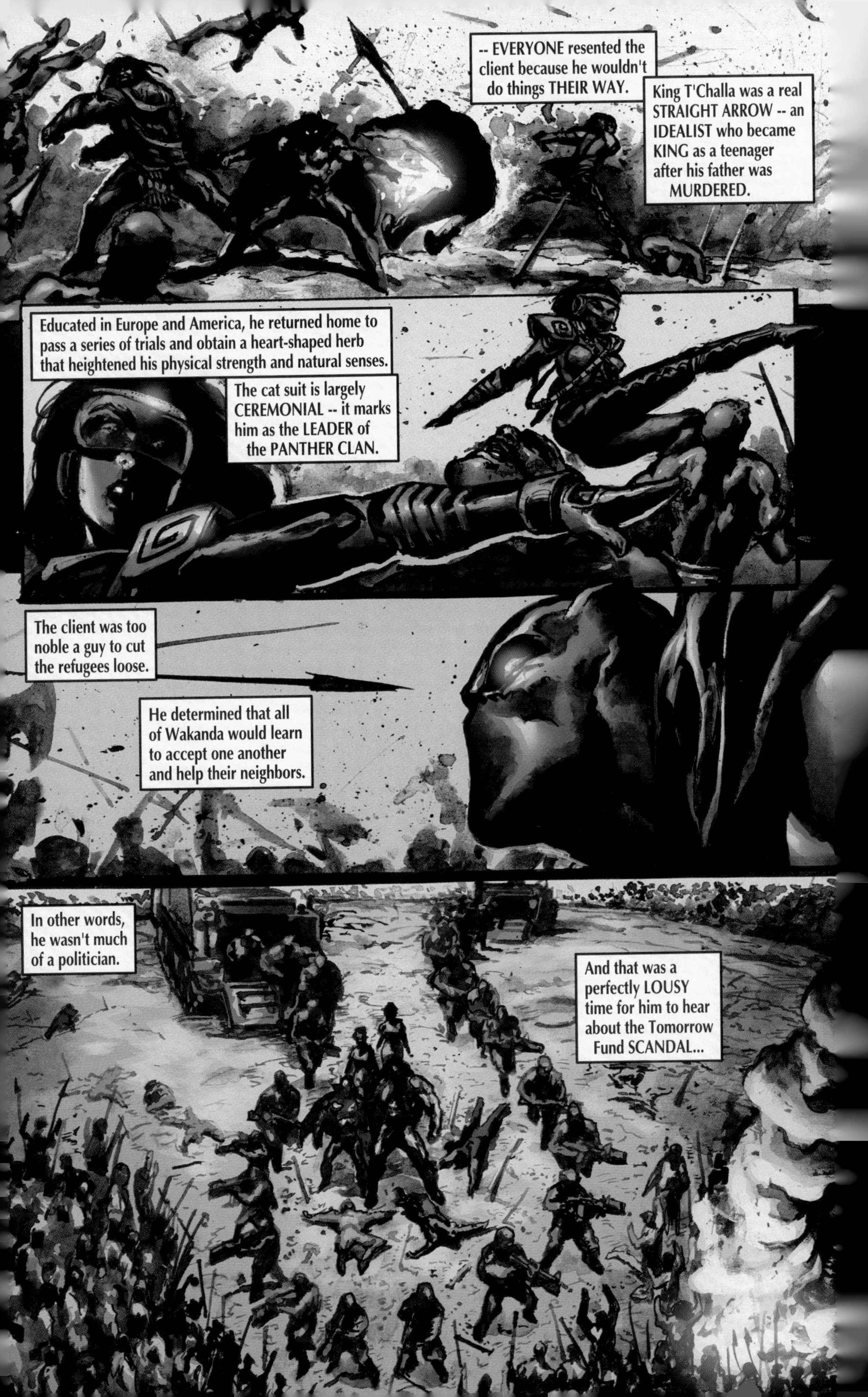
-- EVERYONE resented the client because he wouldn't do things THEIR WAY.
King T'Challa was a real STRAIGHT ARROW -- an IDEALIST who became KING as a teenager after his father was MURDERED.
Educated in Europe and America, he returned home to pass a series of trials and obtain a heart-shaped herb that heightened his physical strength and natural senses.
The cat suit is largely CEREMONIAL -- it marks him as the LEADER of the PANTHER CLAN.
The client was too noble a guy to cut the refugees loose.
He determined that all of Wakanda would learn to accept one another and help their neighbors.
In other words, he wasn't much of a politician.
And that was a perfectly LOUSY time for him to hear about the Tomorrow Fund SCANDAL...

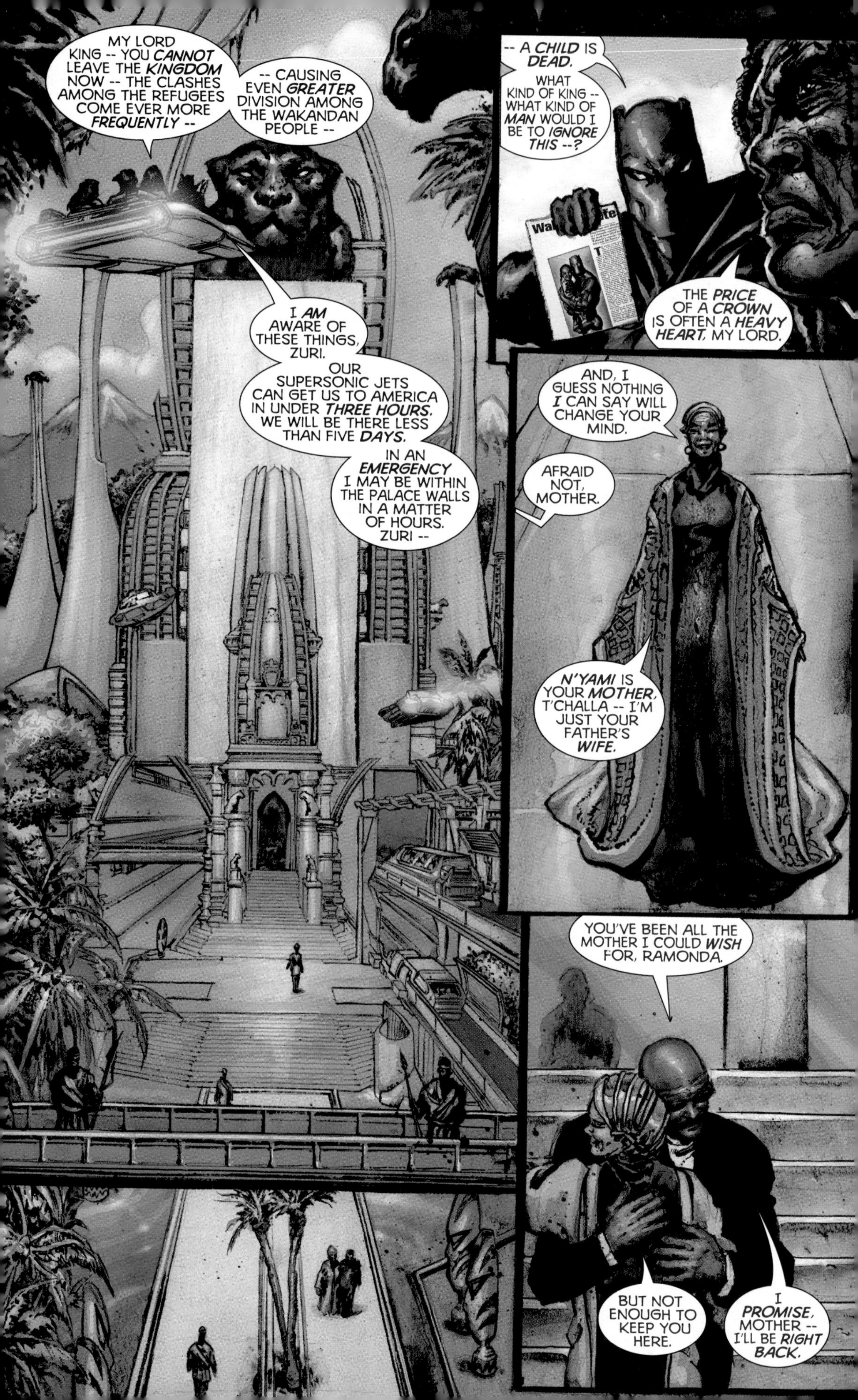

MY LORD KING -- YOU CANNOT LEAVE THE KINGDOM NOW -- THE CLASHES AMONG THE REFUGEES COME EVER MORE FREQUENTLY --
-- CAUSING EVEN GREATER DIVISION AMONG THE WAKANDAN PEOPLE --
I AM AWARE OF THESE THINGS, ZURI.
OUR SUPERSONIC JETS CAN GET US TO AMERICA IN UNDER THREE HOURS. WE WILL BE THERE LESS THAN FIVE DAYS.
IN AN EMERGENCY I MAY BE WITHIN THE PALACE WALLS IN A MATTER OF HOURS. ZURI --
-- A CHILD IS DEAD.
WHAT KIND OF KING -- WHAT KIND OF MAN WOULD I BE TO IGNORE THIS --?
THE PRICE OF A CROWN IS OFTEN A HEAVY HEART, MY LORD.
AND, I GUESS NOTHING I CAN SAY WILL CHANGE YOUR MIND.
AFRAID NOT, MOTHER.
N'YAMI IS YOUR MOTHER, T'CHALLA -- I'M JUST YOUR FATHER'S WIFE.
YOU'VE BEEN ALL THE MOTHER I COULD WISH FOR, RAMONDA.
BUT NOT ENOUGH TO KEEP YOU HERE.
I PROMISE, MOTHER -- I'LL BE RIGHT BACK.

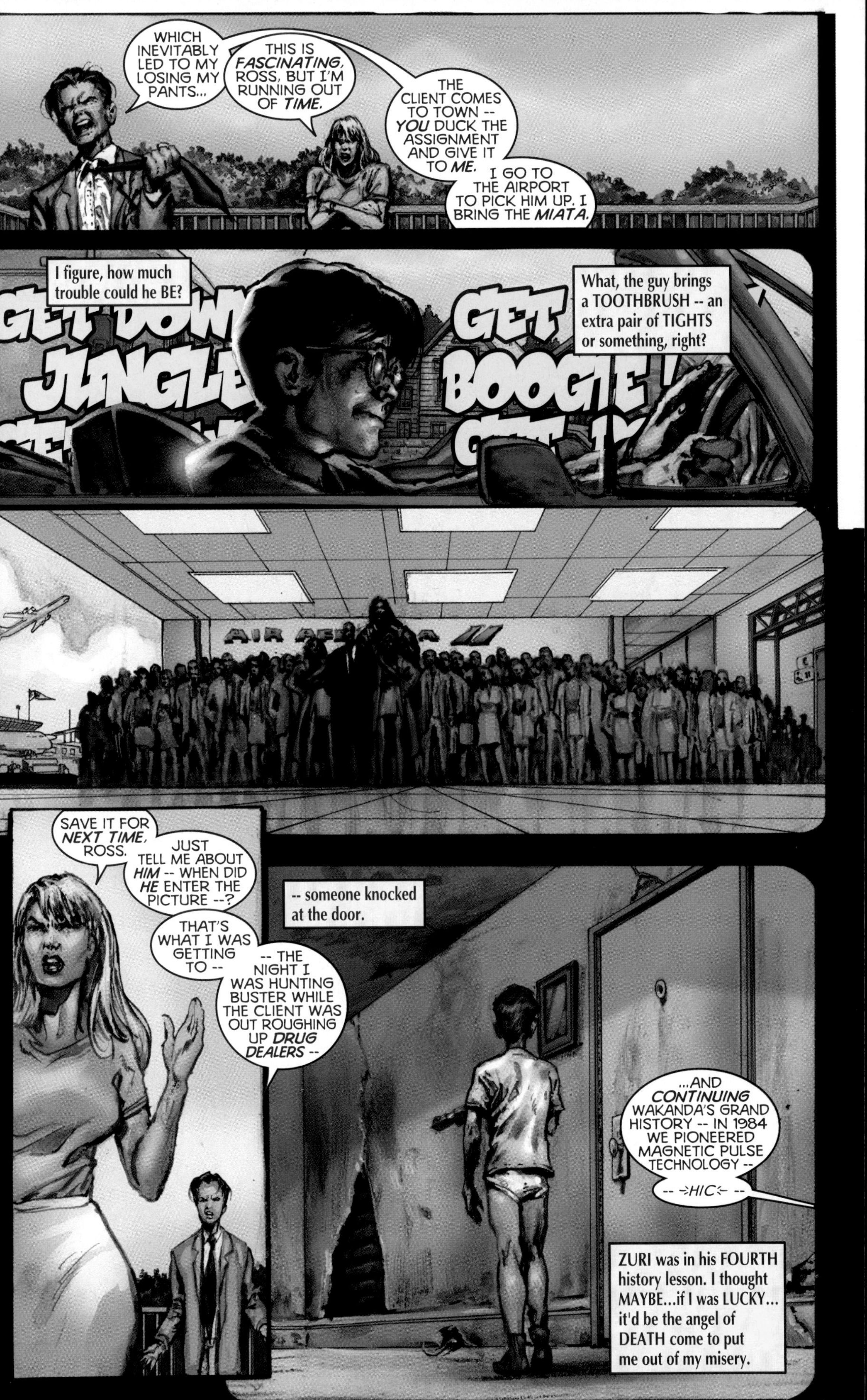
WHICH INEVITABLY LED TO MY LOSING MY PANTS...
THIS IS *FASCINATING*, ROSS, BUT I'M RUNNING OUT OF *TIME*.
THE CLIENT COMES TO TOWN -- *YOU* DUCK THE ASSIGNMENT AND GIVE IT TO *ME*.
I GO TO THE AIRPORT TO PICK HIM UP. I BRING THE *MIATA*.
I figure, how much trouble could he BE?
JUNGLE
What, the guy brings a TOOTHBRUSH -- an extra pair of TIGHTS or something, right?
GET
BOOGIE!
SAVE IT FOR *NEXT TIME*, ROSS.
JUST TELL ME ABOUT *HIM* -- WHEN DID *HE* ENTER THE PICTURE --?
THAT'S WHAT I WAS GETTING TO --
-- THE NIGHT I WAS HUNTING BUSTER WHILE THE CLIENT WAS OUT ROUGHING UP *DRUG DEALERS* --
-- someone knocked at the door.
...AND *CONTINUING* WAKANDA'S GRAND HISTORY -- IN 1984 WE PIONEERED MAGNETIC PULSE TECHNOLOGY --
-- *HIC* --
ZURI was in his FOURTH history lesson. I thought MAYBE...if I was LUCKY... it'd be the angel of DEATH come to put me out of my misery.

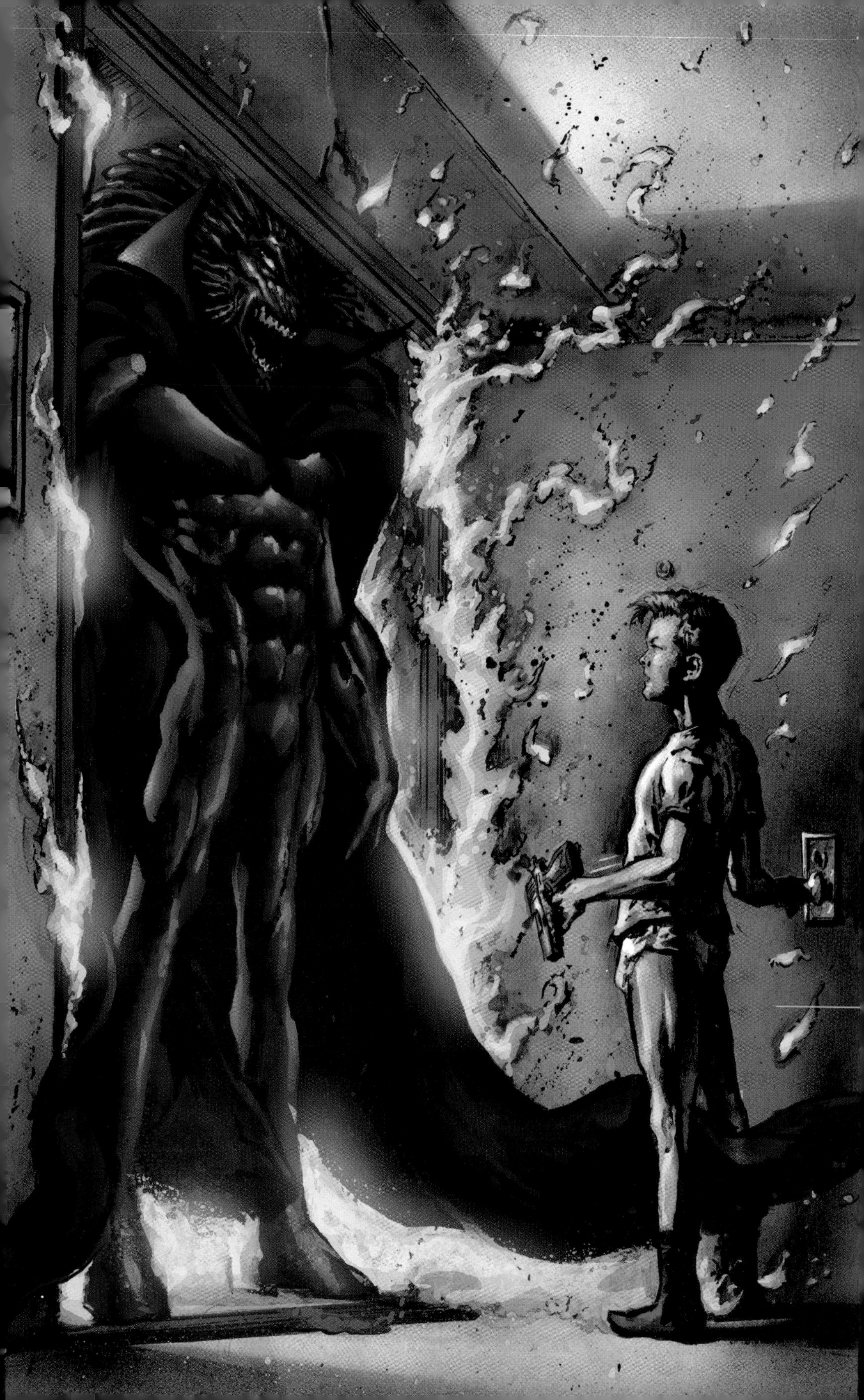

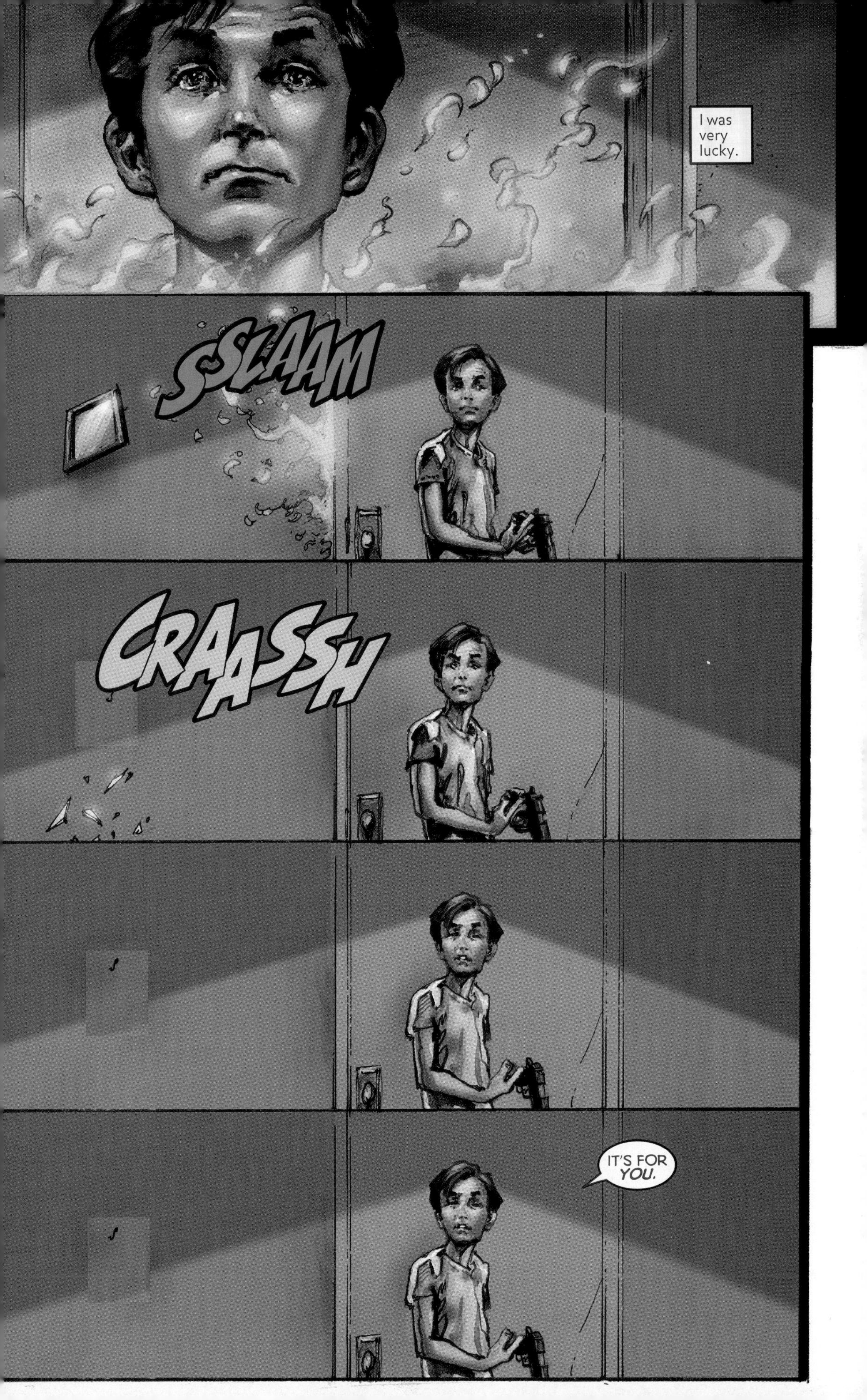
I was very lucky.
SSLAAM
CRAASSH
IT'S FOR *YOU*.

CHAPTER 2

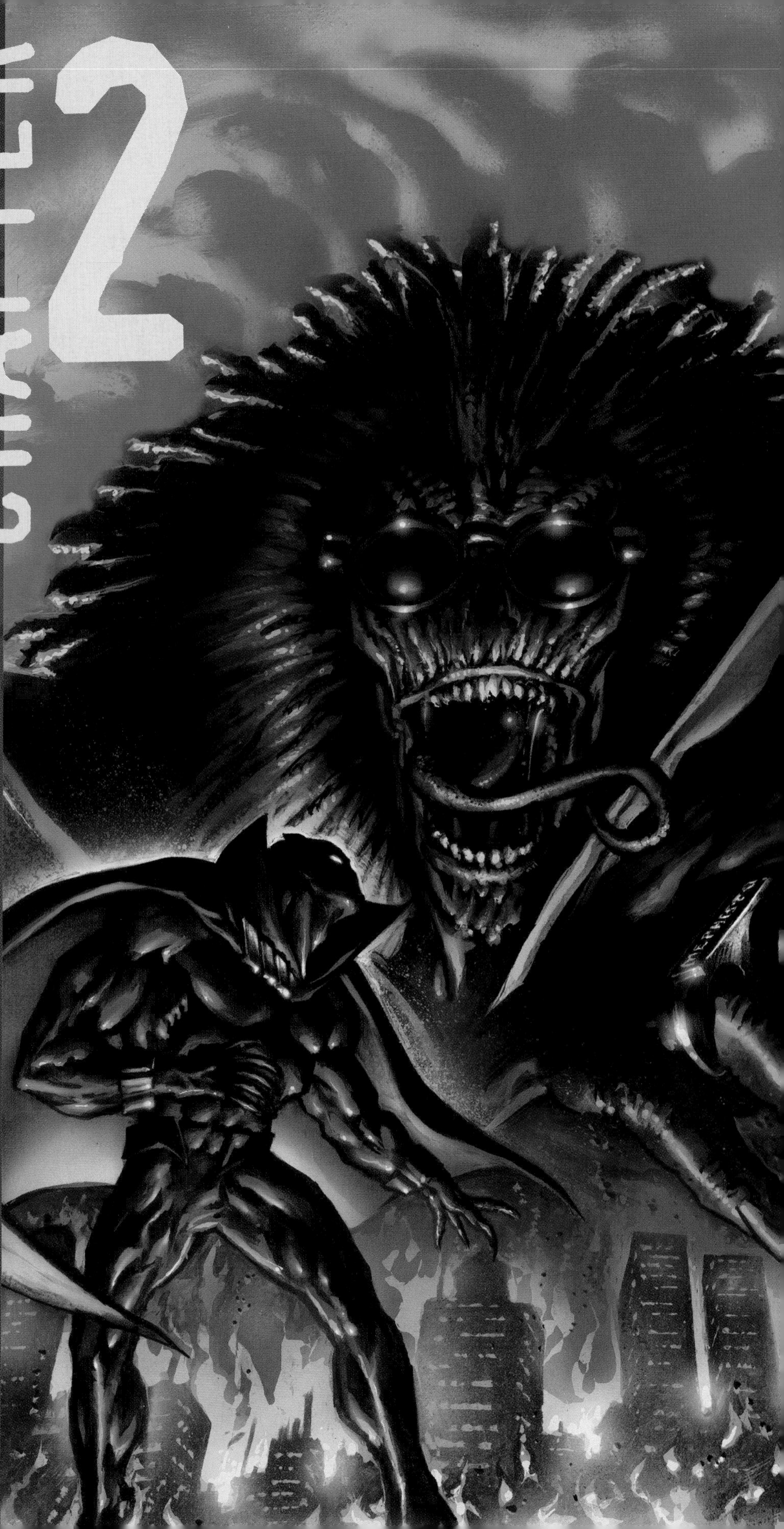

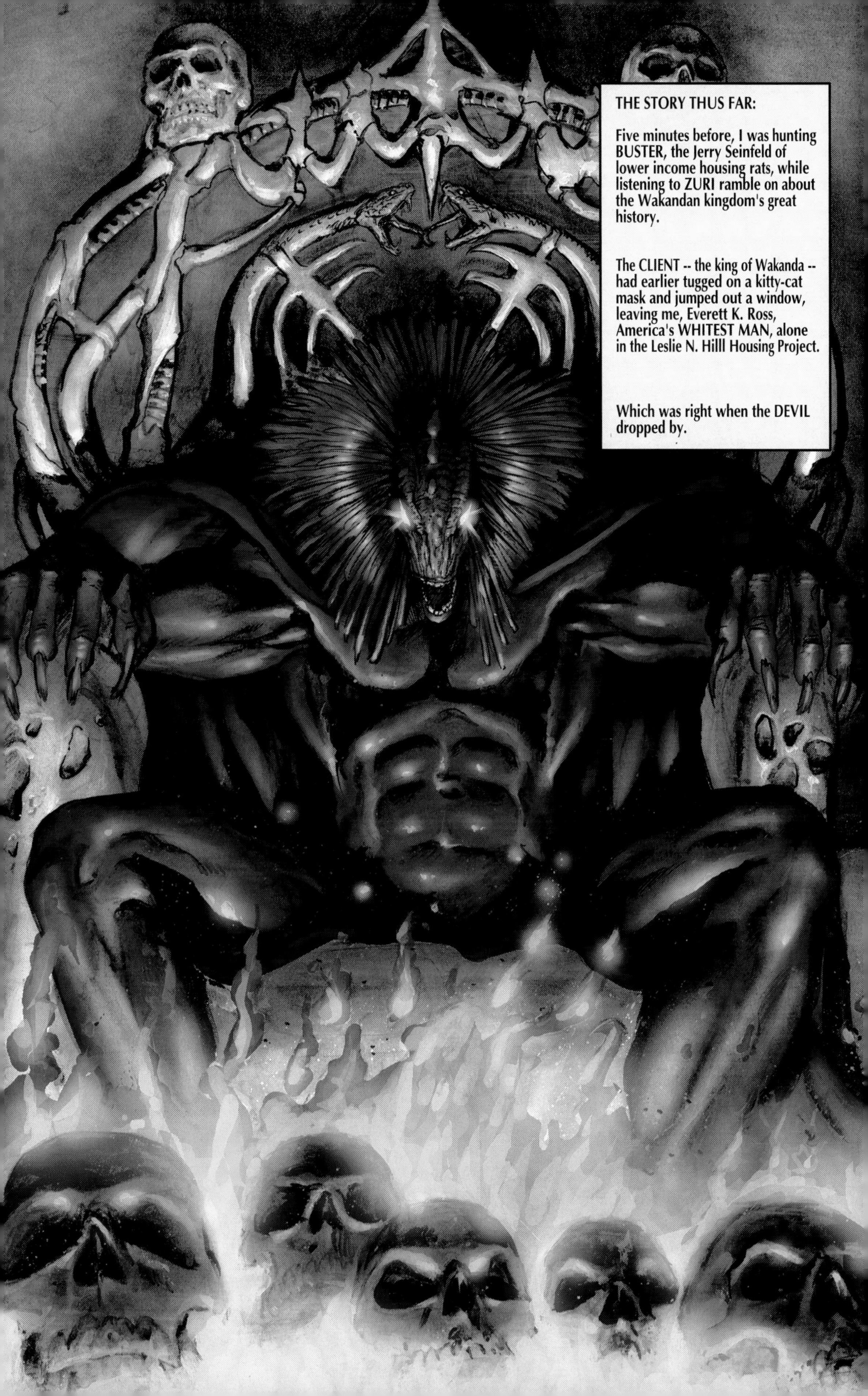
THE STORY THUS FAR:
Five minutes before, I was hunting BUSTER, the Jerry Seinfeld of lower income housing rats, while listening to ZURI ramble on about the Wakandan kingdom's great history.
The CLIENT -- the king of Wakanda -- had earlier tugged on a kitty-cat mask and jumped out a window, leaving me, Everett K. Ross, America's WHITEST MAN, alone in the Leslie N. Hilll Housing Project.
Which was right when the DEVIL dropped by.

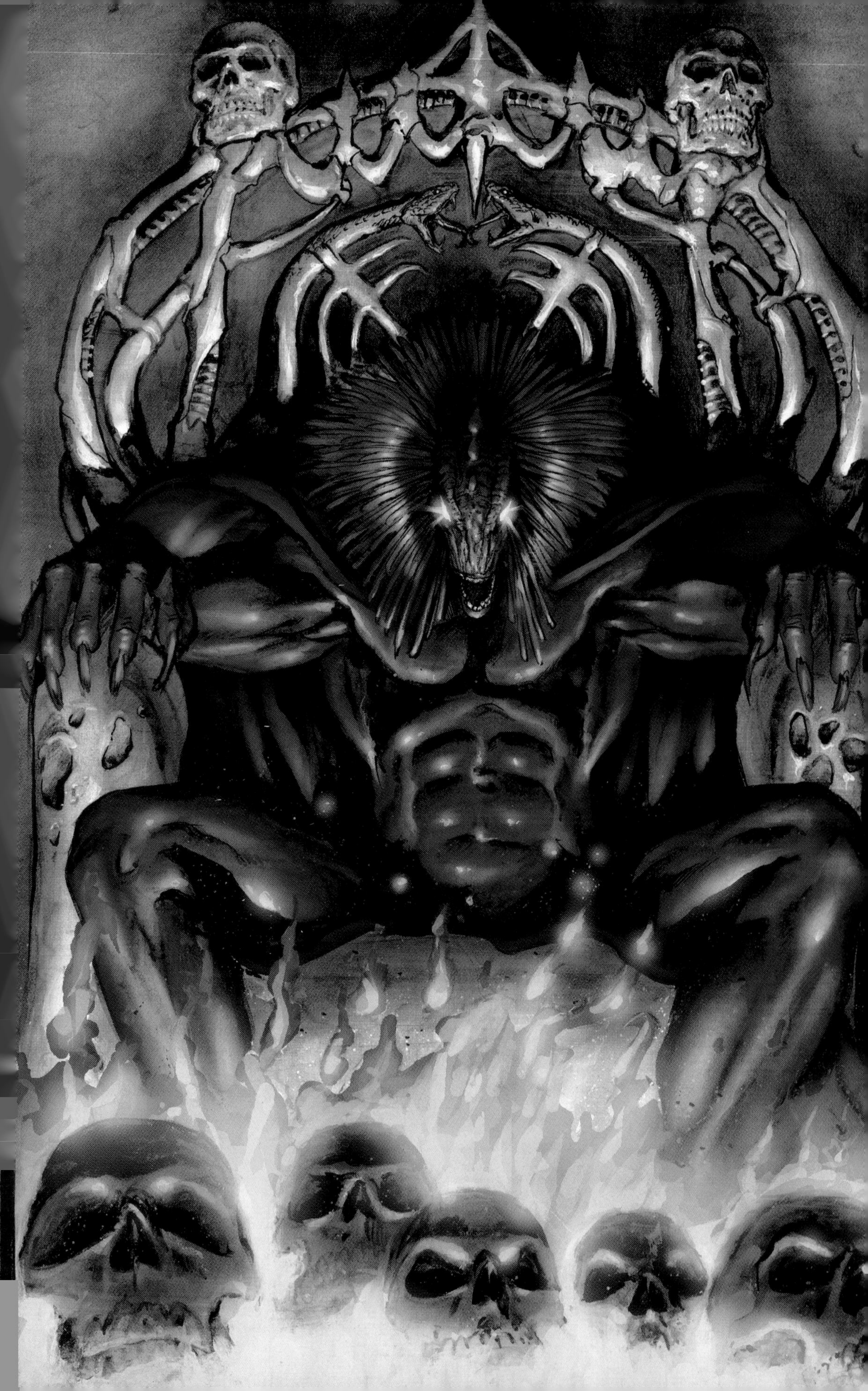

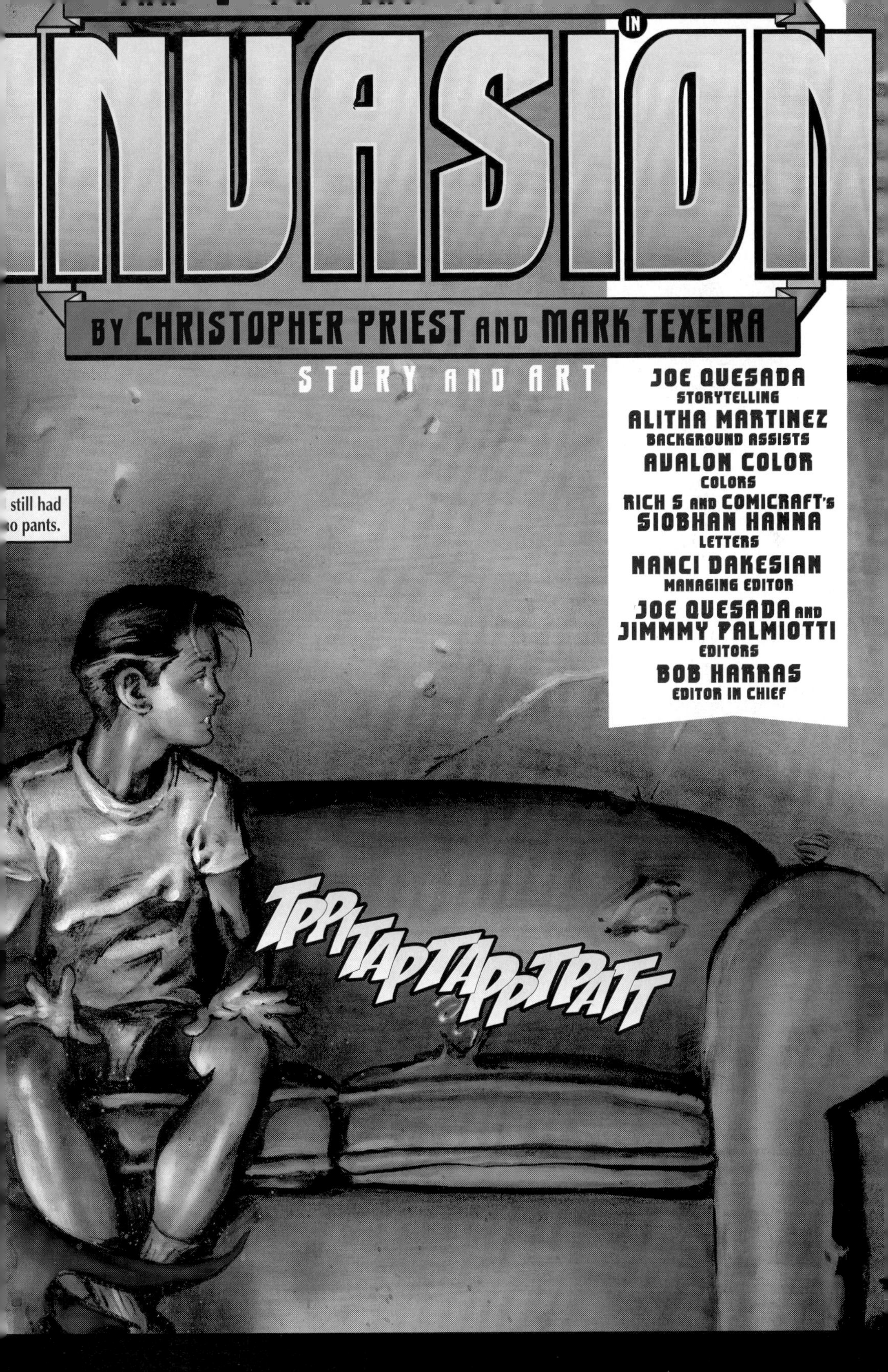
IN
INVASION
BY CHRISTOPHER PRIEST AND MARK TEXEIRA
STORY AND ART
JOE QUESADA
STORYTELLING
ALITHA MARTINEZ
BACKGROUND ASSISTS
AVALON COLOR
COLORS
RICH S AND COMICRAFT's
SIOBHAN HANNA
LETTERS
NANCI DAKESIAN
MANAGING EDITOR
JOE QUESADA AND
JIMMMY PALMIOTTI
EDITORS
BOB HARRAS
EDITOR IN CHIEF
still had
no pants.
TPPITAPTAPPTPATT

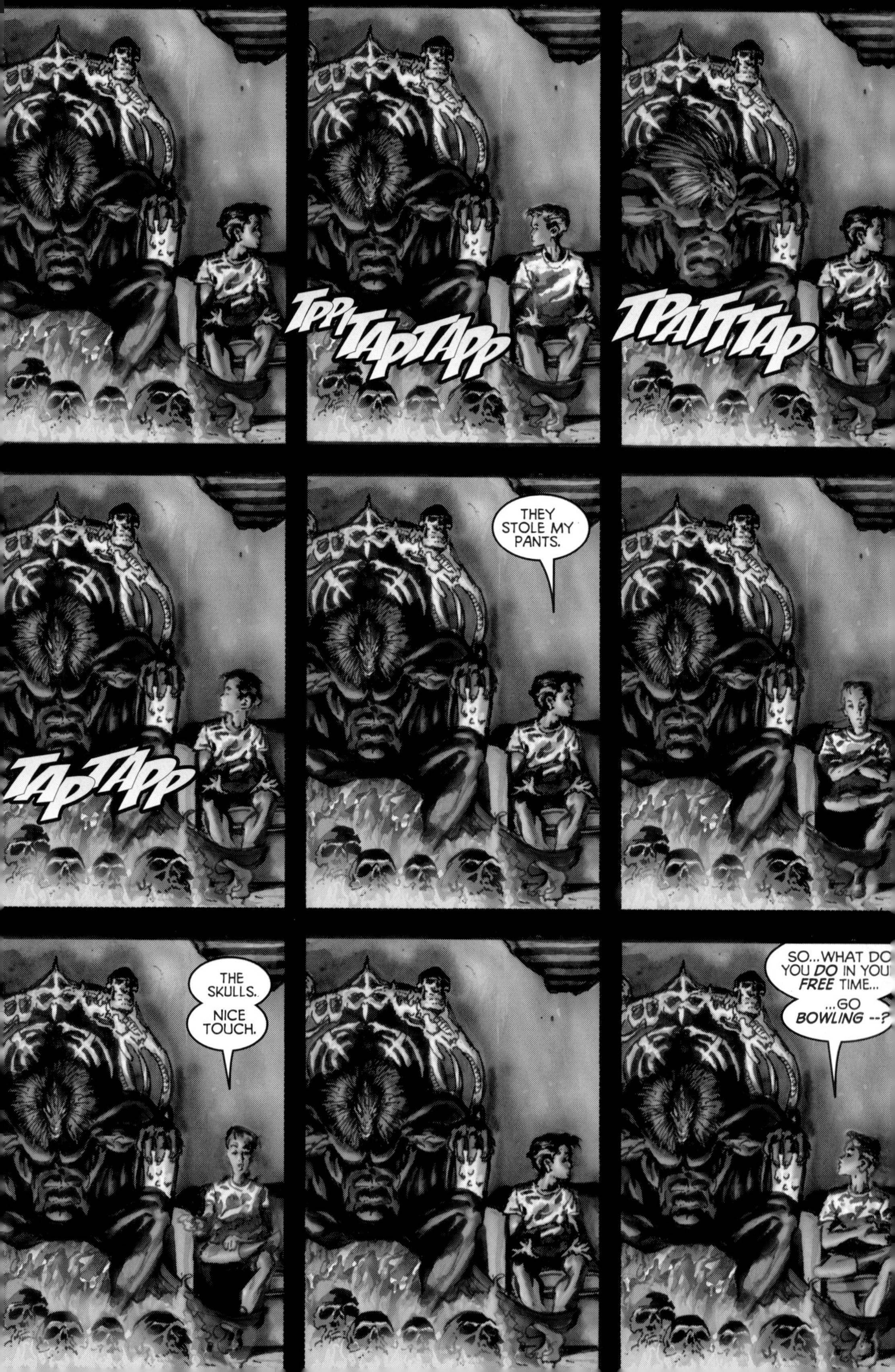
TPPITAPTAPP
TPATTTAP
TAPTAPP
THEY STOLE MY PANTS.
THE SKULLS.
NICE TOUCH.
SO...WHAT DO YOU DO IN YOU FREE TIME...
...GO BOWLING --?

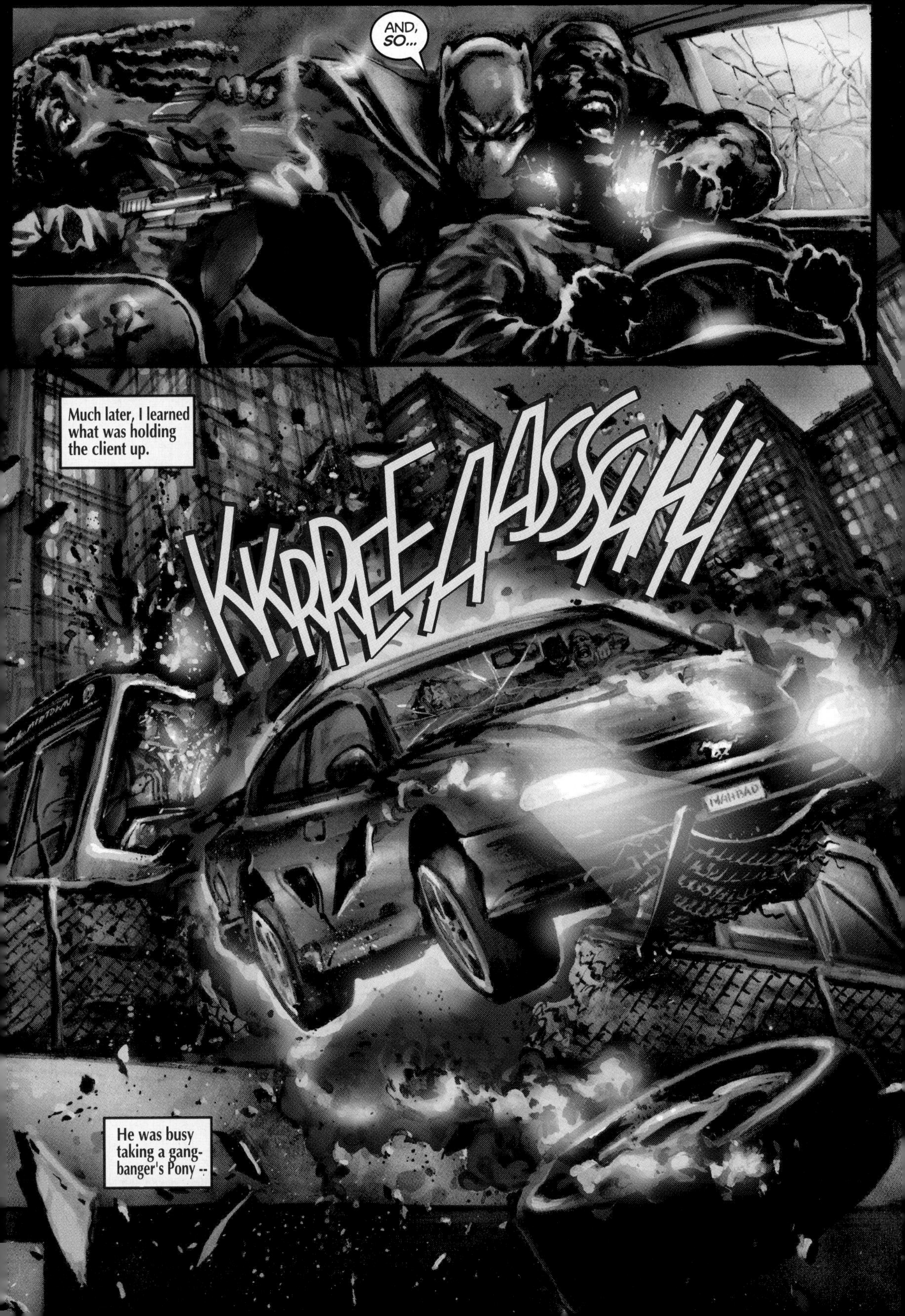
AND, SO...
Much later, I learned what was holding the client up.
KKRREEAASSHH
He was busy taking a gang-banger's Pony --

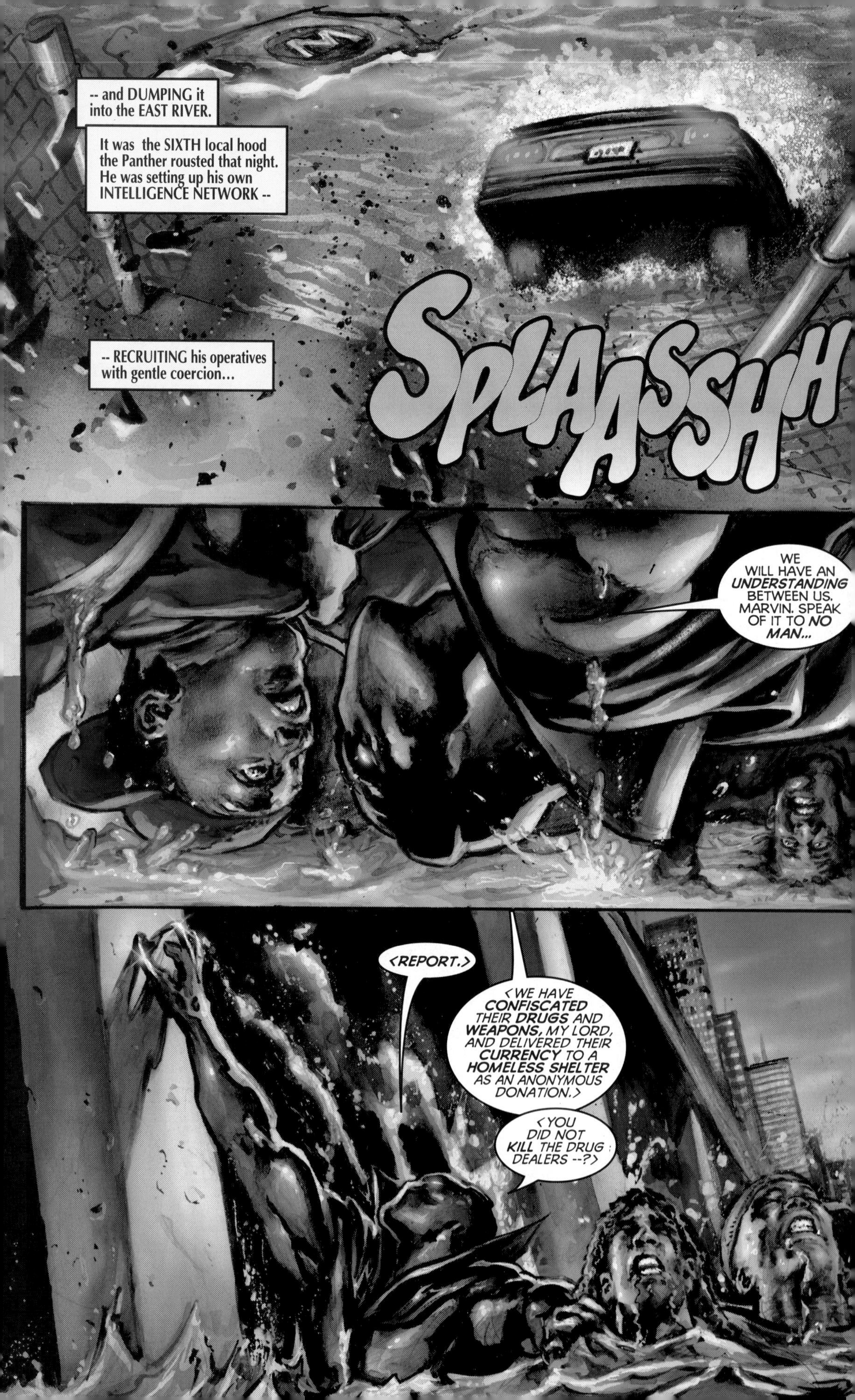
-- and DUMPING it into the EAST RIVER.
It was the SIXTH local hood the Panther rousted that night. He was setting up his own INTELLIGENCE NETWORK --
-- RECRUITING his operatives with gentle coercion...
SPLAASSHH
WE WILL HAVE AN UNDERSTANDING BETWEEN US. MARVIN. SPEAK OF IT TO NO MAN...
<REPORT.>
<WE HAVE CONFISCATED THEIR DRUGS AND WEAPONS, MY LORD, AND DELIVERED THEIR CURRENCY TO A HOMELESS SHELTER AS AN ANONYMOUS DONATION.>
<YOU DID NOT KILL THE DRUG DEALERS --?>

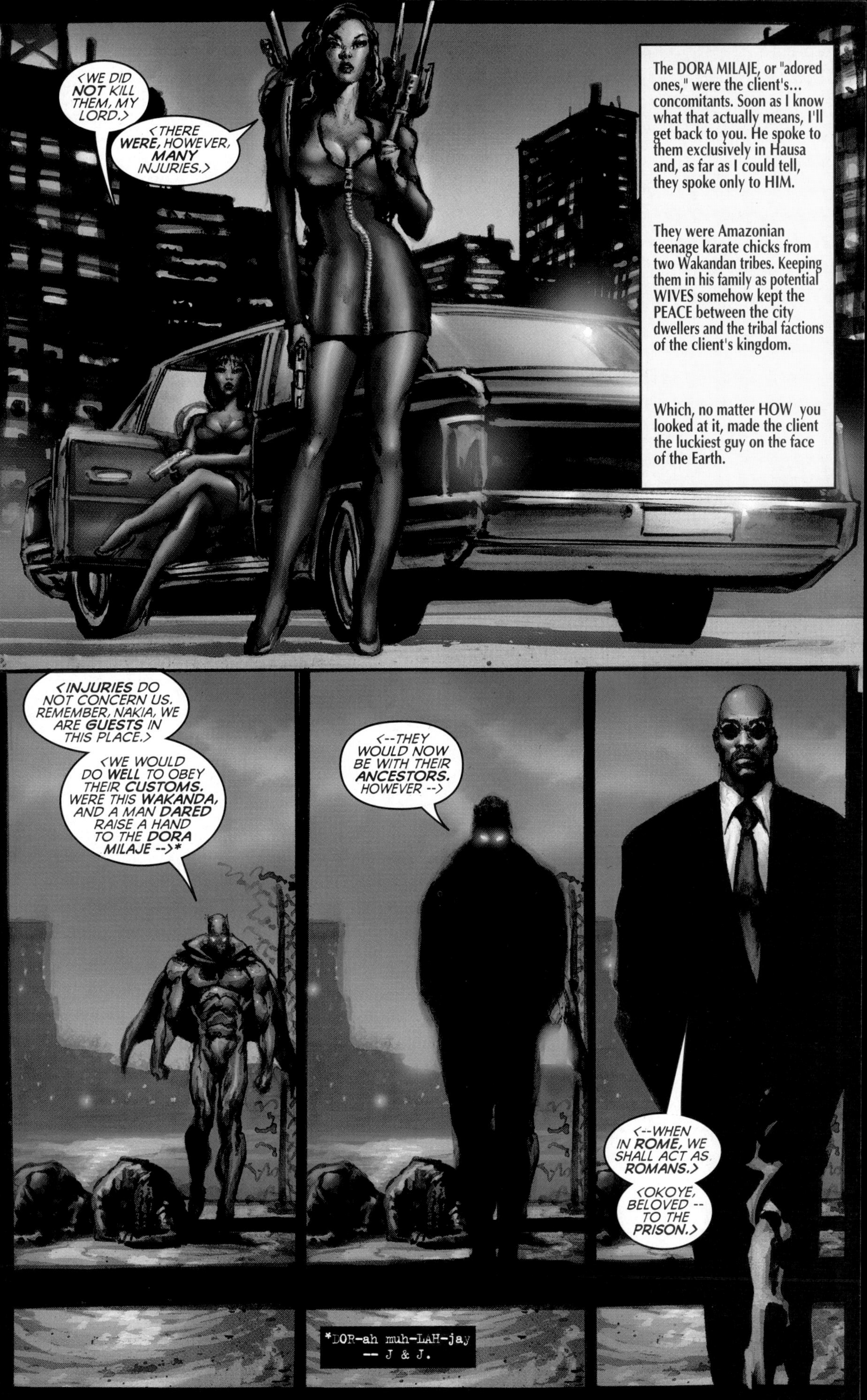
<WE DID NOT KILL THEM, MY LORD.>
<THERE WERE, HOWEVER, MANY INJURIES.>
The DORA MILAJE, or "adored ones," were the client's... concomitants. Soon as I know what that actually means, I'll get back to you. He spoke to them exclusively in Hausa and, as far as I could tell, they spoke only to HIM.
They were Amazonian teenage karate chicks from two Wakandan tribes. Keeping them in his family as potential WIVES somehow kept the PEACE between the city dwellers and the tribal factions of the client's kingdom.
Which, no matter HOW you looked at it, made the client the luckiest guy on the face of the Earth.
<INJURIES DO NOT CONCERN US. REMEMBER, NAKIA, WE ARE GUESTS IN THIS PLACE.>
<WE WOULD DO WELL TO OBEY THEIR CUSTOMS. WERE THIS WAKANDA, AND A MAN DARED RAISE A HAND TO THE DORA MILAJE -->*
<--THEY WOULD NOW BE WITH THEIR ANCESTORS. HOWEVER -->
<--WHEN IN ROME, WE SHALL ACT AS ROMANS.>
<OKOYE, BELOVED -- TO THE PRISON.>
*DOR-ah muh-LAH-jay -- J & J.

NOT TODAY

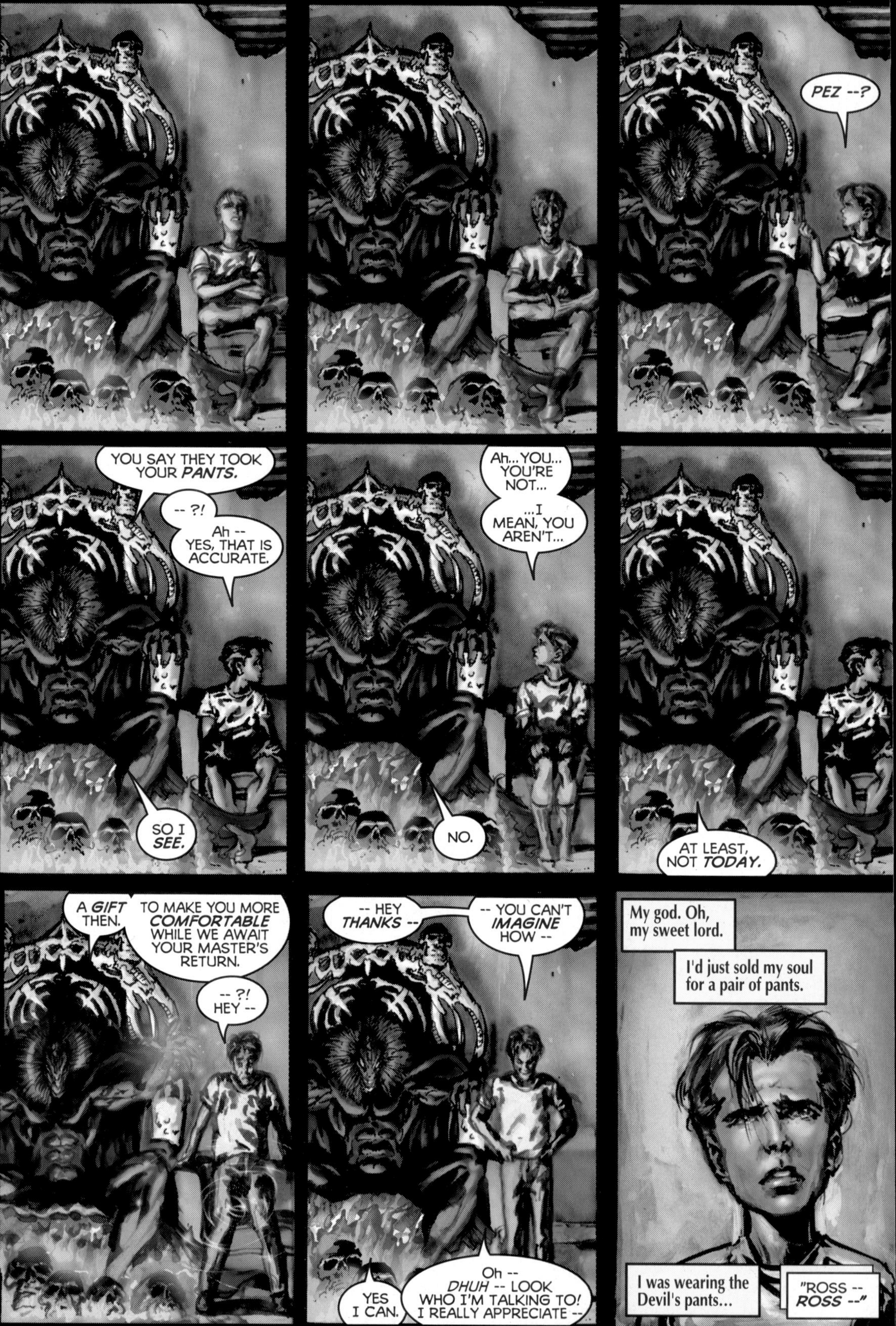

PEZ --?
YOU SAY THEY TOOK YOUR PANTS.
-- ?!
Ah -- YES, THAT IS ACCURATE.
SO I SEE.
Ah... YOU... YOU'RE NOT...
...I MEAN, YOU AREN'T...
NO.
AT LEAST, NOT TODAY.
A GIFT THEN.
TO MAKE YOU MORE COMFORTABLE WHILE WE AWAIT YOUR MASTER'S RETURN.
-- ?! HEY --
-- HEY THANKS --
-- YOU CAN'T IMAGINE HOW --
YES I CAN.
Oh -- DHUH -- LOOK WHO I'M TALKING TO! I REALLY APPRECIATE --
My god. Oh, my sweet lord.
I'd just sold my soul for a pair of pants.
I was wearing the Devil's pants...
"ROSS -- ROSS --"

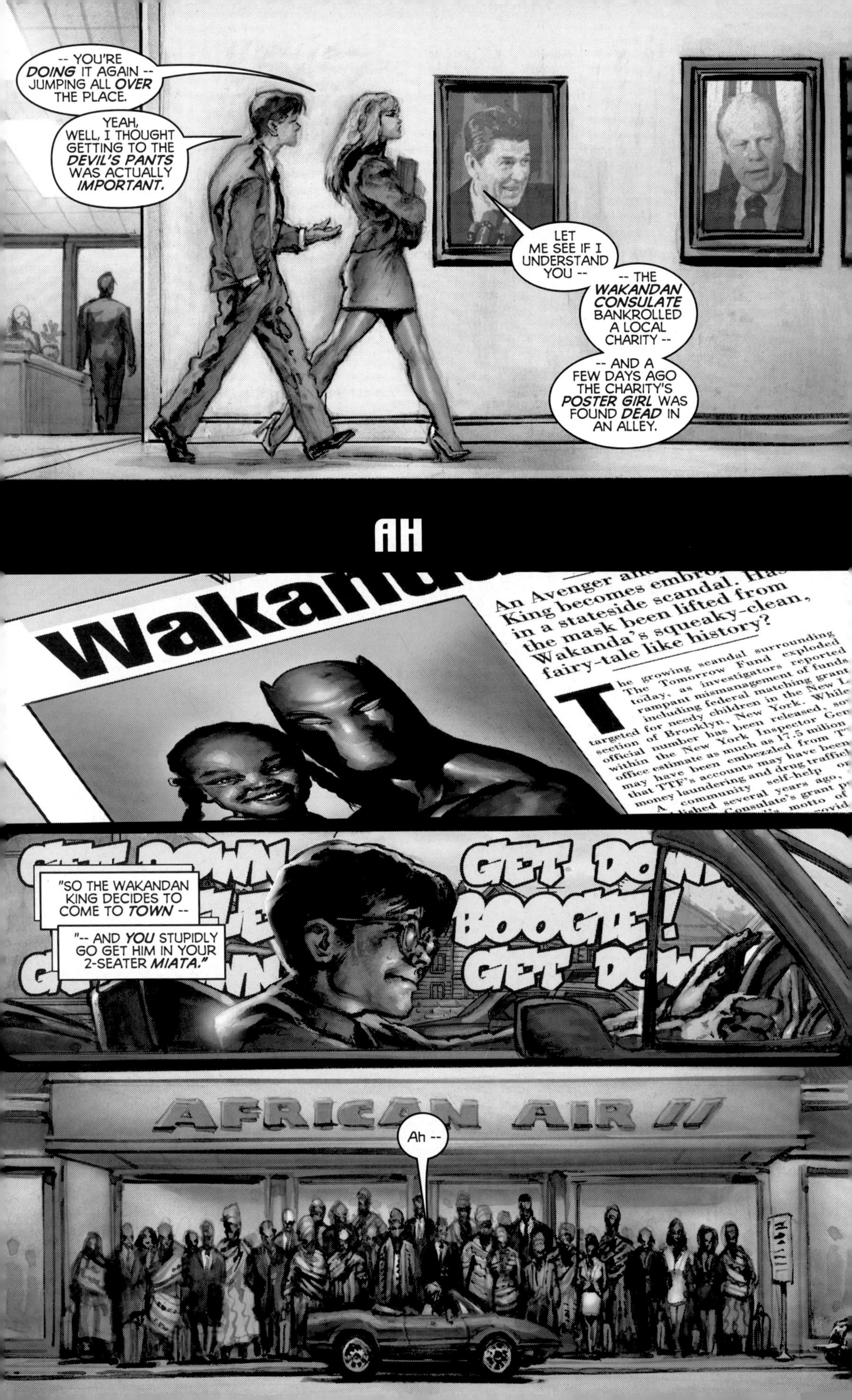
-- YOU'RE DOING IT AGAIN -- JUMPING ALL OVER THE PLACE.
YEAH, WELL, I THOUGHT GETTING TO THE DEVIL'S PANTS WAS ACTUALLY IMPORTANT.
LET ME SEE IF I UNDERSTAND YOU --
-- THE WAKANDAN CONSULATE BANKROLLED A LOCAL CHARITY --
-- AND A FEW DAYS AGO THE CHARITY'S POSTER GIRL WAS FOUND DEAD IN AN ALLEY.
AH
Wakand
An Avenger
King becomes
in a stateside scandal.
the mask been lifted from
Wakanda's squeaky-clean,
fairy-tale like history?
The growing scandal surrounding
The Tomorrow Fund exploded
today, as investigators reported
rampant mismanagement of funds
including federal matching grant
targeted for needy children in the New
section of Brooklyn, New York. While
official number has been released,
within the New York Inspector
office estimate as much as 17.5 milion
may have been embezzled from
that TTF's accounts may have been
money laundering and drug
A community self-help
several years ago,
Consulate's grant
motto
GET DOWN
GET DOWN
BOOGIE!
GET DOWN
"SO THE WAKANDAN KING DECIDES TO COME TO TOWN --
"-- AND YOU STUPIDLY GO GET HIM IN YOUR 2-SEATER MIATA."
AFRICAN AIR II
Ah --

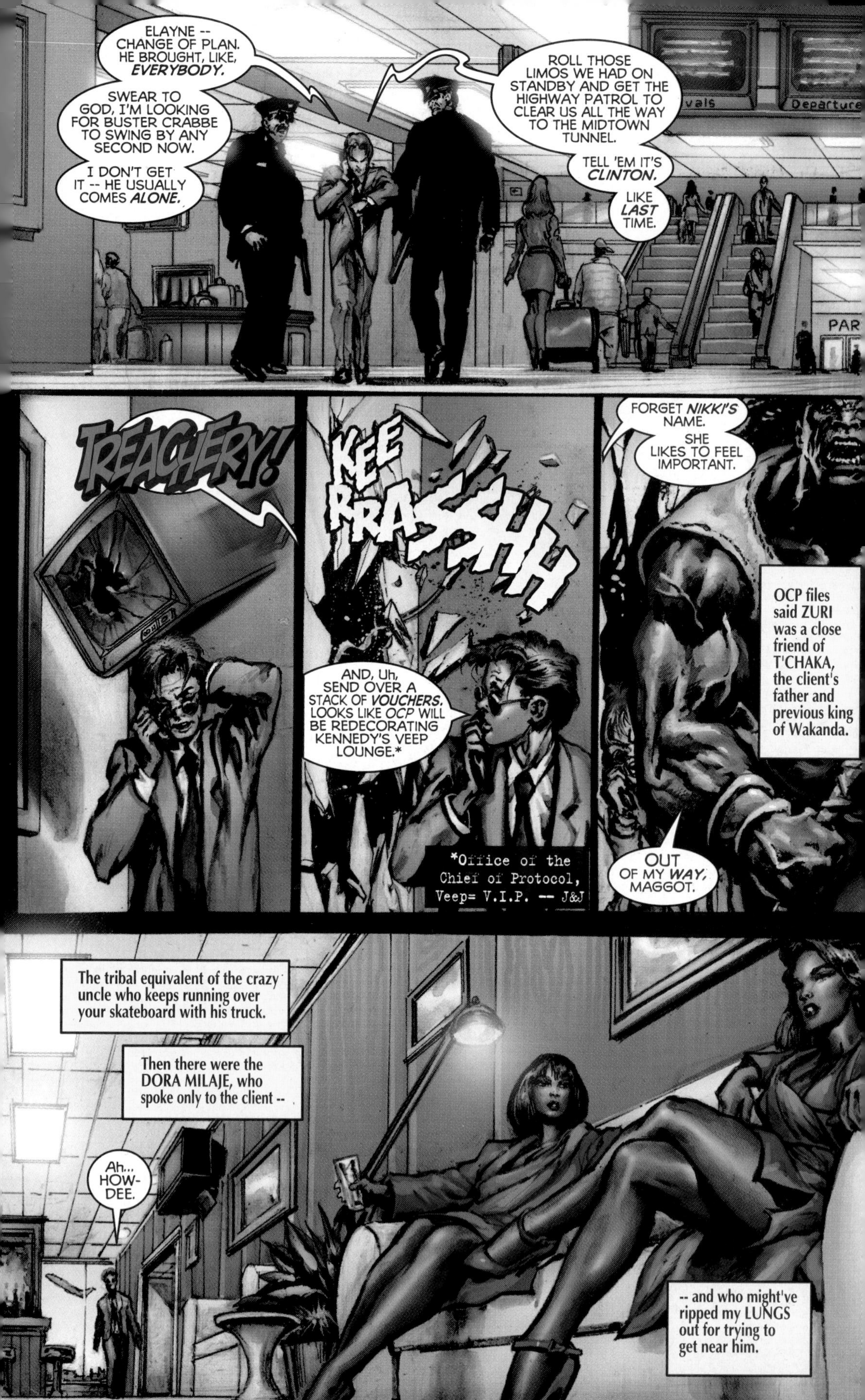
ELAYNE -- CHANGE OF PLAN. HE BROUGHT, LIKE, EVERYBODY.
SWEAR TO GOD, I'M LOOKING FOR BUSTER CRABBE TO SWING BY ANY SECOND NOW.
I DON'T GET IT -- HE USUALLY COMES ALONE.
ROLL THOSE LIMOS WE HAD ON STANDBY AND GET THE HIGHWAY PATROL TO CLEAR US ALL THE WAY TO THE MIDTOWN TUNNEL.
TELL 'EM IT'S CLINTON.
LIKE LAST TIME.
vals
Departure
PAR
TREACHERY!
KEE RRASSHH
AND, Uh, SEND OVER A STACK OF VOUCHERS. LOOKS LIKE OCP WILL BE REDECORATING KENNEDY'S VEEP LOUNGE.*
*Office of the Chief of Protocol, Veep= V.I.P. -- J&J
FORGET NIKKI'S NAME.
SHE LIKES TO FEEL IMPORTANT.
OCP files said ZURI was a close friend of T'CHAKA, the client's father and previous king of Wakanda.
OUT OF MY WAY, MAGGOT.
The tribal equivalent of the crazy uncle who keeps running over your skateboard with his truck.
Then there were the DORA MILAJE, who spoke only to the client --
Ah... HOW-DEE.
-- and who might've ripped my LUNGS out for trying to get near him.

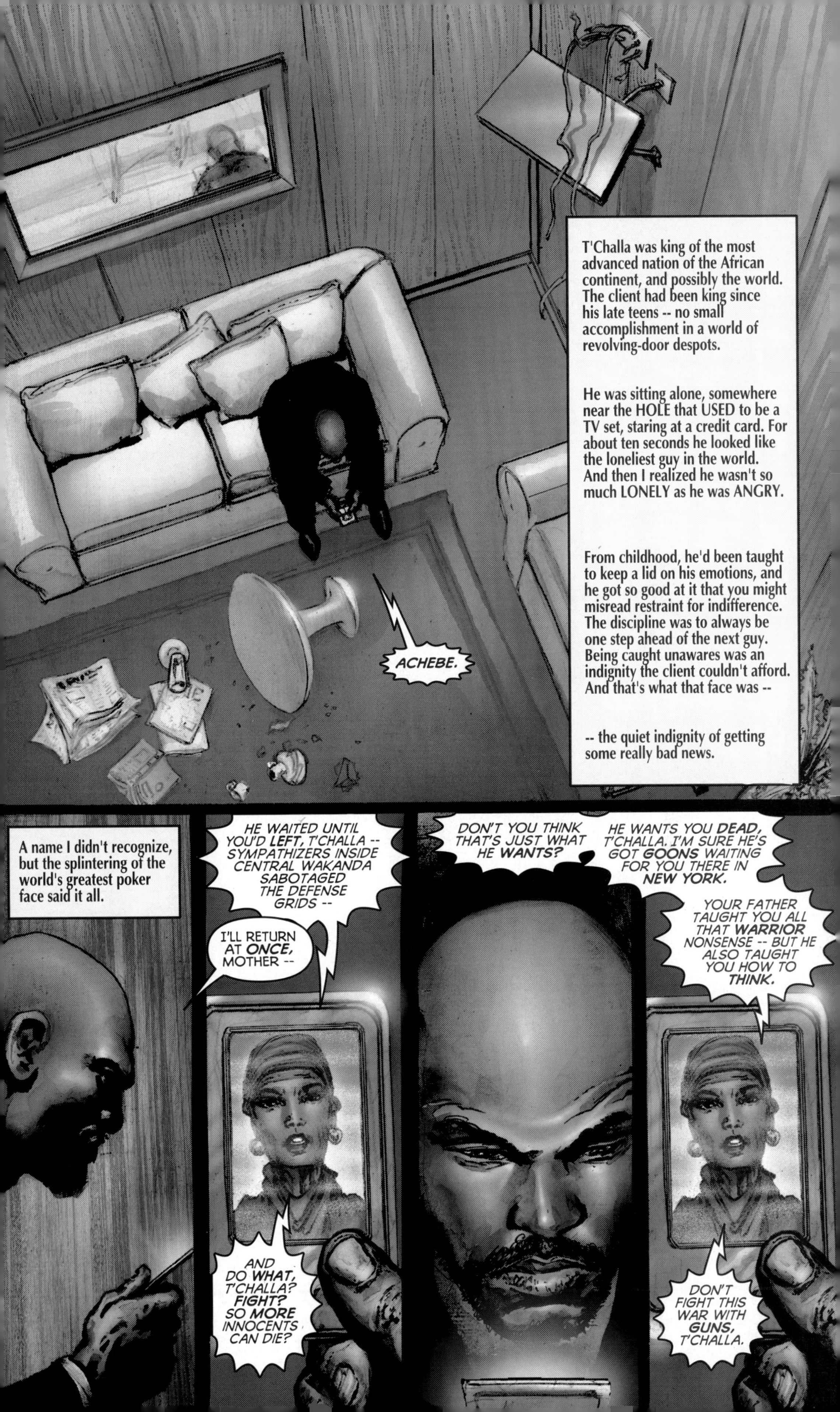

T'Challa was king of the most advanced nation of the African continent, and possibly the world. The client had been king since his late teens -- no small accomplishment in a world of revolving-door despots.
He was sitting alone, somewhere near the HOLE that USED to be a TV set, staring at a credit card. For about ten seconds he looked like the loneliest guy in the world. And then I realized he wasn't so much LONELY as he was ANGRY.
From childhood, he'd been taught to keep a lid on his emotions, and he got so good at it that you might misread restraint for indifference. The discipline was to always be one step ahead of the next guy. Being caught unawares was an indignity the client couldn't afford. And that's what that face was --
-- the quiet indignity of getting some really bad news.
ACHEBE.
A name I didn't recognize, but the splintering of the world's greatest poker face said it all.
HE WAITED UNTIL YOU'D LEFT, T'CHALLA -- SYMPATHIZERS INSIDE CENTRAL WAKANDA SABOTAGED THE DEFENSE GRIDS --
I'LL RETURN AT ONCE, MOTHER --
AND DO WHAT, T'CHALLA? FIGHT? SO MORE INNOCENTS CAN DIE?
DON'T YOU THINK THAT'S JUST WHAT HE WANTS?
HE WANTS YOU DEAD, T'CHALLA. I'M SURE HE'S GOT GOONS WAITING FOR YOU THERE IN NEW YORK.
YOUR FATHER TAUGHT YOU ALL THAT WARRIOR NONSENSE -- BUT HE ALSO TAUGHT YOU HOW TO THINK.
DON'T FIGHT THIS WAR WITH GUNS, T'CHALLA.

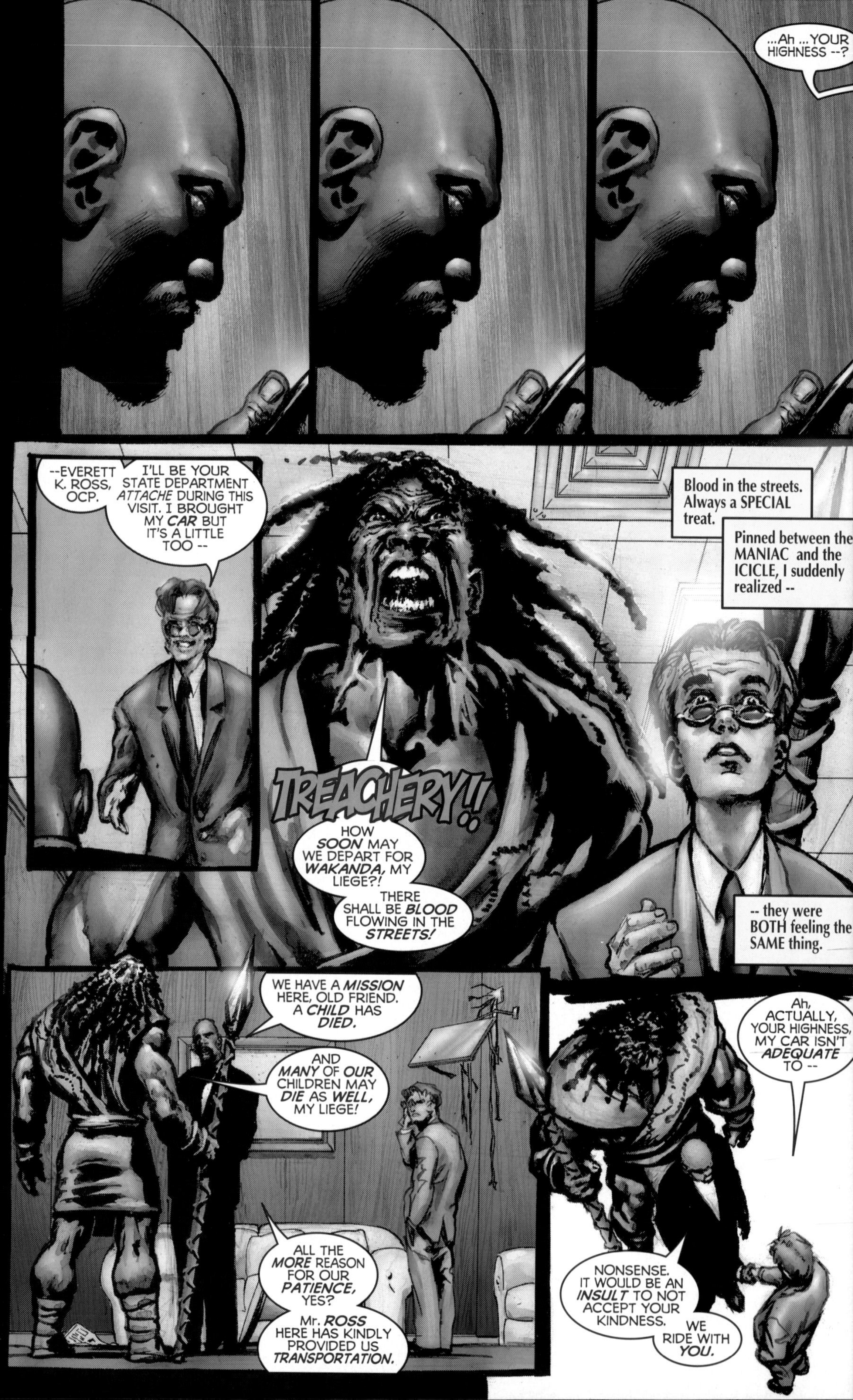
...Ah ...YOUR HIGHNESS --?
--EVERETT K. ROSS, OCP.
I'LL BE YOUR STATE DEPARTMENT ATTACHE DURING THIS VISIT. I BROUGHT MY CAR BUT IT'S A LITTLE TOO --
TREACHERY!!
HOW SOON MAY WE DEPART FOR WAKANDA, MY LIEGE?!
THERE SHALL BE BLOOD FLOWING IN THE STREETS!
Blood in the streets. Always a SPECIAL treat.
Pinned between the MANIAC and the ICICLE, I suddenly realized --
-- they were BOTH feeling the SAME thing.
WE HAVE A MISSION HERE, OLD FRIEND. A CHILD HAS DIED.
AND MANY OF OUR CHILDREN MAY DIE AS WELL, MY LIEGE!
ALL THE MORE REASON FOR OUR PATIENCE, YES?
Mr. ROSS HERE HAS KINDLY PROVIDED US TRANSPORTATION.
Ah, ACTUALLY, YOUR HIGHNESS, MY CAR ISN'T ADEQUATE TO --
NONSENSE. IT WOULD BE AN INSULT TO NOT ACCEPT YOUR KINDNESS.
WE RIDE WITH YOU.

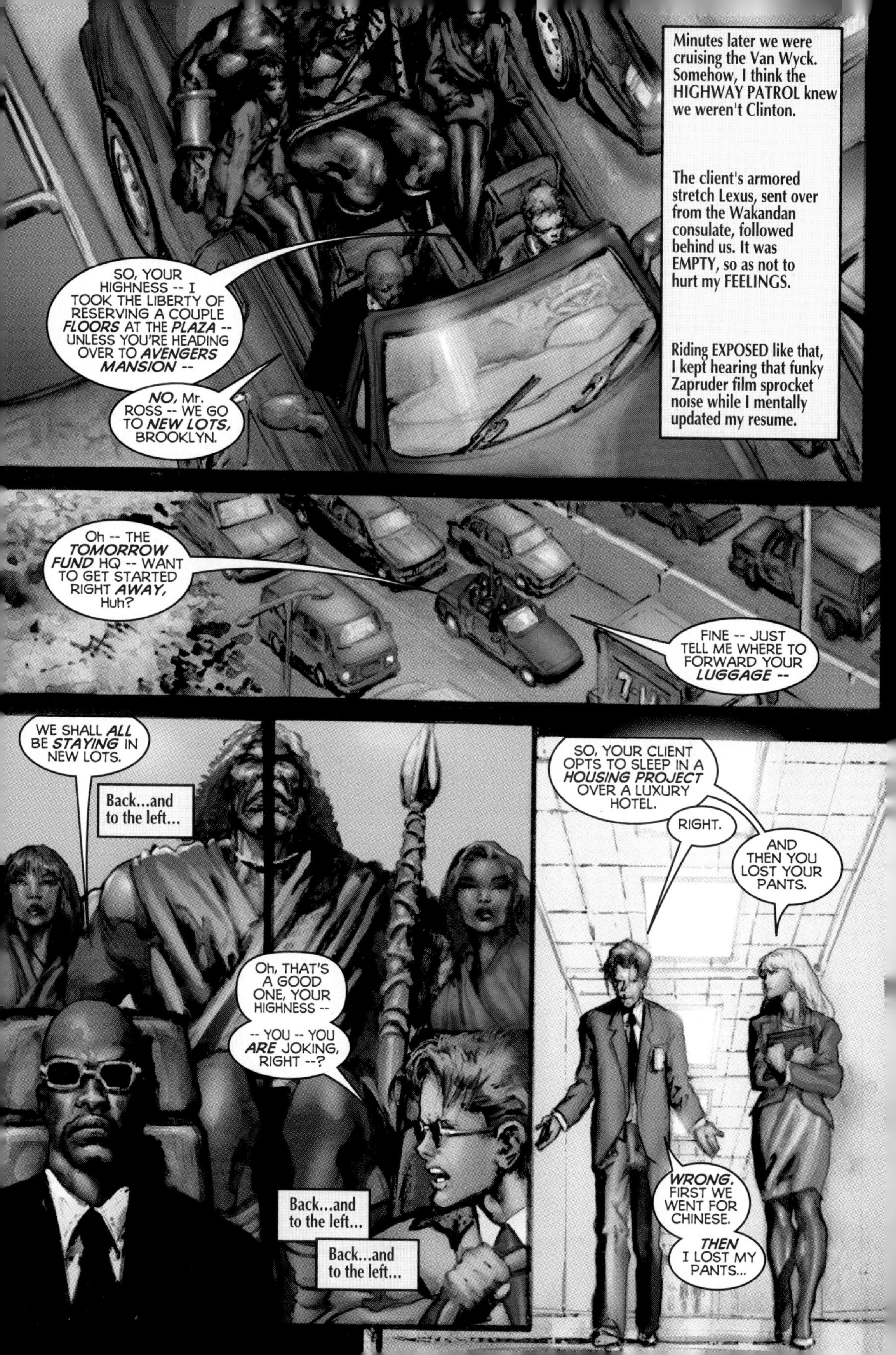

Minutes later we were cruising the Van Wyck. Somehow, I think the HIGHWAY PATROL knew we weren't Clinton.
The client's armored stretch Lexus, sent over from the Wakandan consulate, followed behind us. It was EMPTY, so as not to hurt my FEELINGS.
Riding EXPOSED like that, I kept hearing that funky Zapruder film sprocket noise while I mentally updated my resume.
SO, YOUR HIGHNESS -- I TOOK THE LIBERTY OF RESERVING A COUPLE FLOORS AT THE PLAZA -- UNLESS YOU'RE HEADING OVER TO AVENGERS MANSION --
NO, Mr. ROSS -- WE GO TO NEW LOTS, BROOKLYN.
Oh -- THE TOMORROW FUND HQ -- WANT TO GET STARTED RIGHT AWAY, Huh?
FINE -- JUST TELL ME WHERE TO FORWARD YOUR LUGGAGE --
WE SHALL ALL BE STAYING IN NEW LOTS.
Back...and to the left...
Oh, THAT'S A GOOD ONE, YOUR HIGHNESS --
-- YOU -- YOU ARE JOKING, RIGHT --?
Back...and to the left...
Back...and to the left...
SO, YOUR CLIENT OPTS TO SLEEP IN A HOUSING PROJECT OVER A LUXURY HOTEL.
RIGHT.
AND THEN YOU LOST YOUR PANTS.
WRONG. FIRST WE WENT FOR CHINESE.
THEN I LOST MY PANTS...

KUMUSTA KA

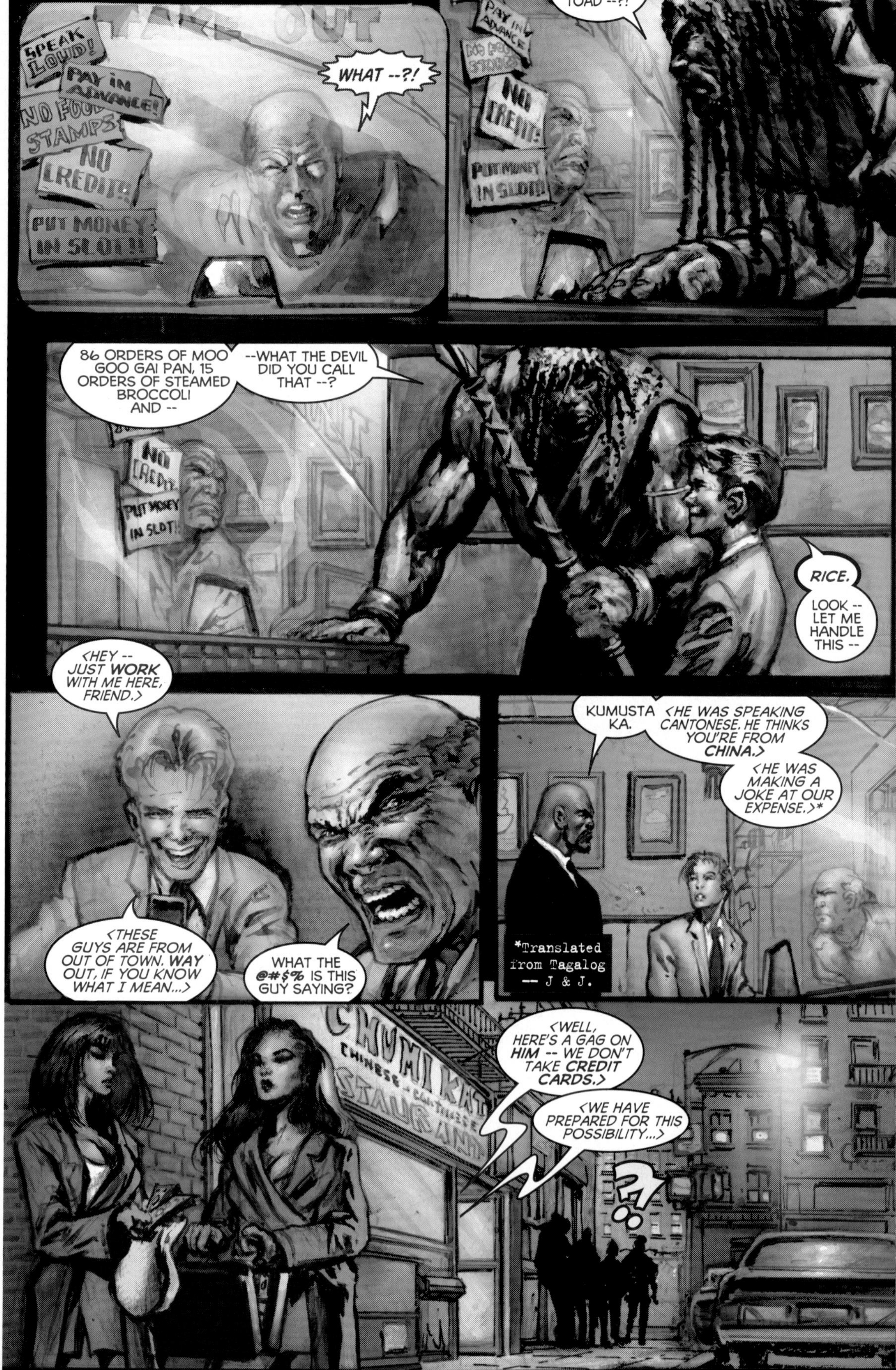
SPEAK LOUD!
PAY IN ADVANCE!
NO FOOD STAMPS!
NO CREDIT!!
PUT MONEY IN SLOT!!
WHAT --?!
ARE YOU *DEAF*, TOAD --?!
86 ORDERS OF MOO GOO GAI PAN, 15 ORDERS OF STEAMED BROCCOLI AND --
--WHAT THE DEVIL DID YOU CALL THAT --?
RICE.
LOOK -- LET ME HANDLE THIS --
<HEY -- JUST **WORK** WITH ME HERE, FRIEND.>
<THESE GUYS ARE FROM OUT OF TOWN. **WAY** OUT, IF YOU KNOW WHAT I MEAN...>
WHAT THE @#$% IS THIS GUY SAYING?
KUMUSTA KA.
<HE WAS SPEAKING CANTONESE. HE THINKS YOU'RE FROM **CHINA.**>
<HE WAS MAKING A JOKE AT OUR EXPENSE.>*
*Translated from Tagalog -- J & J.
<WELL, HERE'S A GAG ON **HIM** -- WE DON'T TAKE **CREDIT CARDS.**>
<WE HAVE PREPARED FOR THIS POSSIBILITY...>
?!

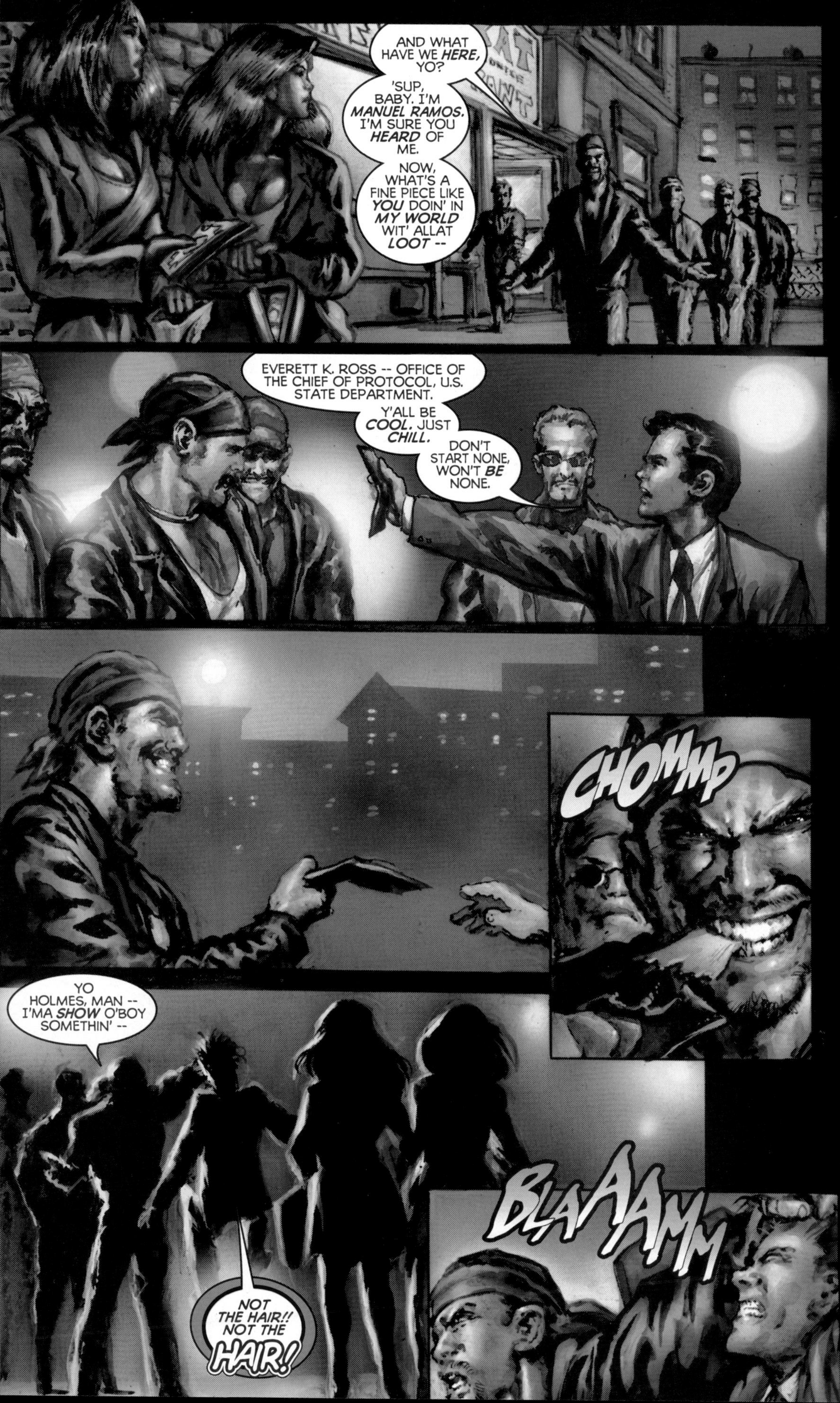

AND WHAT HAVE WE *HERE,* YO?
'SUP, BABY. I'M *MANUEL RAMOS.* I'M SURE YOU *HEARD* OF ME.
NOW, WHAT'S A FINE PIECE LIKE *YOU* DOIN' IN *MY WORLD* WIT' ALLAT *LOOT* --
EVERETT K. ROSS -- OFFICE OF THE CHIEF OF PROTOCOL, U.S. STATE DEPARTMENT.
Y'ALL BE *COOL.* JUST *CHILL.*
DON'T START NONE, WON'T *BE* NONE.
CHOMMP
YO HOLMES, MAN -- I'MA *SHOW* O'BOY SOMETHIN' --
BLAAAMM
NOT THE HAIR!! NOT THE HAIR!

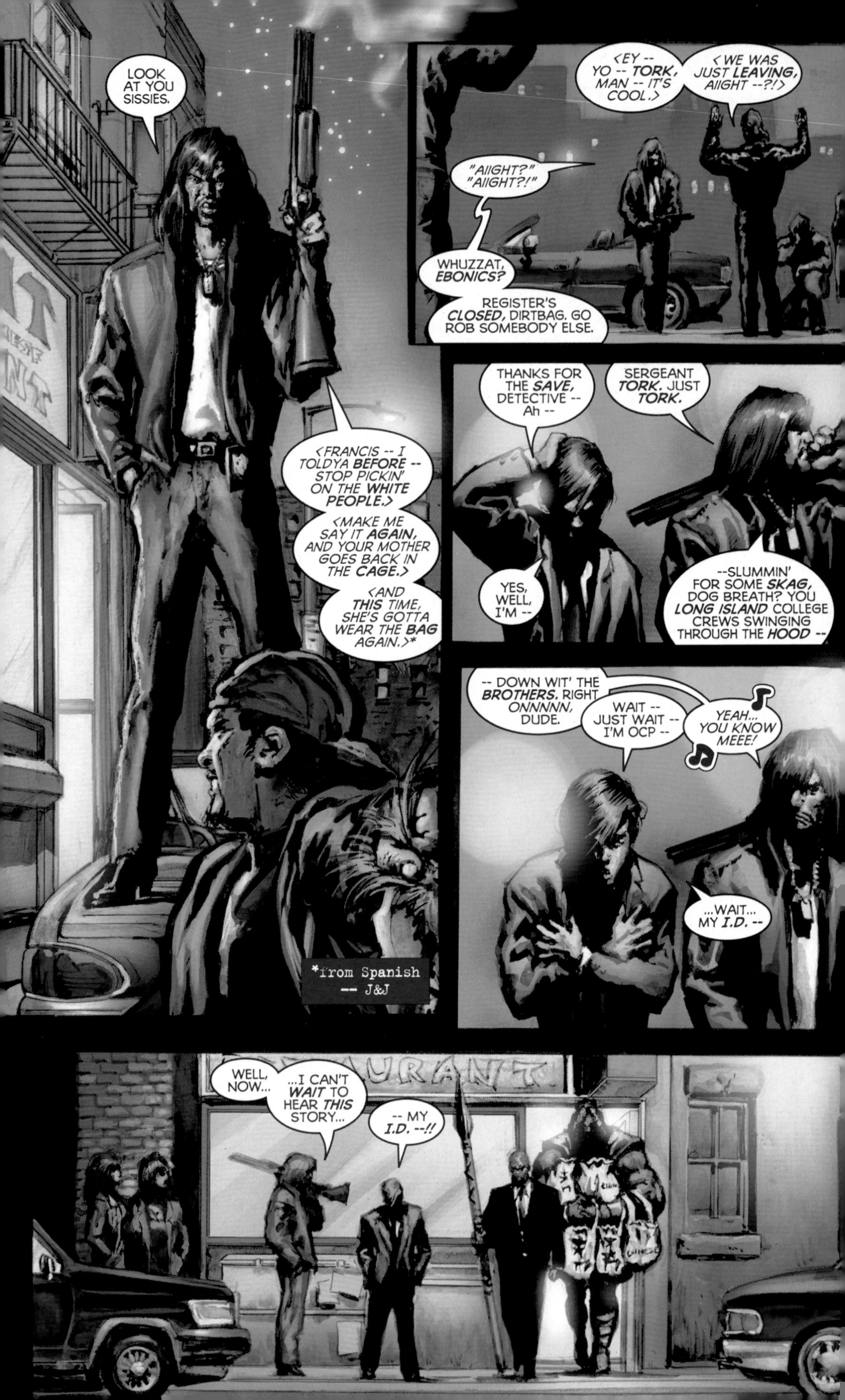
LOOK AT YOU SISSIES.
<EY -- YO -- TORK, MAN -- IT'S COOL.>
< WE WAS JUST LEAVING, AIIGHT --?!>
"AIIGHT?" "AIIGHT?!"
WHUZZAT, EBONICS?
REGISTER'S CLOSED, DIRTBAG. GO ROB SOMEBODY ELSE.
<FRANCIS -- I TOLDYA BEFORE -- STOP PICKIN' ON THE WHITE PEOPLE.>
<MAKE ME SAY IT AGAIN, AND YOUR MOTHER GOES BACK IN THE CAGE.>
<AND THIS TIME, SHE'S GOTTA WEAR THE BAG AGAIN.>*
*from Spanish -- J&J
THANKS FOR THE SAVE, DETECTIVE -- Ah --
SERGEANT TORK. JUST TORK.
YES, WELL, I'M --
--SLUMMIN' FOR SOME SKAG, DOG BREATH? YOU LONG ISLAND COLLEGE CREWS SWINGING THROUGH THE HOOD --
-- DOWN WIT' THE BROTHERS. RIGHT ONNNNN, DUDE.
WAIT -- JUST WAIT -- I'M OCP --
YEAH... YOU KNOW MEEE!
...WAIT... MY I.D. --
WELL, NOW...
...I CAN'T WAIT TO HEAR THIS STORY...
-- MY I.D. --!!

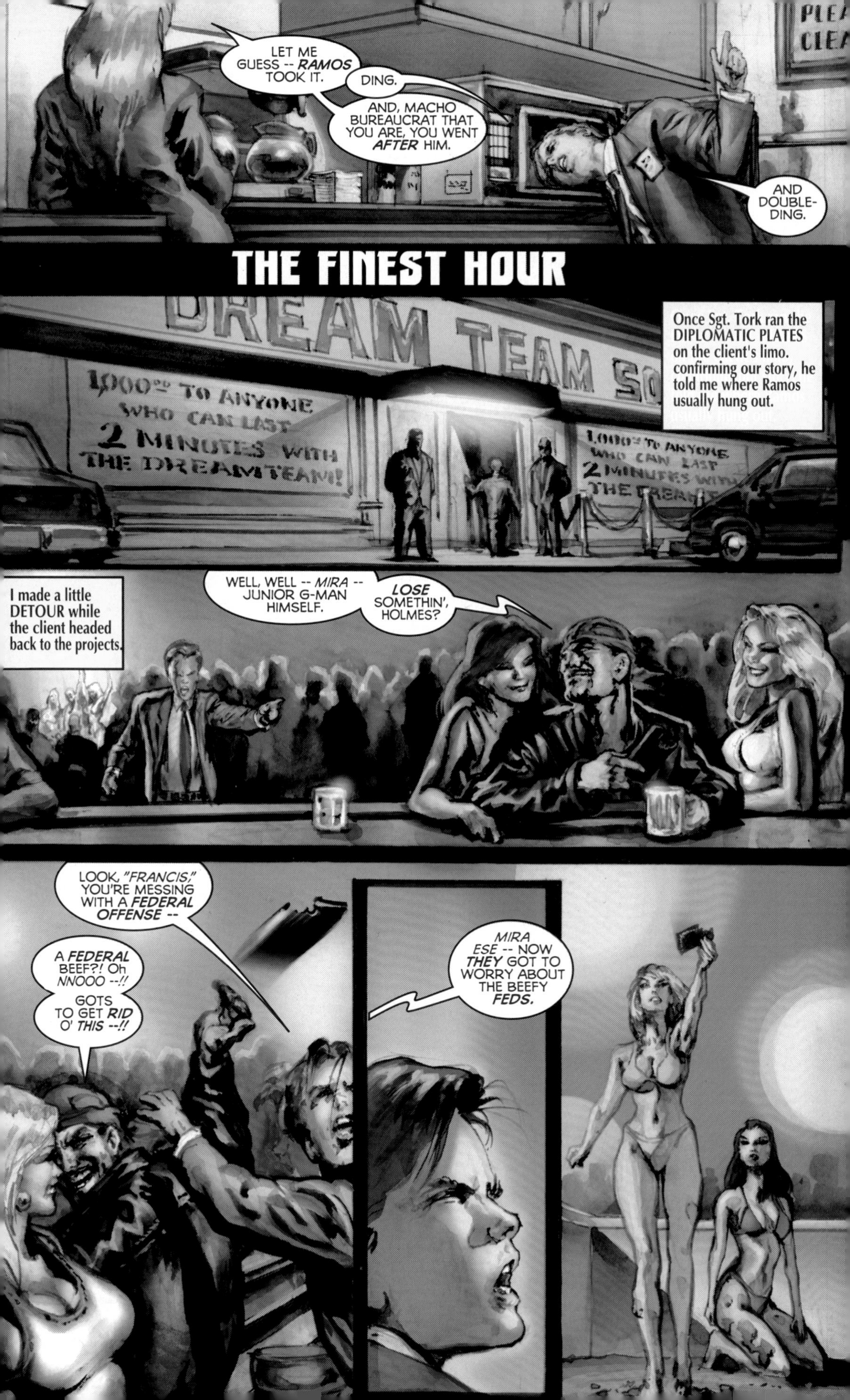

LET ME GUESS -- RAMOS TOOK IT.
DING.
AND, MACHO BUREAUCRAT THAT YOU ARE, YOU WENT AFTER HIM.
AND DOUBLE-DING.
THE FINEST HOUR
DREAM TEAM
Once Sgt. Tork ran the DIPLOMATIC PLATES on the client's limo. confirming our story, he told me where Ramos usually hung out.
1,000.00 TO ANYONE WHO CAN LAST 2 MINUTES WITH THE DREAMTEAM!
I made a little DETOUR while the client headed back to the projects.
WELL, WELL -- MIRA -- JUNIOR G-MAN HIMSELF.
LOSE SOMETHIN', HOLMES?
LOOK, "FRANCIS," YOU'RE MESSING WITH A FEDERAL OFFENSE --
A FEDERAL BEEF?! Oh NNOOO --!!
GOTS TO GET RID O' THIS --!!
MIRA ESE -- NOW THEY GOT TO WORRY ABOUT THE BEEFY FEDS.

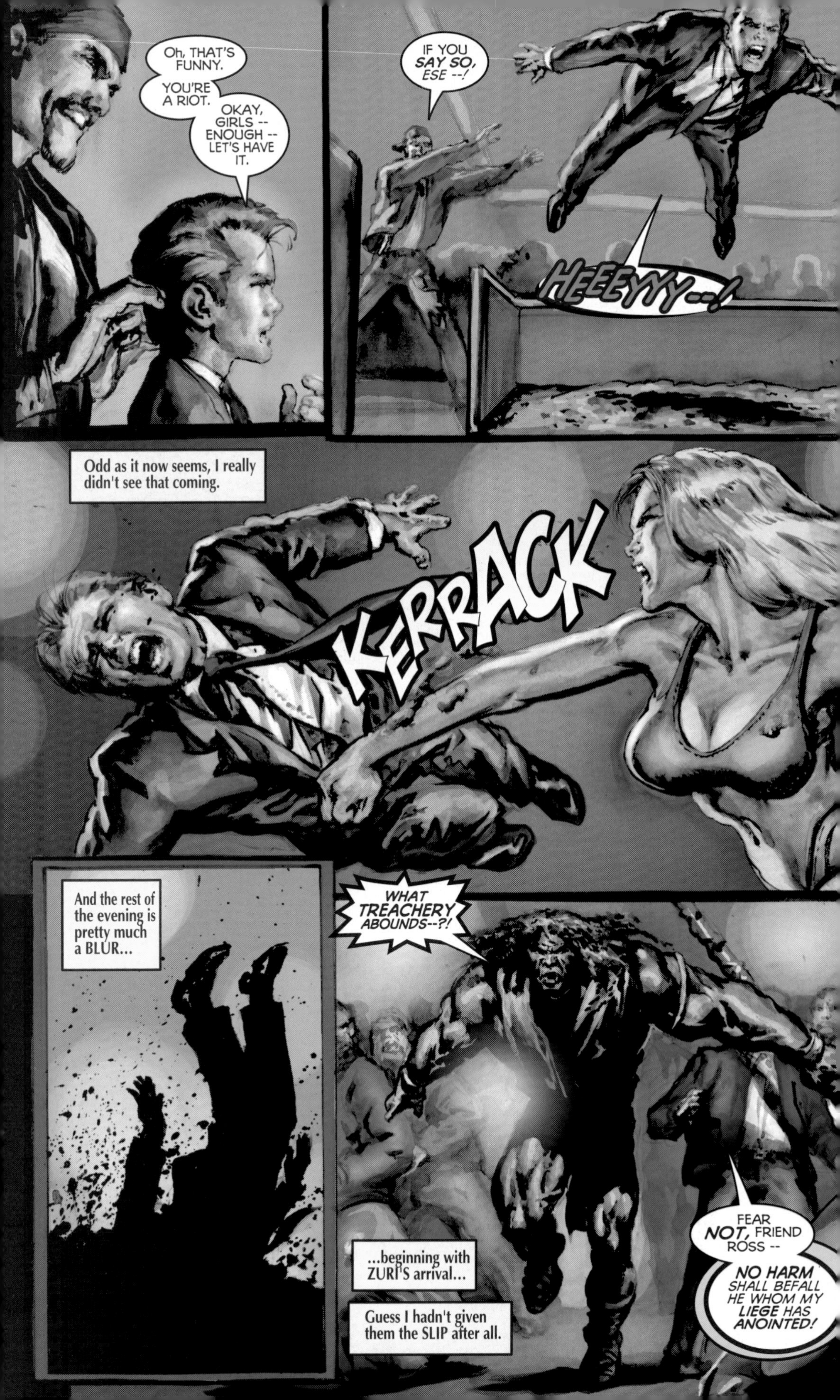
Oh, THAT'S FUNNY.
YOU'RE A RIOT.
OKAY, GIRLS -- ENOUGH -- LET'S HAVE IT.
IF YOU SAY SO, ESE --!
HEEEYYY--!
Odd as it now seems, I really didn't see that coming.
KERRACK
And the rest of the evening is pretty much a BLUR...
WHAT TREACHERY ABOUNDS--?!
...beginning with ZURI'S arrival...
Guess I hadn't given them the SLIP after all.
FEAR NOT, FRIEND ROSS --
NO HARM SHALL BEFALL HE WHOM MY LIEGE HAS ANOINTED!

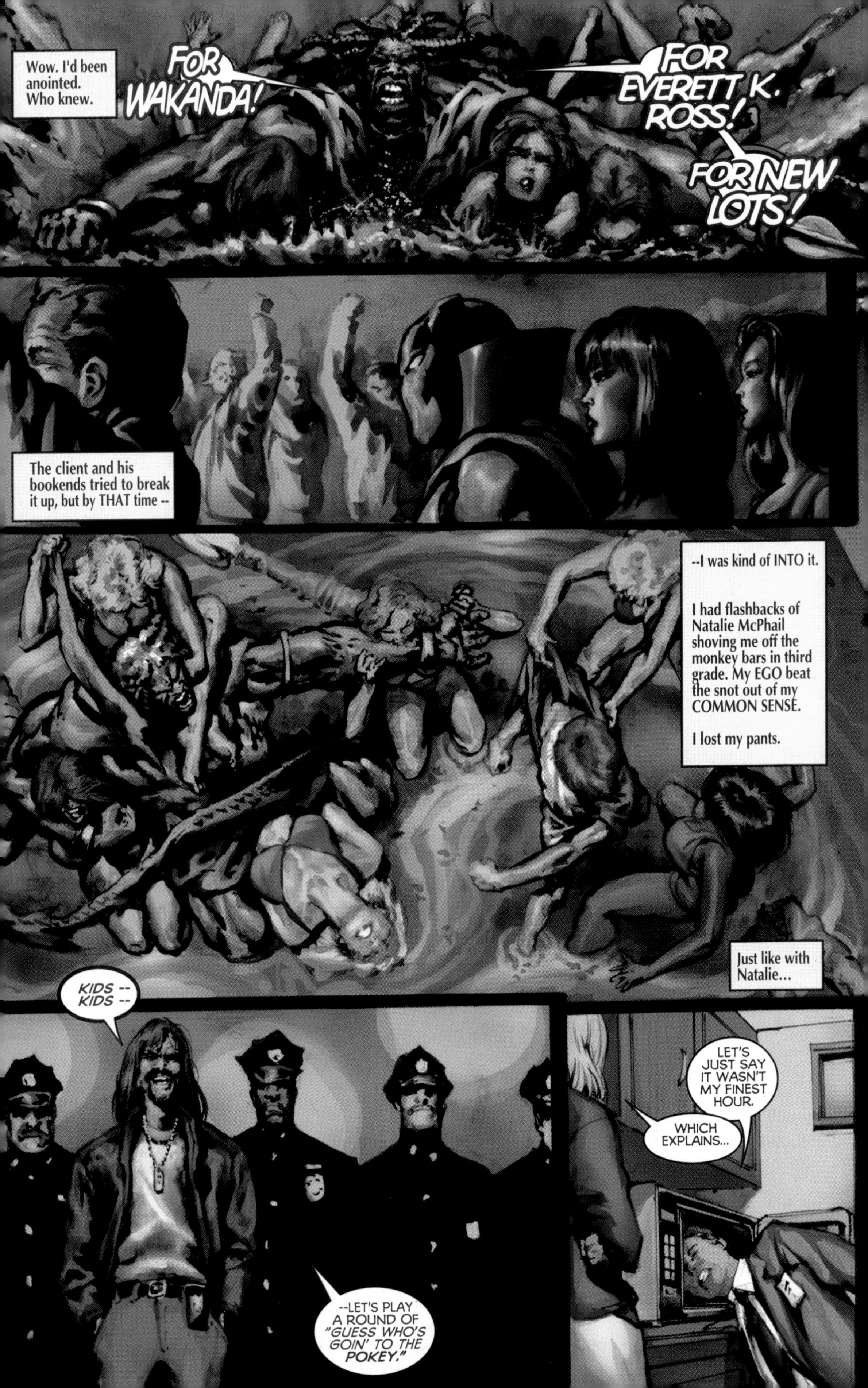
Wow. I'd been anointed. Who knew.
FOR WAKANDA!
FOR EVERETT K. ROSS!
FOR NEW LOTS!
The client and his bookends tried to break it up, but by THAT time --
--I was kind of INTO it.
I had flashbacks of Natalie McPhail shoving me off the monkey bars in third grade. My EGO beat the snot out of my COMMON SENSE.
I lost my pants.
Just like with Natalie...
KIDS -- KIDS --
--LET'S PLAY A ROUND OF "GUESS WHO'S GOIN' TO THE POKEY."
LET'S JUST SAY IT WASN'T MY FINEST HOUR.
WHICH EXPLAINS...

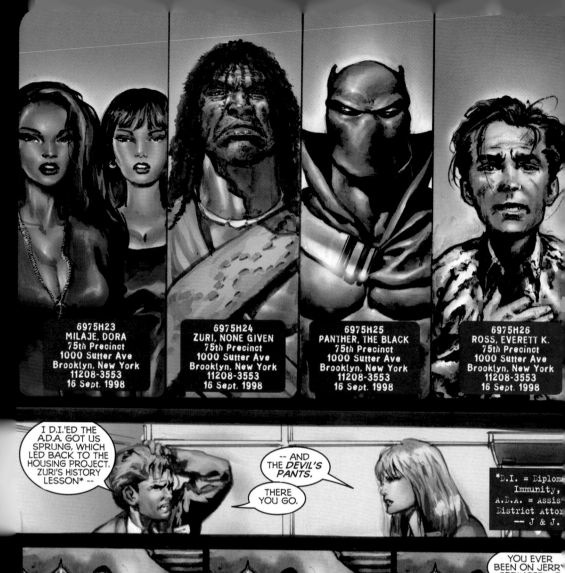

6975H23
MILAJE, DORA
75th Precinct
1000 Sutter Ave
Brooklyn, New York
11208-3553
16 Sept. 1998

6975H24
ZURI, NONE GIVEN
75th Precinct
1000 Sutter Ave
Brooklyn, New York
11208-3553
16 Sept. 1998

6975H25
PANTHER, THE BLACK
75th Precinct
1000 Sutter Ave
Brooklyn, New York
11208-3553
16 Sept. 1998

6975H26
ROSS, EVERETT K.
75th Precinct
1000 Sutter Ave
Brooklyn, New York
11208-3553
16 Sept. 1998

I D.I.'ED THE A.D.A GOT US SPRUNG, WHICH LED BACK TO THE HOUSING PROJECT. ZURI'S HISTORY LESSON* --

-- AND THE *DEVIL'S PANTS.*

THERE YOU GO.

*D.I. = Diploma[tic] Immunity, A.D.A. = Assis[tant] District Attor[ney] -- J & J.

YOU EVER BEEN ON JERR[Y] SPRINGER --?

SO -- WHERE *WAS* THE CLIENT --?

STILL INVESTIGATING THE *TOMORROW FUND* THING.

HE DECIDED TO PAY A VISIT TO THE FUND'S *DIRECTOR* -- *AFTER* VISITING HOURS...

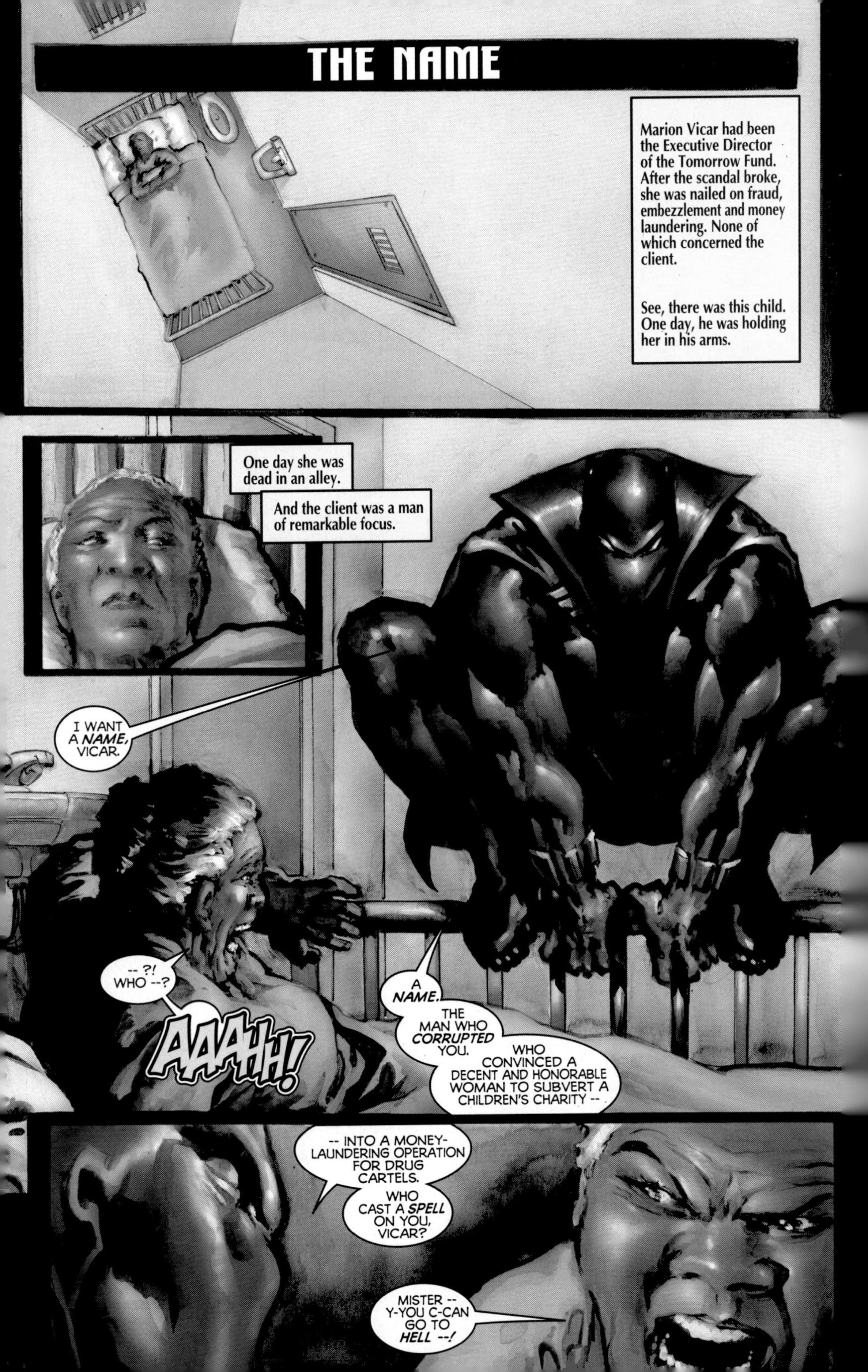
THE NAME
Marion Vicar had been the Executive Director of the Tomorrow Fund. After the scandal broke, she was nailed on fraud, embezzlement and money laundering. None of which concerned the client.
See, there was this child. One day, he was holding her in his arms.
One day she was dead in an alley.
And the client was a man of remarkable focus.
I WANT A NAME, VICAR.
-- ?! WHO --?
AAAHH!
A NAME.
THE MAN WHO CORRUPTED YOU.
WHO CONVINCED A DECENT AND HONORABLE WOMAN TO SUBVERT A CHILDREN'S CHARITY --
-- INTO A MONEY-LAUNDERING OPERATION FOR DRUG CARTELS.
WHO CAST A SPELL ON YOU, VICAR?
MISTER -- Y-YOU C-CAN GO TO HELL --!

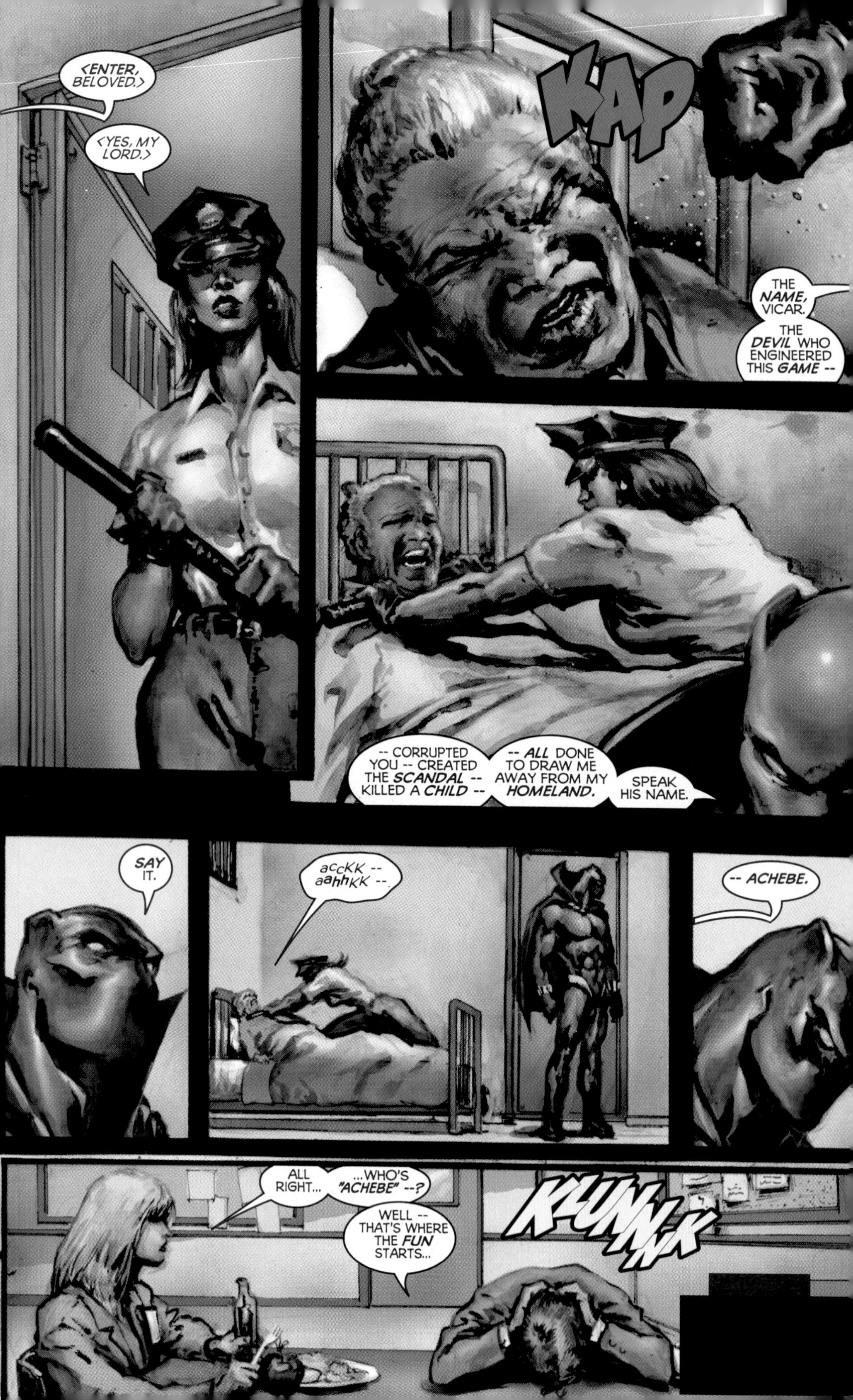

<ENTER, BELOVED.>
<YES, MY LORD.>
KAP
THE NAME, VICAR.
THE DEVIL WHO ENGINEERED THIS GAME --
-- CORRUPTED YOU -- CREATED THE SCANDAL -- KILLED A CHILD --
-- ALL DONE TO DRAW ME AWAY FROM MY HOMELAND.
SPEAK HIS NAME.
SAY IT.
acckk -- aahhkk --.
-- ACHEBE.
ALL RIGHT...
...WHO'S "ACHEBE" --?
WELL -- THAT'S WHERE THE FUN STARTS...
KLUNNNK

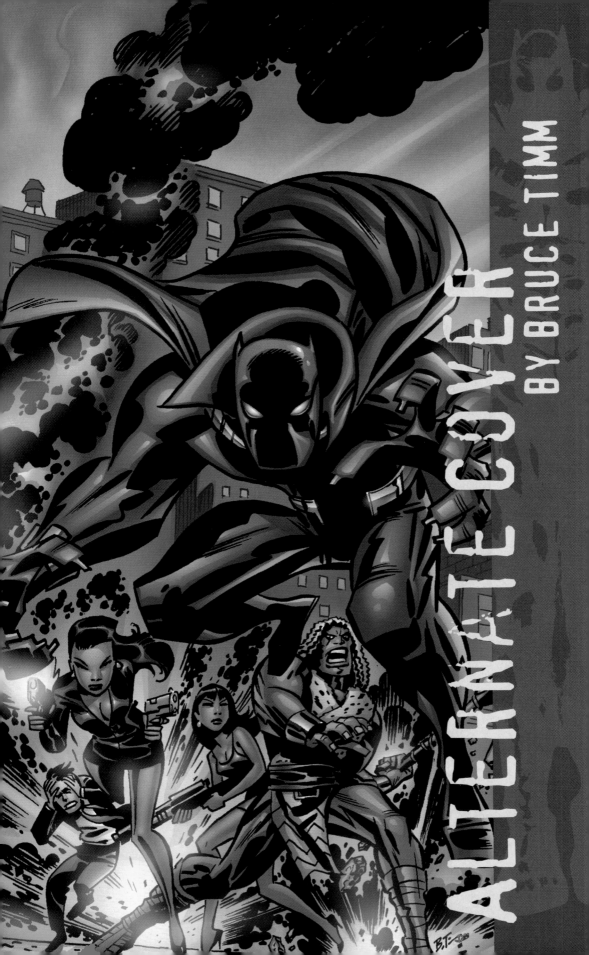

ALTERNATE COVER BY BRUCE TIMM

CHAPTER 3

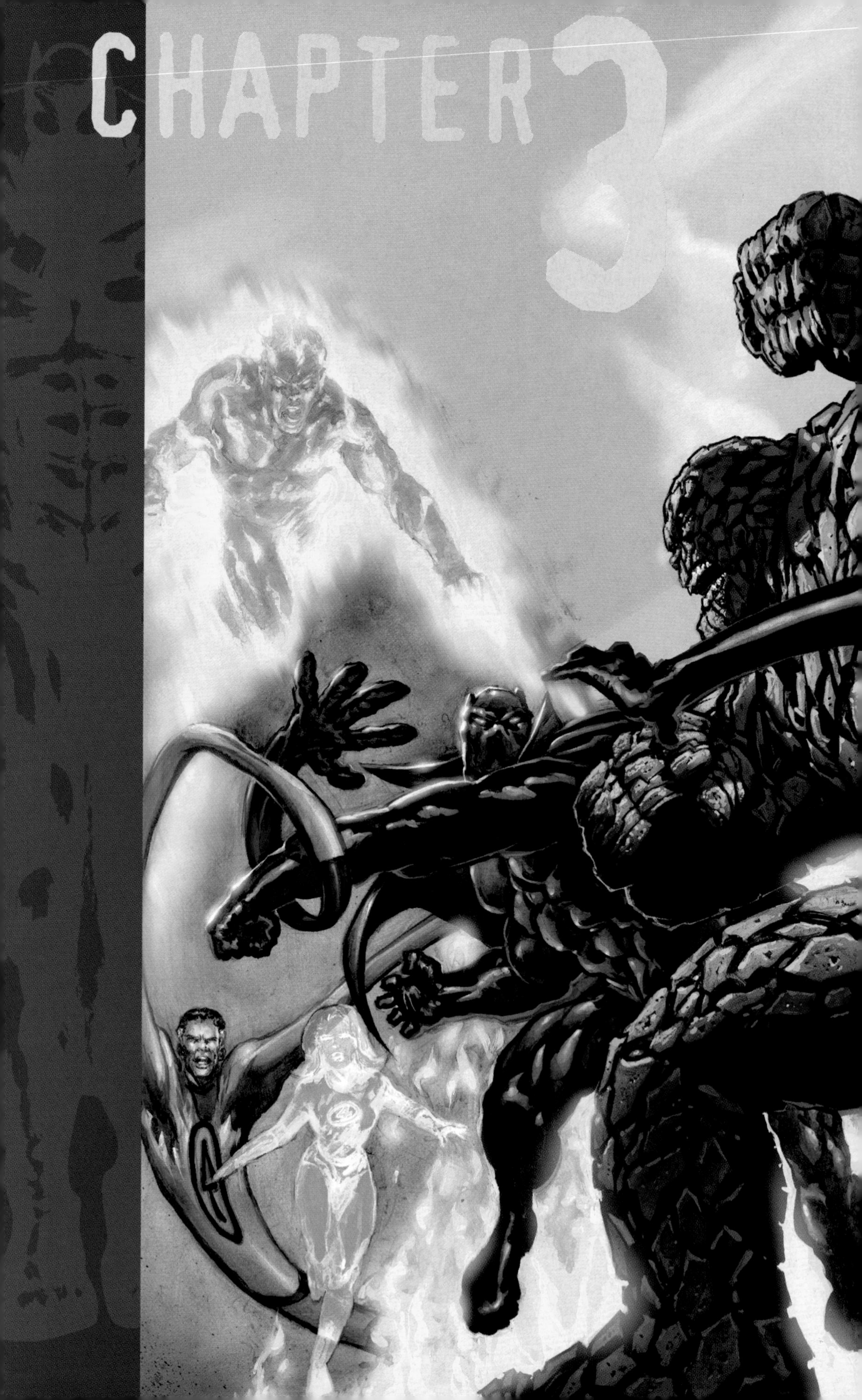

HEART AND SOLE

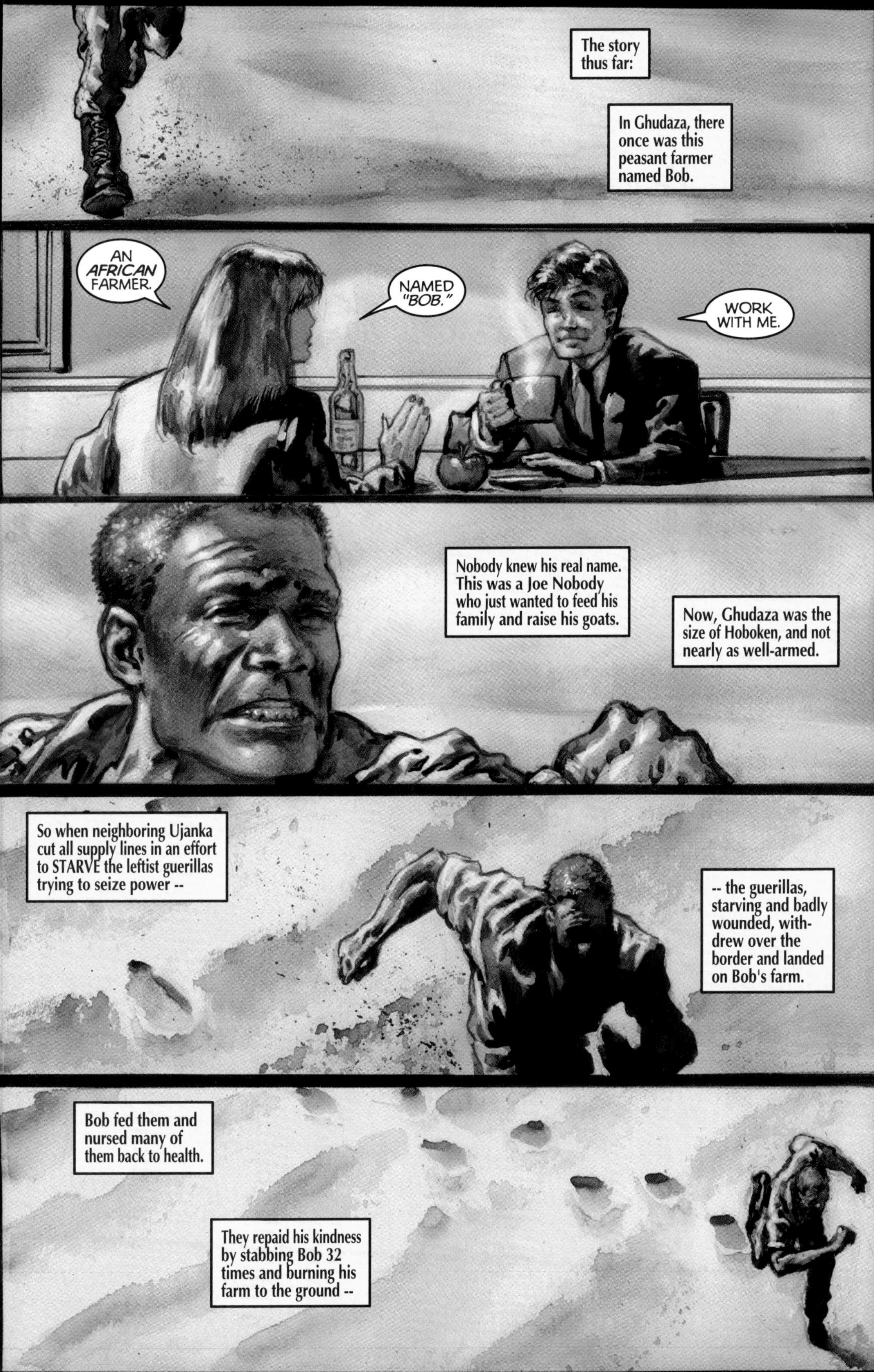
The story thus far:
In Ghudaza, there once was this peasant farmer named Bob.
AN AFRICAN FARMER.
NAMED "BOB."
WORK WITH ME.
Nobody knew his real name. This was a Joe Nobody who just wanted to feed his family and raise his goats.
Now, Ghudaza was the size of Hoboken, and not nearly as well-armed.
So when neighboring Ujanka cut all supply lines in an effort to STARVE the leftist guerillas trying to seize power --
-- the guerillas, starving and badly wounded, withdrew over the border and landed on Bob's farm.
Bob fed them and nursed many of them back to health.
They repaid his kindness by stabbing Bob 32 times and burning his farm to the ground --

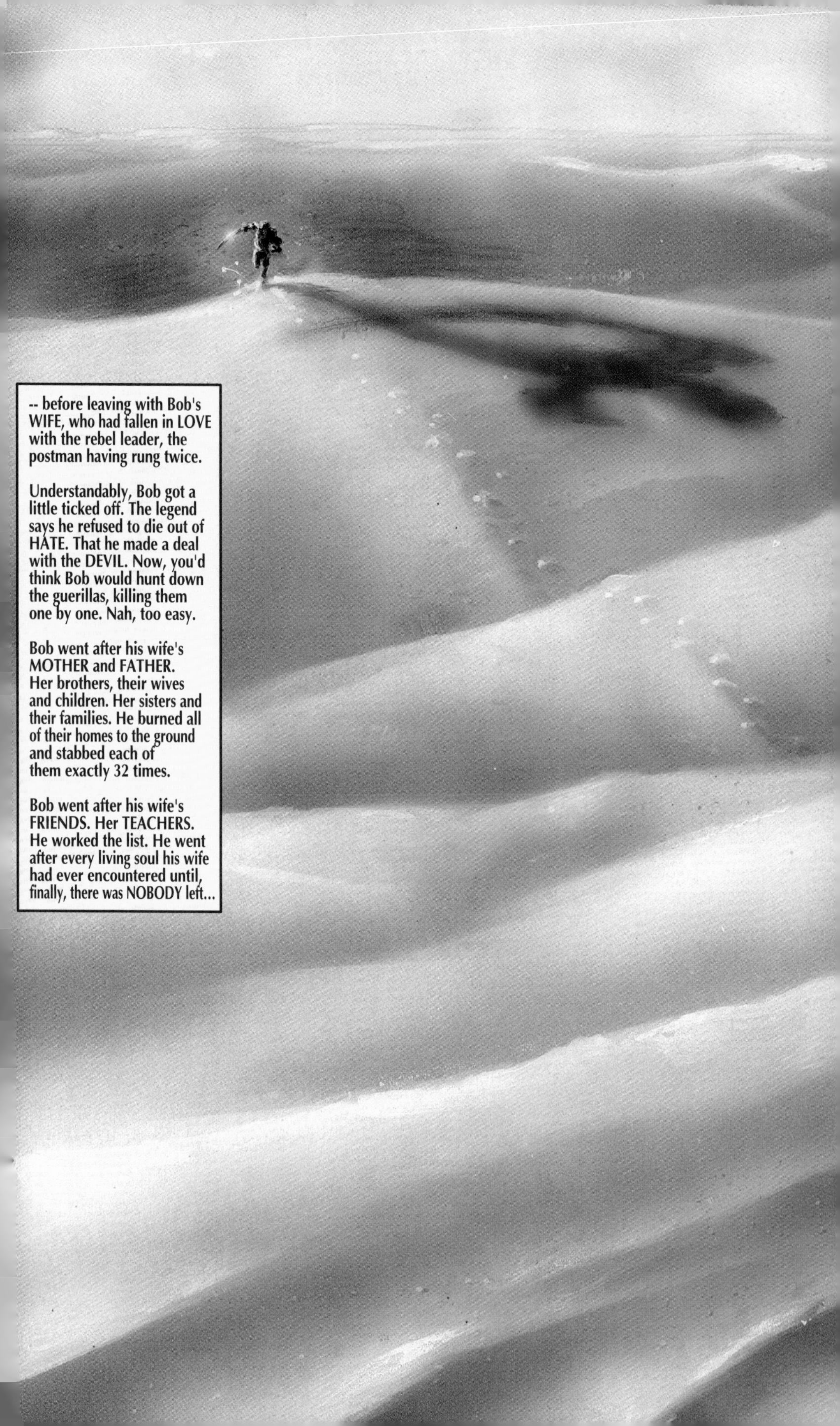
-- before leaving with Bob's WIFE, who had fallen in LOVE with the rebel leader, the postman having rung twice.
Understandably, Bob got a little ticked off. The legend says he refused to die out of HATE. That he made a deal with the DEVIL. Now, you'd think Bob would hunt down the guerillas, killing them one by one. Nah, too easy.
Bob went after his wife's MOTHER and FATHER. Her brothers, their wives and children. Her sisters and their families. He burned all of their homes to the ground and stabbed each of them exactly 32 times.
Bob went after his wife's FRIENDS. Her TEACHERS. He worked the list. He went after every living soul his wife had ever encountered until, finally, there was NOBODY left...

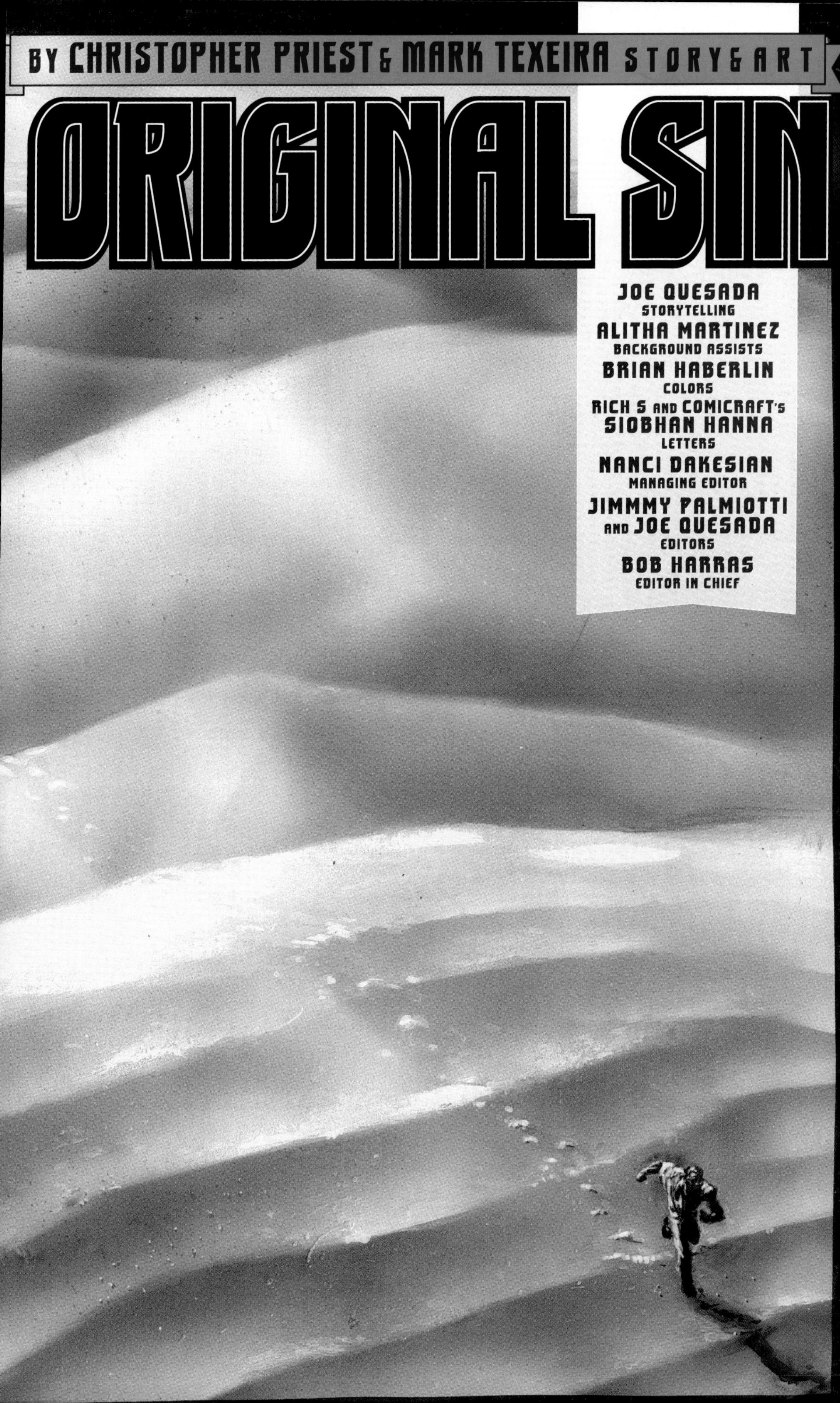
BY CHRISTOPHER PRIEST & MARK TEXEIRA STORY & ART
ORIGINAL SIN
JOE QUESADA
STORYTELLING
ALITHA MARTINEZ
BACKGROUND ASSISTS
BRIAN HABERLIN
COLORS
RICH S AND COMICRAFT'S
SIOBHAN HANNA
LETTERS
NANCI DAKESIAN
MANAGING EDITOR
JIMMMY PALMIOTTI
AND JOE QUESADA
EDITORS
BOB HARRAS
EDITOR IN CHIEF

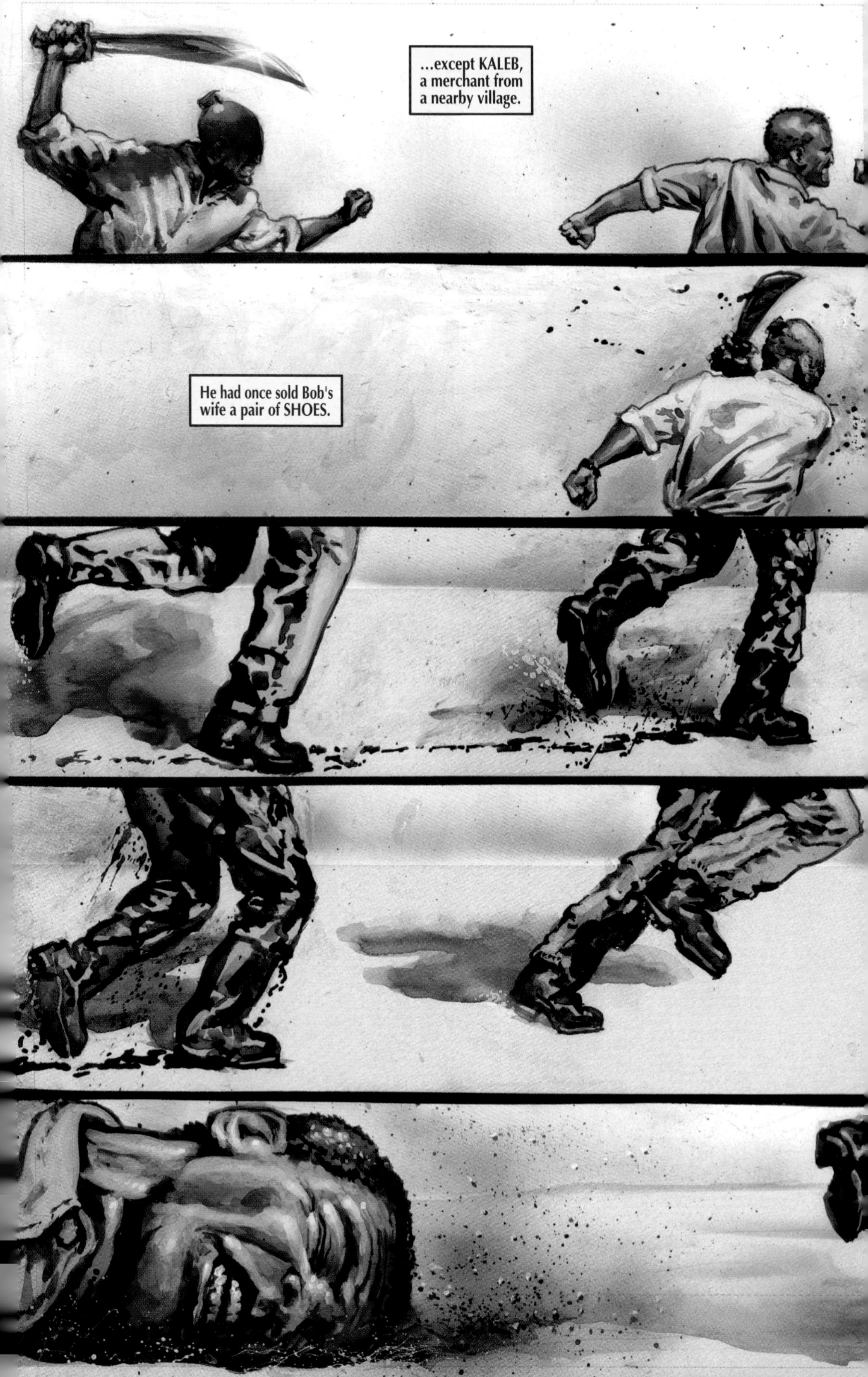
...except KALEB, a merchant from a nearby village.
He had once sold Bob's wife a pair of SHOES.

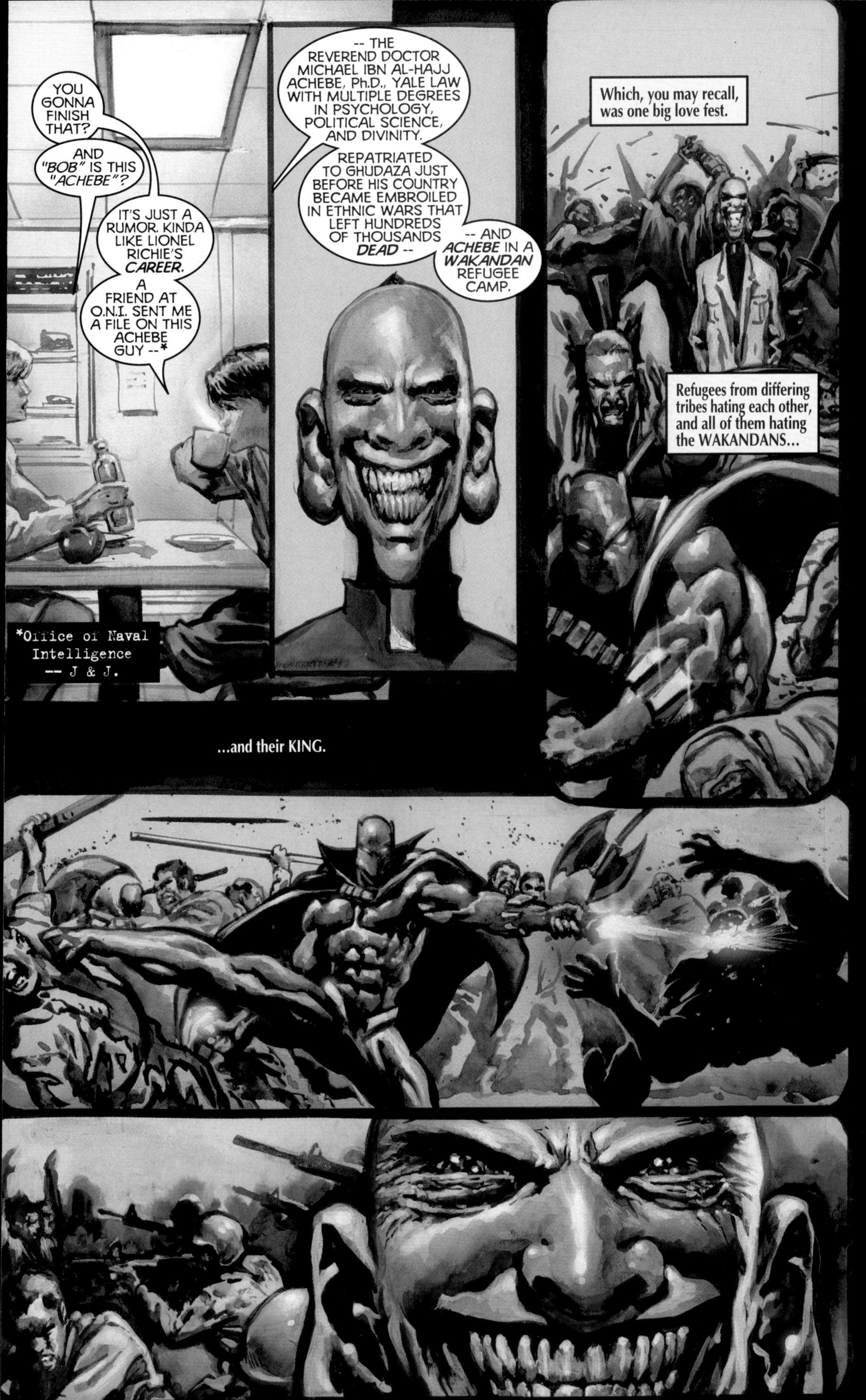
YOU GONNA FINISH THAT?
AND "BOB" IS THIS "ACHEBE"?
IT'S JUST A RUMOR. KINDA LIKE LIONEL RICHIE'S CAREER.
A FRIEND AT O.N.I. SENT ME A FILE ON THIS ACHEBE GUY --*
*Office of Naval Intelligence -- J & J.
-- THE REVEREND DOCTOR MICHAEL IBN AL-HAJJ ACHEBE, Ph.D., YALE LAW WITH MULTIPLE DEGREES IN PSYCHOLOGY, POLITICAL SCIENCE, AND DIVINITY.
REPATRIATED TO GHUDAZA JUST BEFORE HIS COUNTRY BECAME EMBROILED IN ETHNIC WARS THAT LEFT HUNDREDS OF THOUSANDS DEAD --
-- AND ACHEBE IN A WAKANDAN REFUGEE CAMP.
Which, you may recall, was one big love fest.
Refugees from differing tribes hating each other, and all of them hating the WAKANDANS...
...and their KING.

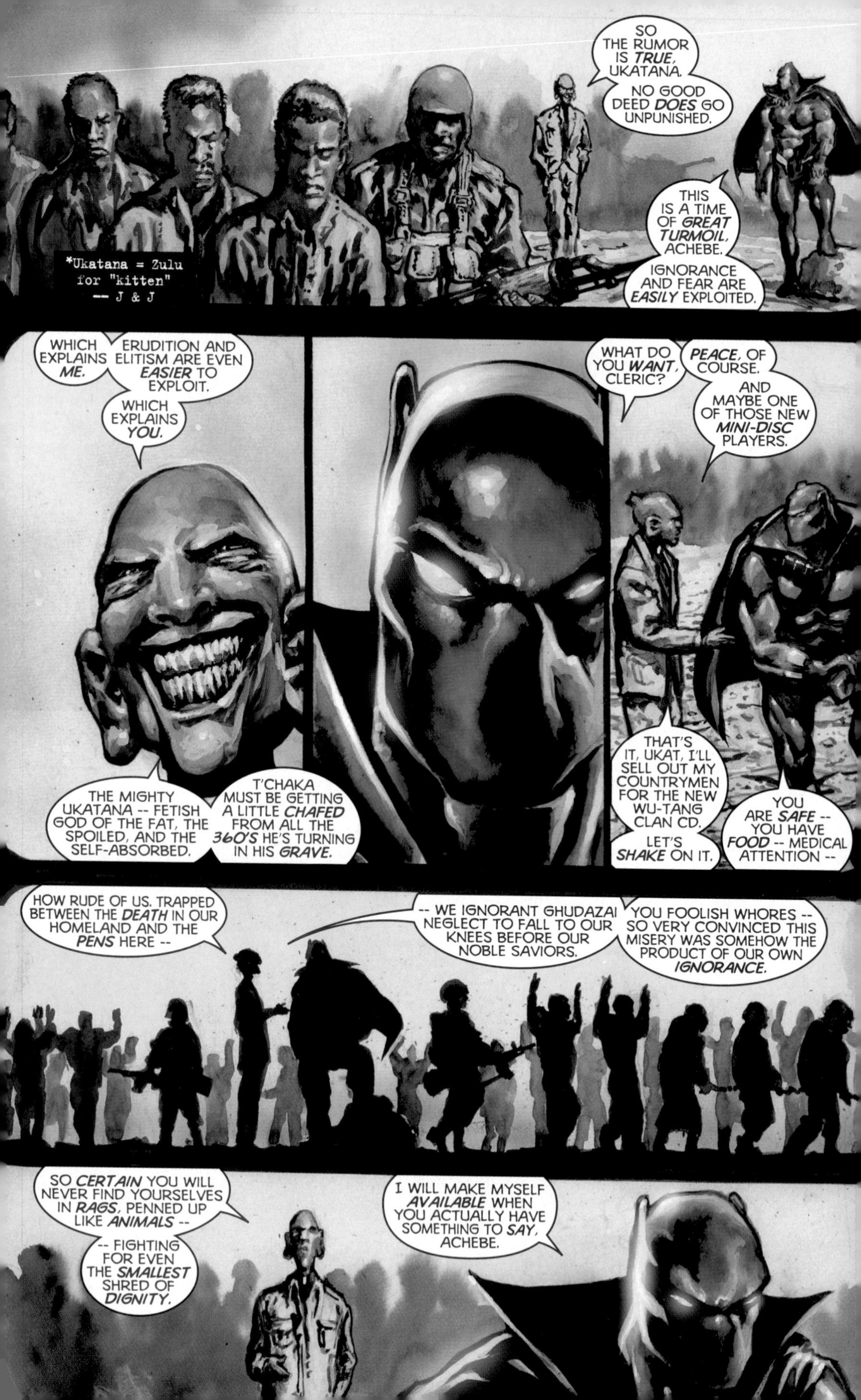
*Ukatana = Zulu for "kitten" -- J & J
SO THE RUMOR IS TRUE, UKATANA.
NO GOOD DEED DOES GO UNPUNISHED.
THIS IS A TIME OF GREAT TURMOIL, ACHEBE.
IGNORANCE AND FEAR ARE EASILY EXPLOITED.
WHICH EXPLAINS ME.
ERUDITION AND ELITISM ARE EVEN EASIER TO EXPLOIT.
WHICH EXPLAINS YOU.
THE MIGHTY UKATANA -- FETISH GOD OF THE FAT, THE SPOILED, AND THE SELF-ABSORBED.
T'CHAKA MUST BE GETTING A LITTLE CHAFED FROM ALL THE 360'S HE'S TURNING IN HIS GRAVE.
WHAT DO YOU WANT, CLERIC?
PEACE, OF COURSE.
AND MAYBE ONE OF THOSE NEW MINI-DISC PLAYERS.
THAT'S IT, UKAT, I'LL SELL OUT MY COUNTRYMEN FOR THE NEW WU-TANG CLAN CD.
LET'S SHAKE ON IT.
YOU ARE SAFE -- YOU HAVE FOOD -- MEDICAL ATTENTION --
HOW RUDE OF US. TRAPPED BETWEEN THE DEATH IN OUR HOMELAND AND THE PENS HERE --
-- WE IGNORANT GHUDAZAI NEGLECT TO FALL TO OUR KNEES BEFORE OUR NOBLE SAVIORS.
YOU FOOLISH WHORES -- SO VERY CONVINCED THIS MISERY WAS SOMEHOW THE PRODUCT OF OUR OWN IGNORANCE.
SO CERTAIN YOU WILL NEVER FIND YOURSELVES IN RAGS, PENNED UP LIKE ANIMALS --
-- FIGHTING FOR EVEN THE SMALLEST SHRED OF DIGNITY.
I WILL MAKE MYSELF AVAILABLE WHEN YOU ACTUALLY HAVE SOMETHING TO SAY, ACHEBE.

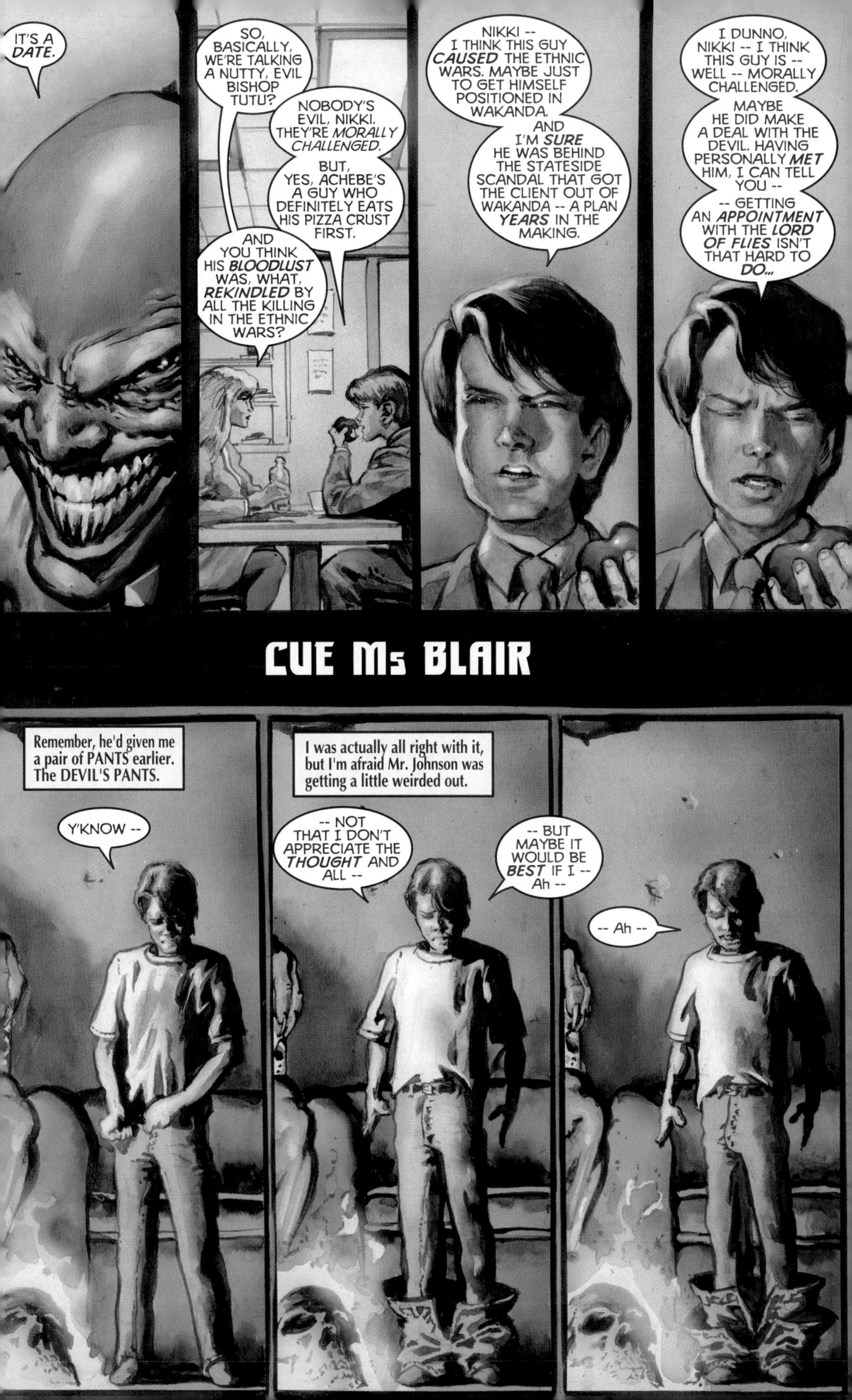

IT'S A DATE.
SO, BASICALLY, WE'RE TALKING A NUTTY, EVIL BISHOP TUTU?
NOBODY'S EVIL, NIKKI. THEY'RE MORALLY CHALLENGED.
BUT, YES, ACHEBE'S A GUY WHO DEFINITELY EATS HIS PIZZA CRUST FIRST.
AND YOU THINK HIS BLOODLUST WAS, WHAT, REKINDLED BY ALL THE KILLING IN THE ETHNIC WARS?
NIKKI -- I THINK THIS GUY CAUSED THE ETHNIC WARS. MAYBE JUST TO GET HIMSELF POSITIONED IN WAKANDA.
AND I'M SURE HE WAS BEHIND THE STATESIDE SCANDAL THAT GOT THE CLIENT OUT OF WAKANDA -- A PLAN YEARS IN THE MAKING.
I DUNNO, NIKKI -- I THINK THIS GUY IS -- WELL -- MORALLY CHALLENGED.
MAYBE HE DID MAKE A DEAL WITH THE DEVIL. HAVING PERSONALLY MET HIM, I CAN TELL YOU --
-- GETTING AN APPOINTMENT WITH THE LORD OF FLIES ISN'T THAT HARD TO DO...
CUE Ms BLAIR
Remember, he'd given me a pair of PANTS earlier. The DEVIL'S PANTS.
Y'KNOW --
I was actually all right with it, but I'm afraid Mr. Johnson was getting a little weirded out.
-- NOT THAT I DON'T APPRECIATE THE THOUGHT AND ALL --
-- BUT MAYBE IT WOULD BE BEST IF I -- Ah --
-- Ah --

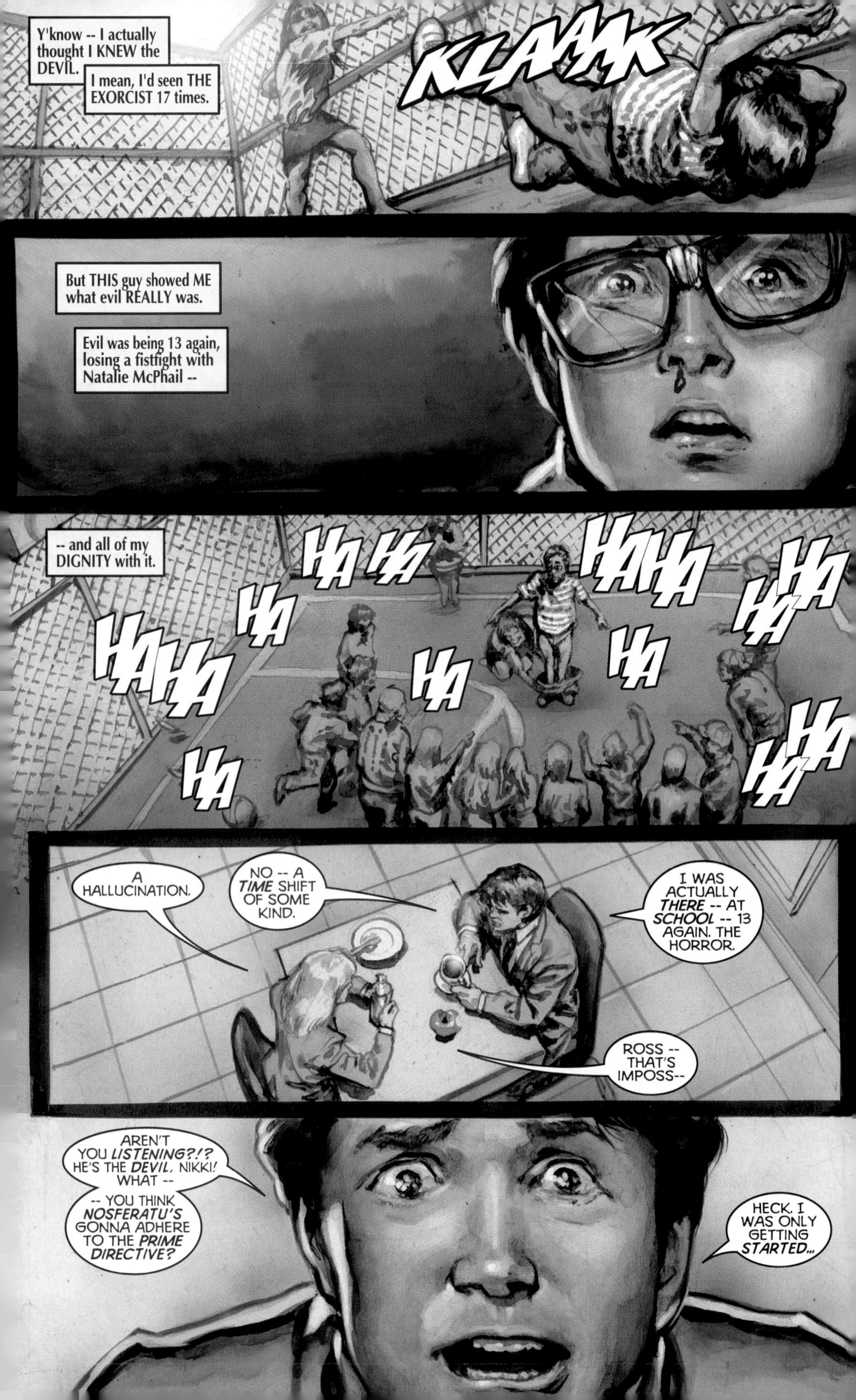

Y'know -- I actually thought I KNEW the DEVIL.
I mean, I'd seen THE EXORCIST 17 times.
KLAAAK
But THIS guy showed ME what evil REALLY was.
Evil was being 13 again, losing a fistfight with Natalie McPhail --
-- and all of my DIGNITY with it.
HA HA
HAHAHA
HA
HAHA
HA
HA
HA
HAHA
HA
HAHA
A HALLUCINATION.
NO -- A TIME SHIFT OF SOME KIND.
I WAS ACTUALLY THERE -- AT SCHOOL -- 13 AGAIN. THE HORROR.
ROSS -- THAT'S IMPOSS--
AREN'T YOU LISTENING?!? HE'S THE DEVIL, NIKKI! WHAT --
-- YOU THINK NOSFERATU'S GONNA ADHERE TO THE PRIME DIRECTIVE?
HECK, I WAS ONLY GETTING STARTED...

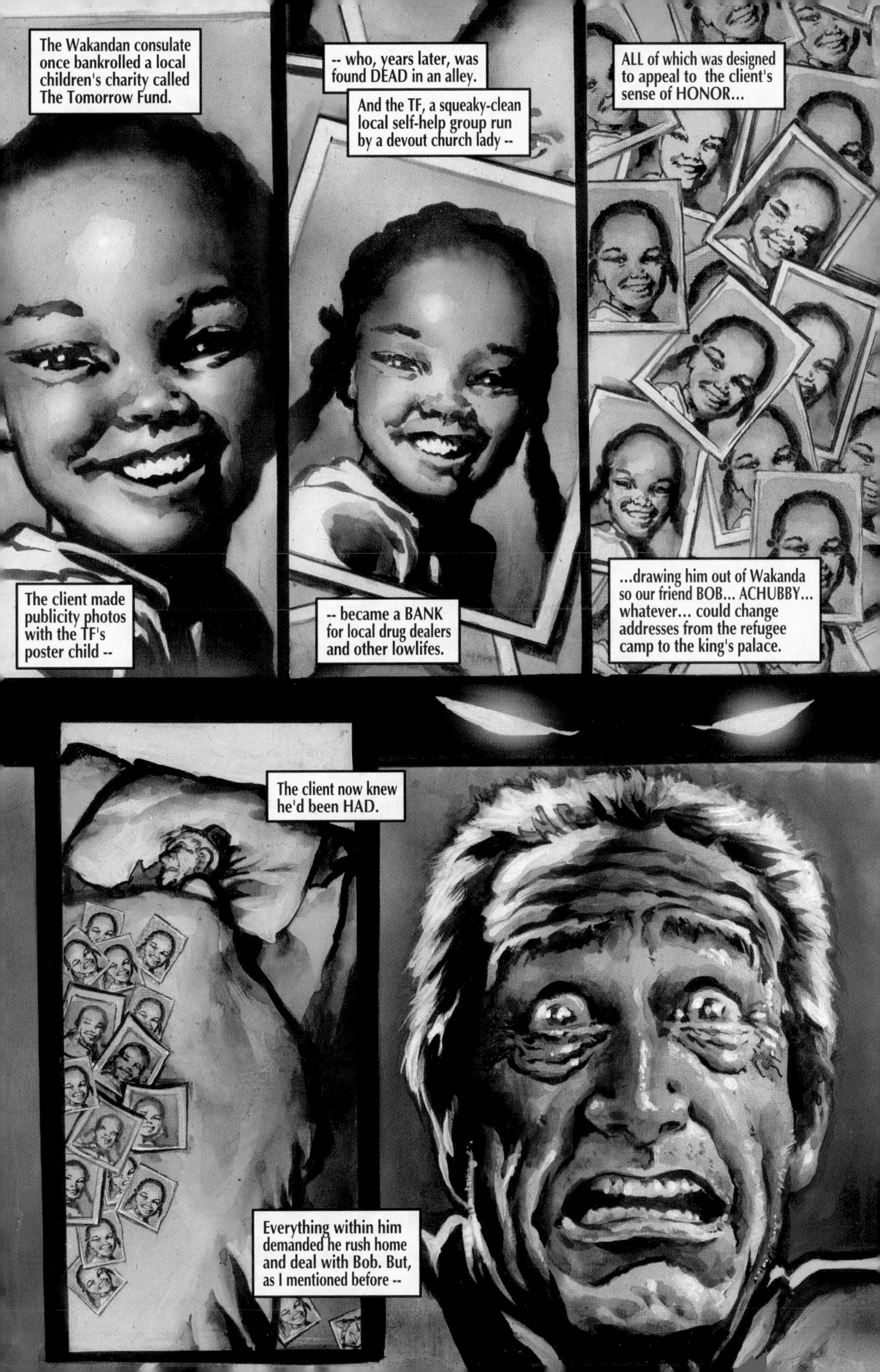
The Wakandan consulate once bankrolled a local children's charity called The Tomorrow Fund.
The client made publicity photos with the TF's poster child --
-- who, years later, was found DEAD in an alley.
And the TF, a squeaky-clean local self-help group run by a devout church lady --
-- became a BANK for local drug dealers and other lowlifes.
ALL of which was designed to appeal to the client's sense of HONOR...
...drawing him out of Wakanda so our friend BOB... ACHUBBY... whatever... could change addresses from the refugee camp to the king's palace.
The client now knew he'd been HAD.
Everything within him demanded he rush home and deal with Bob. But, as I mentioned before --

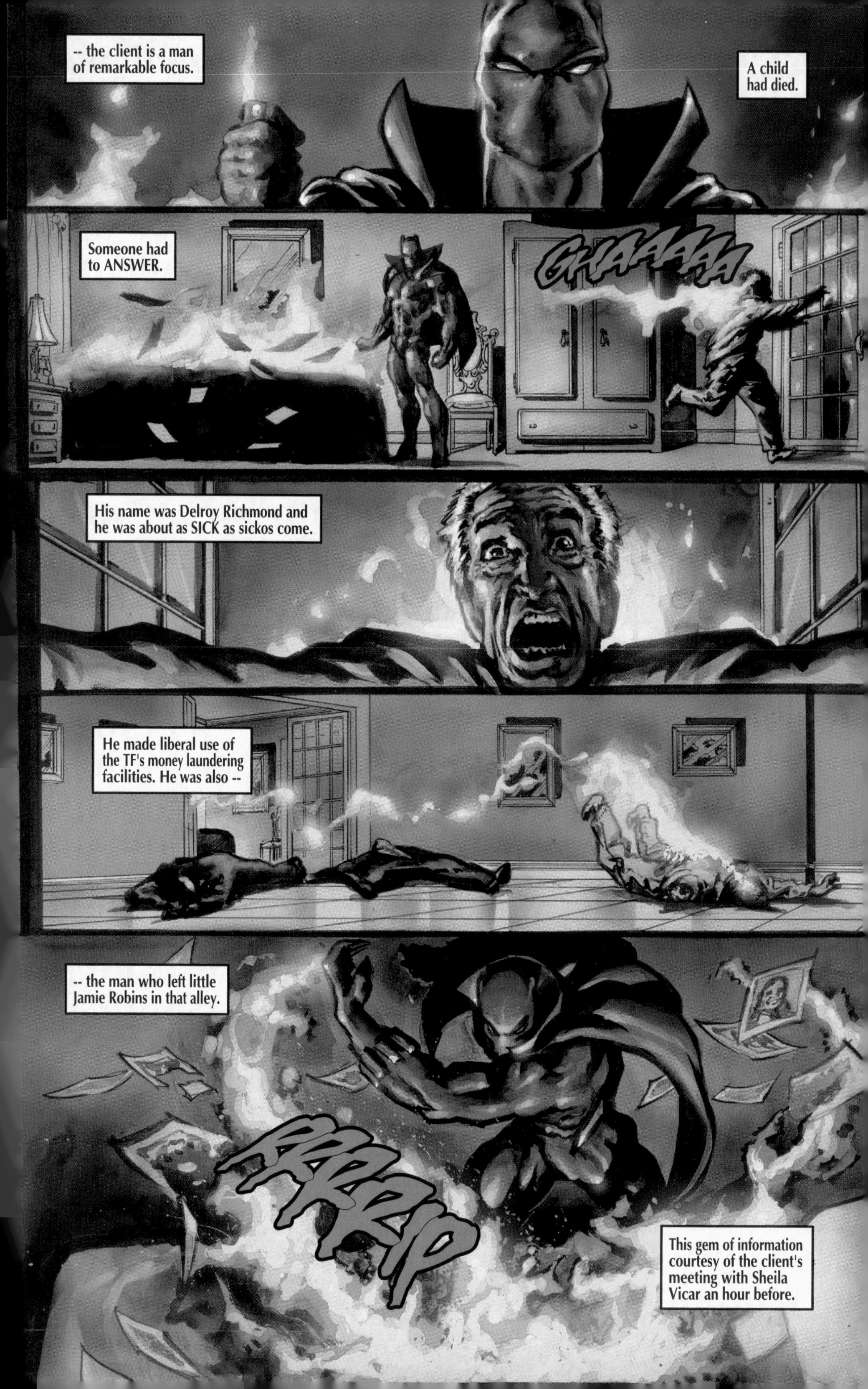
-- the client is a man of remarkable focus.
A child had died.
Someone had to ANSWER.
GHAAAAA
His name was Delroy Richmond and he was about as SICK as sickos come.
He made liberal use of the TF's money laundering facilities. He was also --
-- the man who left little Jamie Robins in that alley.
RRRRIP
This gem of information courtesy of the client's meeting with Sheila Vicar an hour before.

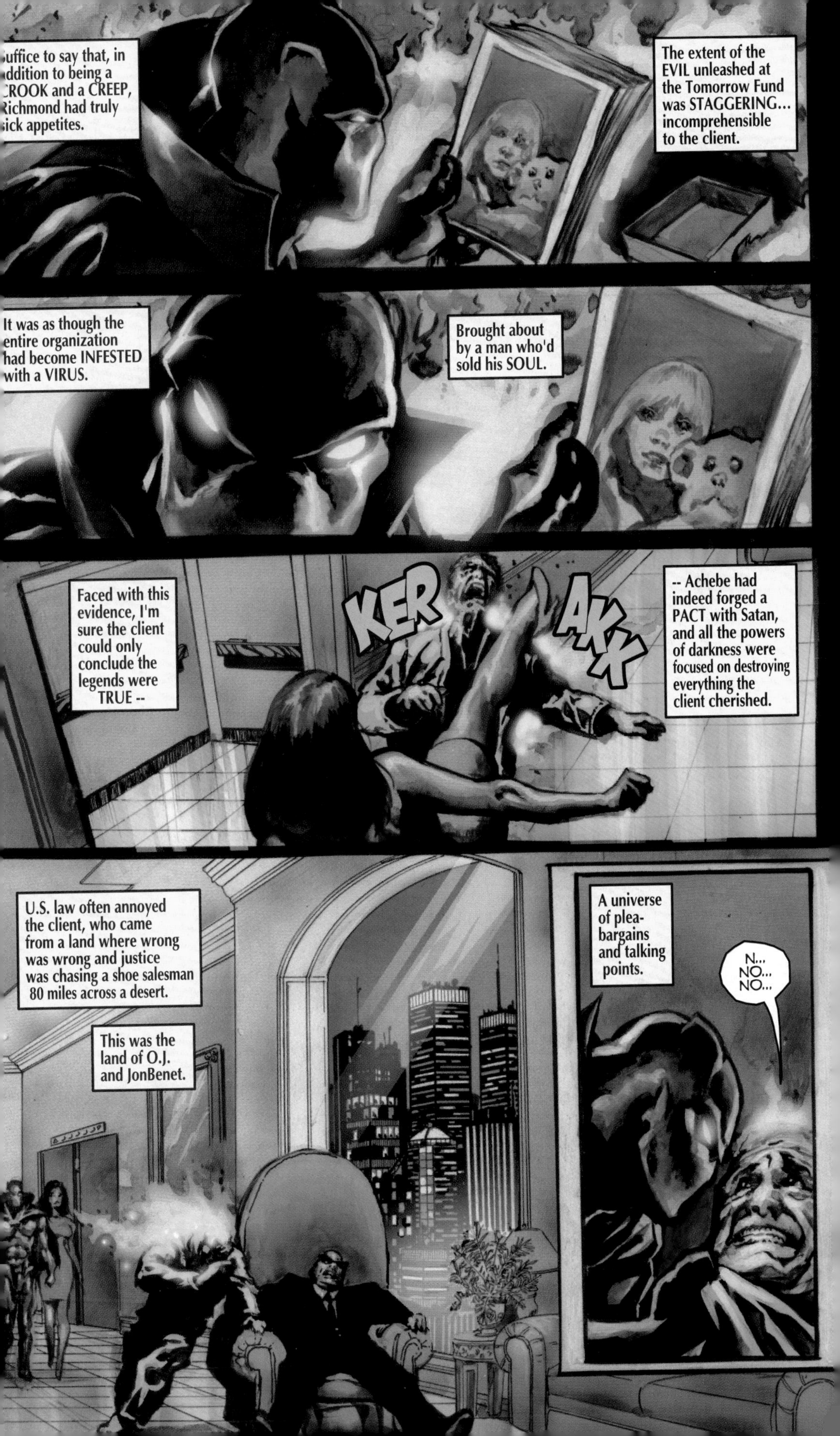
uffice to say that, in addition to being a CROOK and a CREEP, Richmond had truly sick appetites.
The extent of the EVIL unleashed at the Tomorrow Fund was STAGGERING... incomprehensible to the client.
It was as though the entire organization had become INFESTED with a VIRUS.
Brought about by a man who'd sold his SOUL.
Faced with this evidence, I'm sure the client could only conclude the legends were TRUE --
KER
AKK
-- Achebe had indeed forged a PACT with Satan, and all the powers of darkness were focused on destroying everything the client cherished.
U.S. law often annoyed the client, who came from a land where wrong was wrong and justice was chasing a shoe salesman 80 miles across a desert.
This was the land of O.J. and JonBenet.
A universe of plea-bargains and talking points.
N... NO... NO...

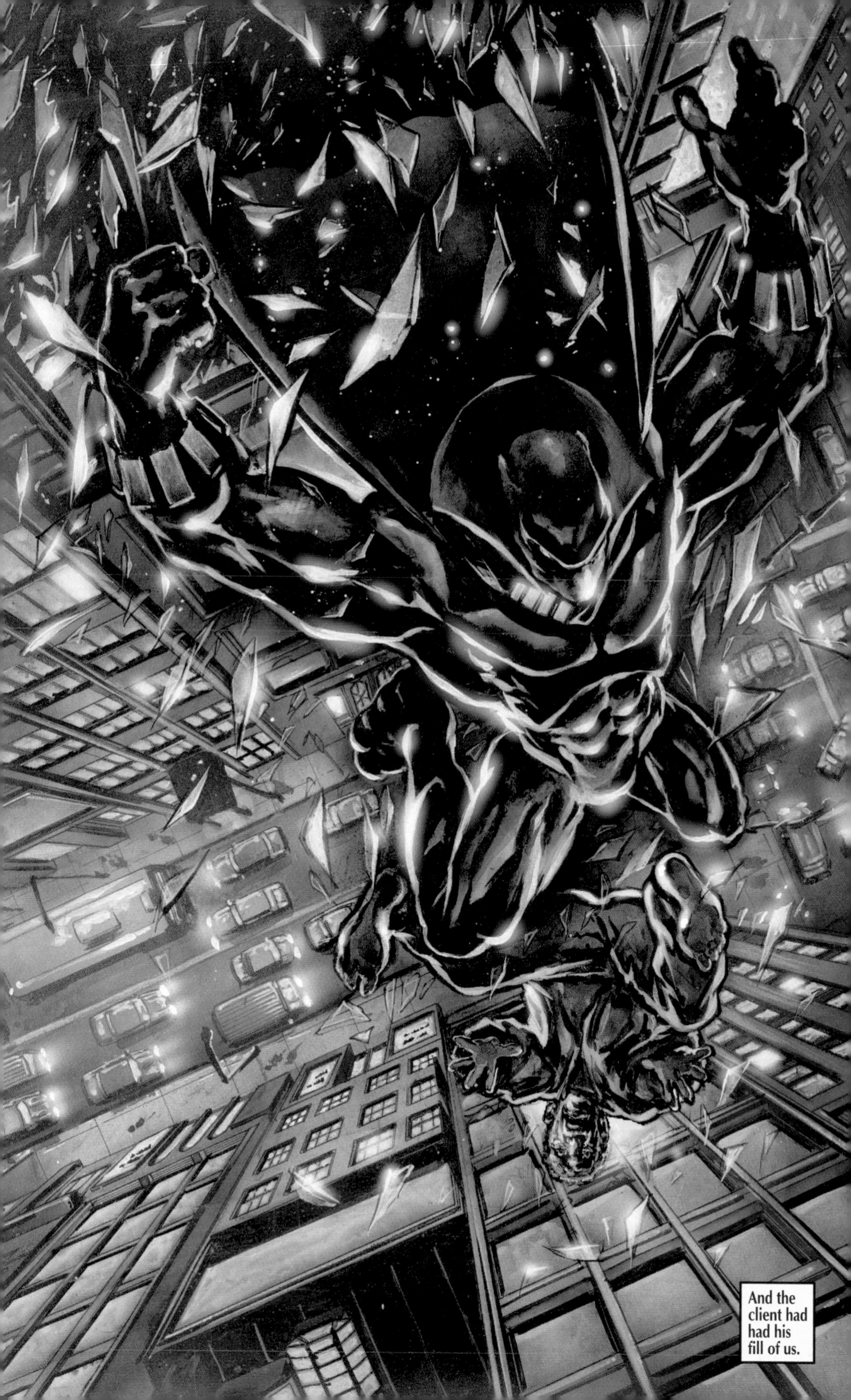
And the client had had his fill of us.

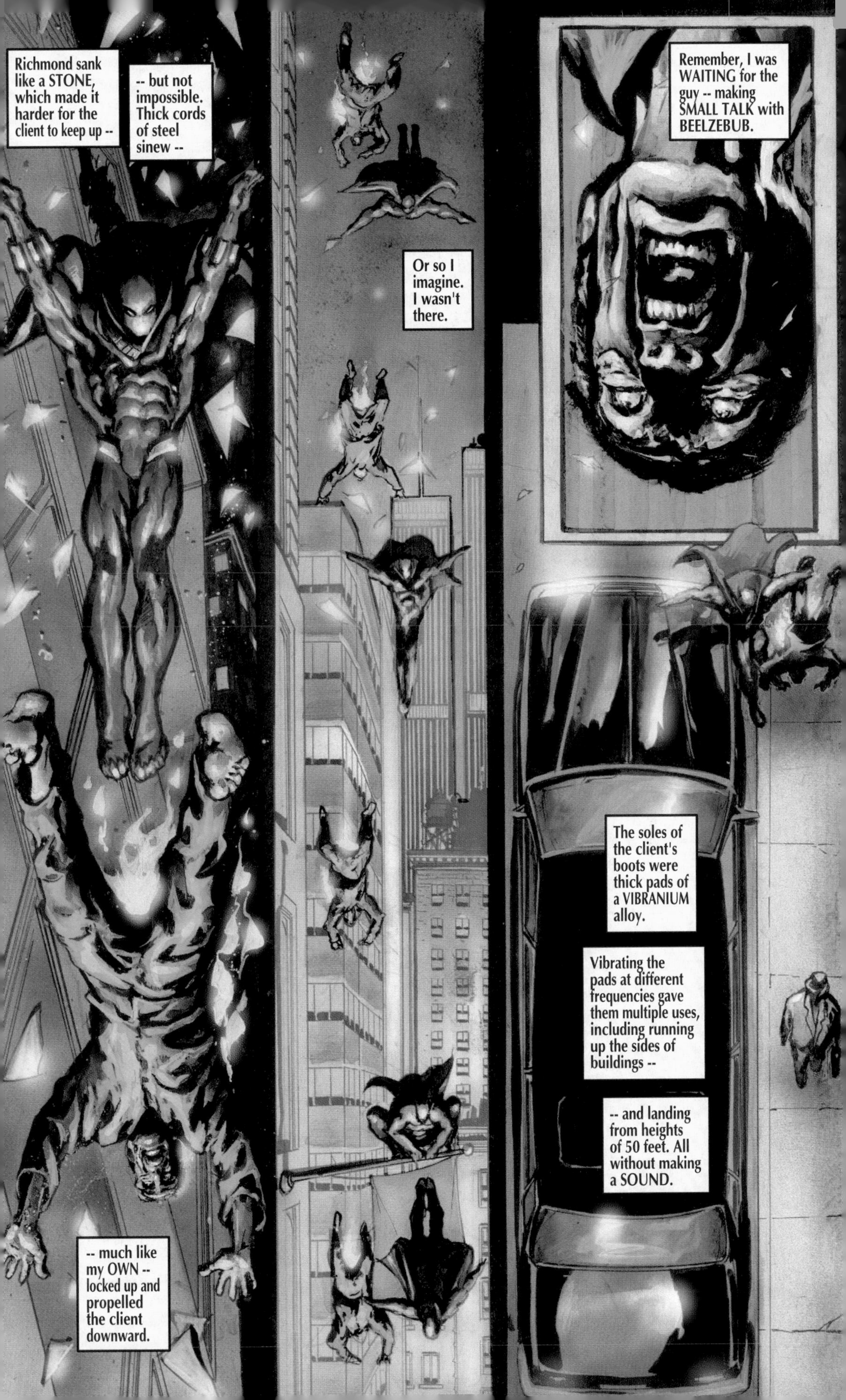
Richmond sank like a STONE, which made it harder for the client to keep up --
-- but not impossible. Thick cords of steel sinew --
-- much like my OWN -- locked up and propelled the client downward.
Or so I imagine. I wasn't there.
Remember, I was WAITING for the guy -- making SMALL TALK with BEELZEBUB.
The soles of the client's boots were thick pads of a VIBRANIUM alloy.
Vibrating the pads at different frequencies gave them multiple uses, including running up the sides of buildings --
-- and landing from heights of 50 feet. All without making a SOUND.

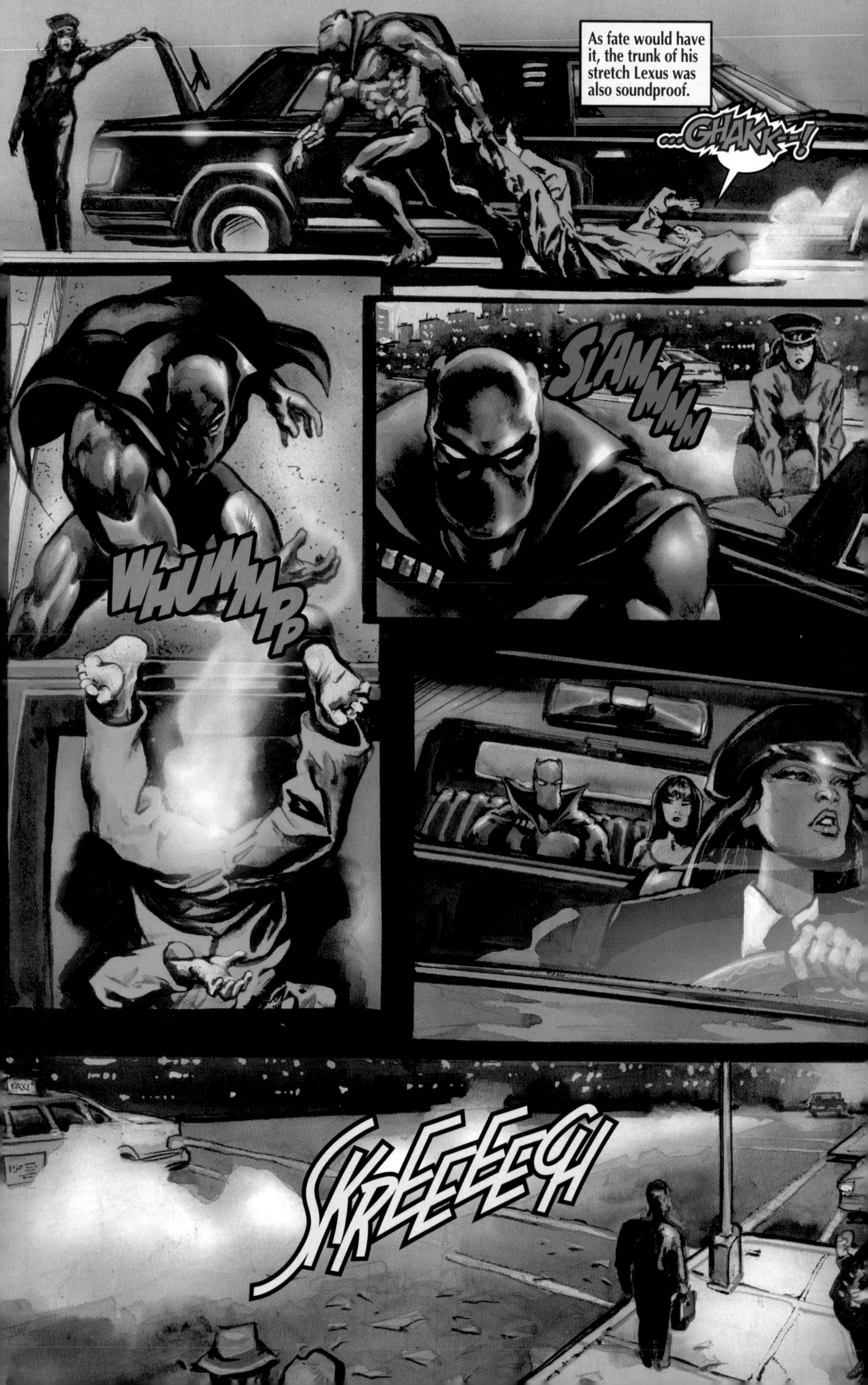
As fate would have it, the trunk of his stretch Lexus was also soundproof.
...GHAKK--!
WHUMMPP
SLAMMMM
SKREEEECH
TAXI

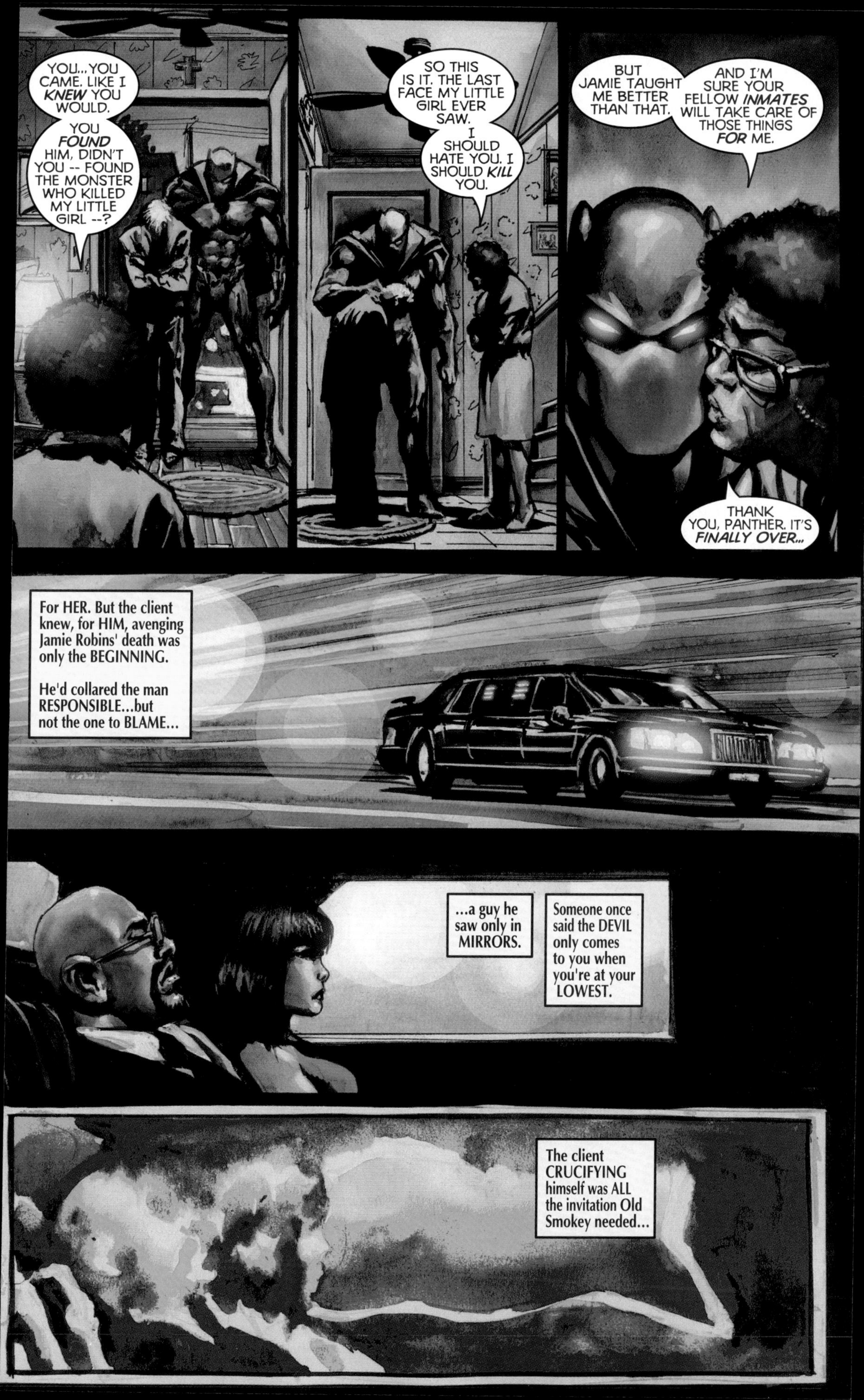
YOU...YOU CAME. LIKE I KNEW YOU WOULD.
YOU FOUND HIM, DIDN'T YOU -- FOUND THE MONSTER WHO KILLED MY LITTLE GIRL --?
SO THIS IS IT. THE LAST FACE MY LITTLE GIRL EVER SAW.
I SHOULD HATE YOU. I SHOULD KILL YOU.
BUT JAMIE TAUGHT ME BETTER THAN THAT.
AND I'M SURE YOUR FELLOW INMATES WILL TAKE CARE OF THOSE THINGS FOR ME.
THANK YOU, PANTHER. IT'S FINALLY OVER...
For HER. But the client knew, for HIM, avenging Jamie Robins' death was only the BEGINNING.
He'd collared the man RESPONSIBLE...but not the one to BLAME...
...a guy he saw only in MIRRORS.
Someone once said the DEVIL only comes to you when you're at your LOWEST.
The client CRUCIFYING himself was ALL the invitation Old Smokey needed...

THE CONSCIENCE OF THE KING

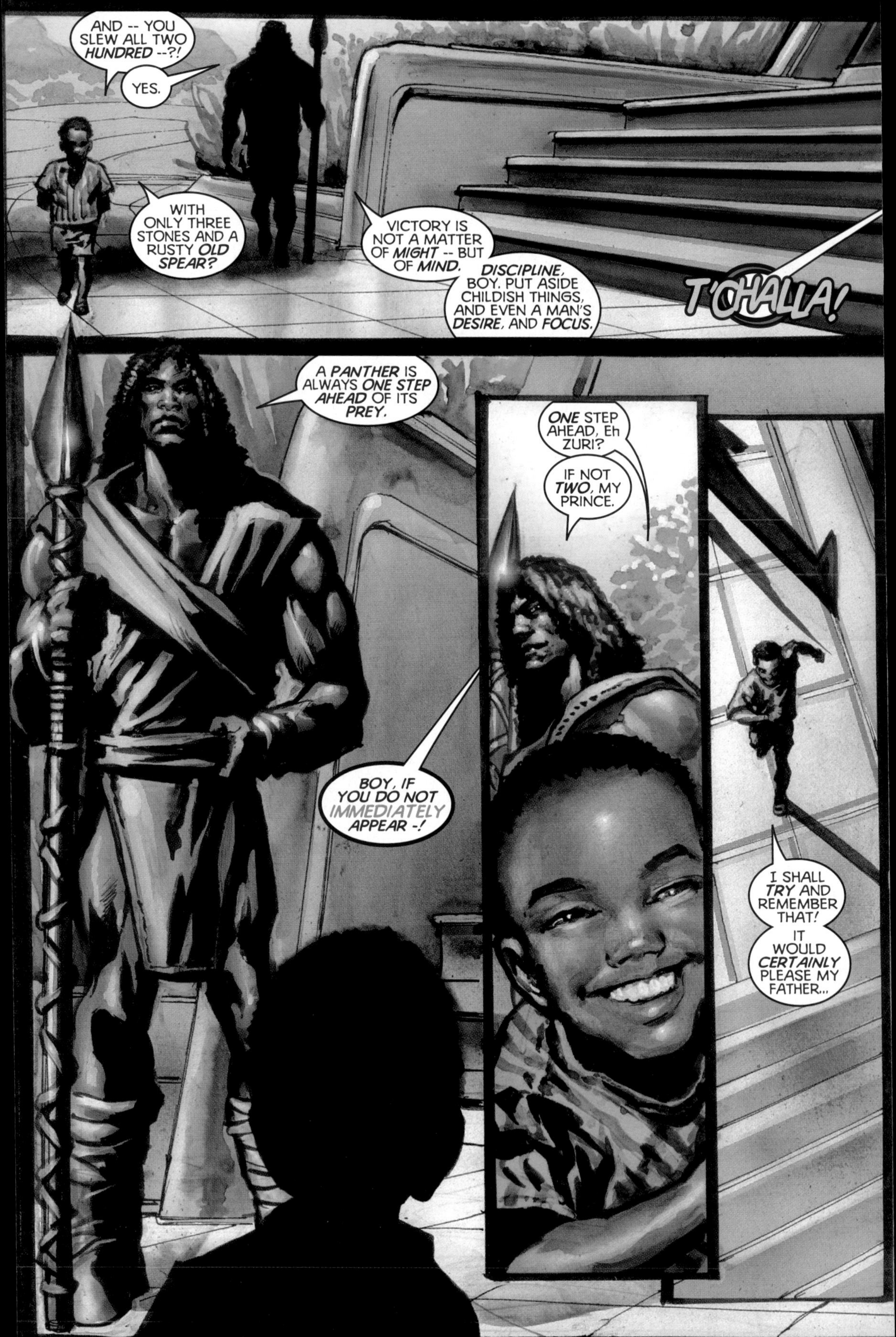

AND -- YOU SLEW ALL TWO HUNDRED --?!
YES.
WITH ONLY THREE STONES AND A RUSTY OLD SPEAR?
VICTORY IS NOT A MATTER OF MIGHT -- BUT OF MIND.
DISCIPLINE, BOY. PUT ASIDE CHILDISH THINGS, AND EVEN A MAN'S DESIRE, AND FOCUS.
T'CHALLA!
A PANTHER IS ALWAYS ONE STEP AHEAD OF ITS PREY.
BOY, IF YOU DO NOT IMMEDIATELY APPEAR -!
ONE STEP AHEAD, Eh ZURI?
IF NOT TWO, MY PRINCE.
I SHALL TRY AND REMEMBER THAT! IT WOULD CERTAINLY PLEASE MY FATHER...

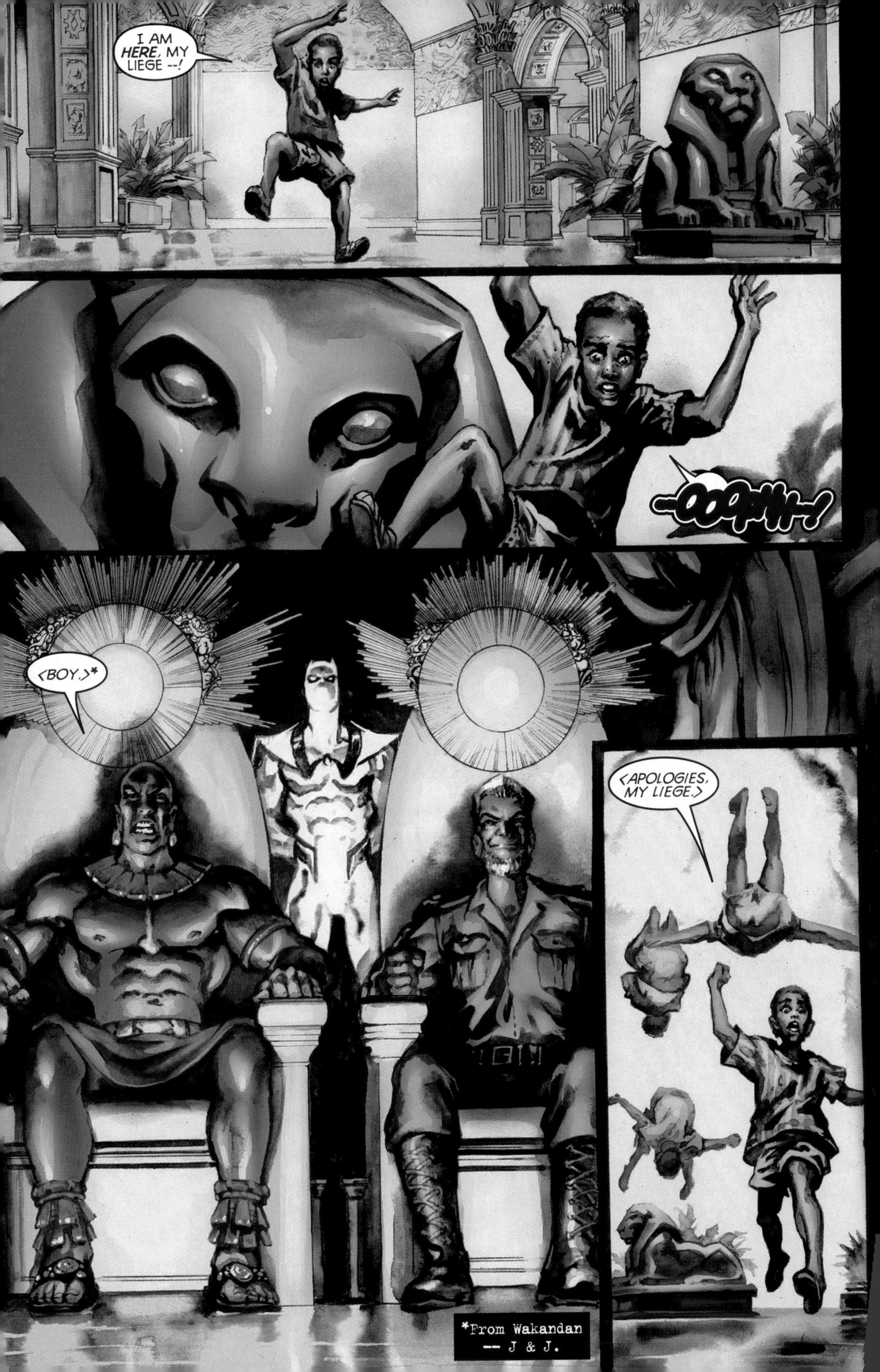
I AM HERE, MY LIEGE --!
--OOOPHH--!
<BOY.>*
<APOLOGIES, MY LIEGE.>
*From Wakandan -- J & J.

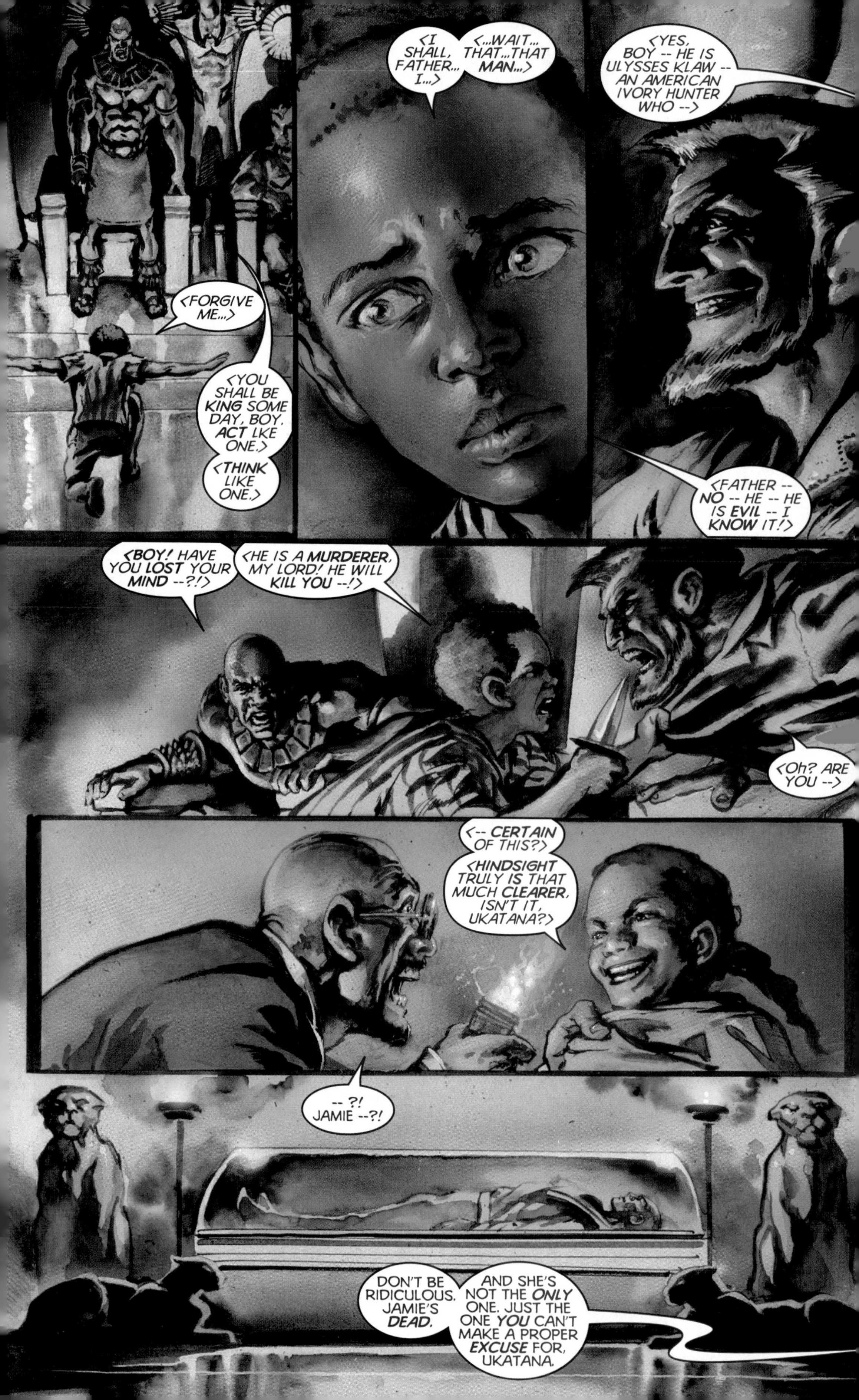

<FORGIVE ME...>
<YOU SHALL BE KING SOME DAY, BOY. ACT LIKE ONE.>
<THINK LIKE ONE.>
<I SHALL, FATHER... I...>
<...WAIT... THAT...THAT MAN...>
<YES, BOY -- HE IS ULYSSES KLAW -- AN AMERICAN IVORY HUNTER WHO -->
<FATHER -- NO -- HE -- HE IS EVIL -- I KNOW IT!>
<BOY! HAVE YOU LOST YOUR MIND --?!>
<HE IS A MURDERER, MY LORD! HE WILL KILL YOU --!>
<Oh? ARE YOU -->
<-- CERTAIN OF THIS?>
<HINDSIGHT TRULY IS THAT MUCH CLEARER, ISN'T IT, UKATANA?>
-- ?! JAMIE --?!
DON'T BE RIDICULOUS. JAMIE'S DEAD.
AND SHE'S NOT THE ONLY ONE. JUST THE ONE YOU CAN'T MAKE A PROPER EXCUSE FOR, UKATANA.

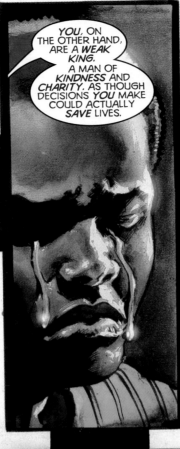

YOU, ON THE OTHER HAND, ARE A *WEAK KING.* A MAN OF *KINDNESS* AND *CHARITY,* AS THOUGH DECISIONS *YOU* MAKE COULD ACTUALLY *SAVE* LIVES.

BLOOD IS *BLOOD,* YOU ARROGANT FOOL. ONLY YOUR *FOCUS* -- YOUR *STRENGTH OF WILL* -- DETERMINES *WHO* SHALL DIE.

LOST SOULS -- ACCEPTABLE LOSSES -- CASUALTIES OF *POLITICAL PROCESS.* YOUR *FATHER* COULD SLEEP AT NIGHT BECAUSE HE UNDERSTOOD THESE THINGS.

THE *CROWN* IS *NOT* FOR IDEALISTS AND ARTISTS AND DREAMERS, BUT FOR MEN OF *IRON.* MEN *SMART* ENOUGH TO SEE THE *WIND BLOWING.*

WHO ARE YOU? DO YOU SERVE *ACHEBE* --?

I AM CALLED *MANY* THINGS, BUT MY *TRUE* NAME IS UNPRON-OUNCEABLE.

AND *ACHEBE* IS MERELY A MEANS TO MY END --

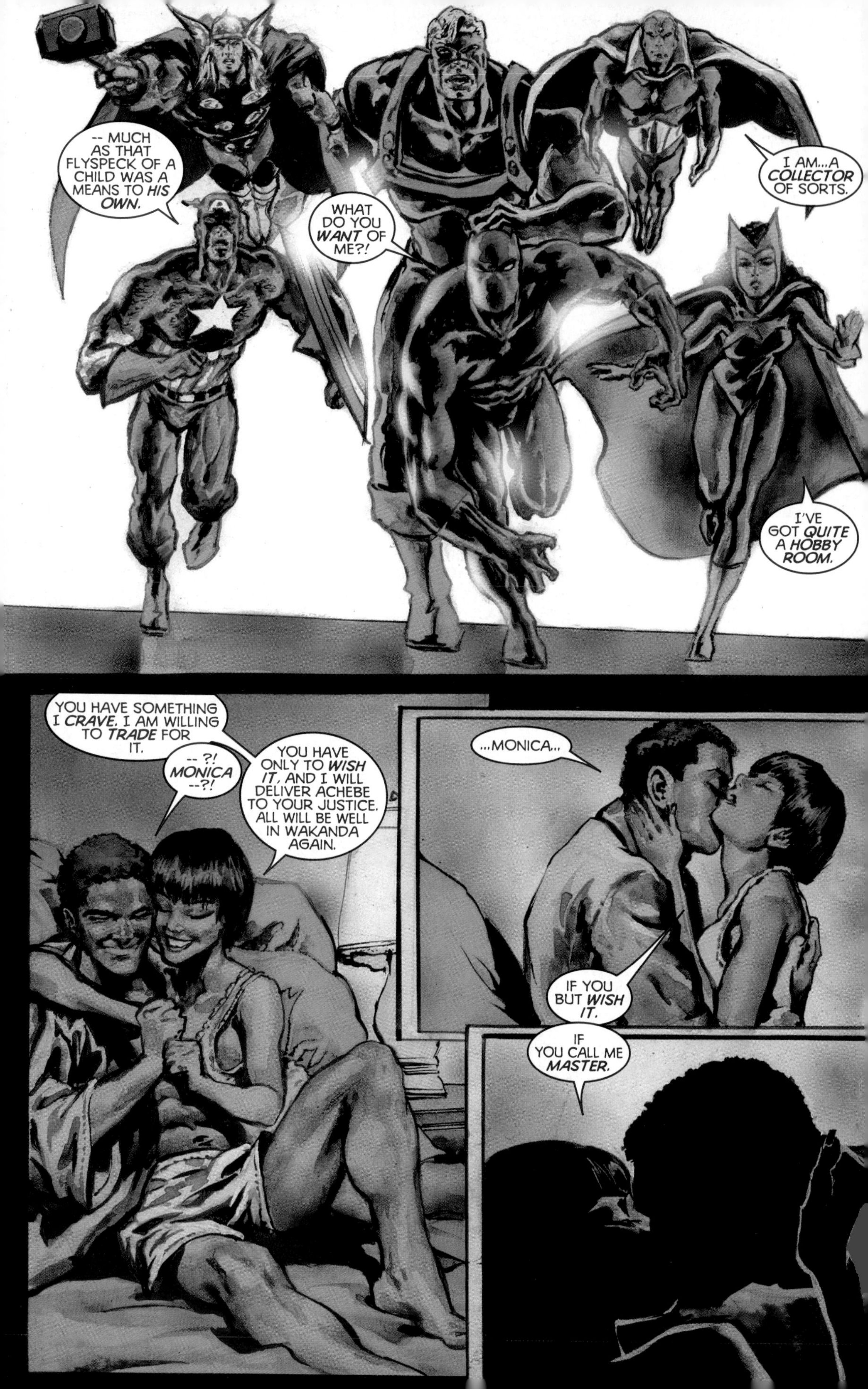
-- MUCH AS THAT FLYSPECK OF A CHILD WAS A MEANS TO HIS OWN.
WHAT DO YOU WANT OF ME?!
I AM...A COLLECTOR OF SORTS.
I'VE GOT QUITE A HOBBY ROOM.
YOU HAVE SOMETHING I CRAVE. I AM WILLING TO TRADE FOR IT.
-- ?! MONICA --?!
YOU HAVE ONLY TO WISH IT, AND I WILL DELIVER ACHEBE TO YOUR JUSTICE. ALL WILL BE WELL IN WAKANDA AGAIN.
...MONICA...
IF YOU BUT WISH IT.
IF YOU CALL ME MASTER.

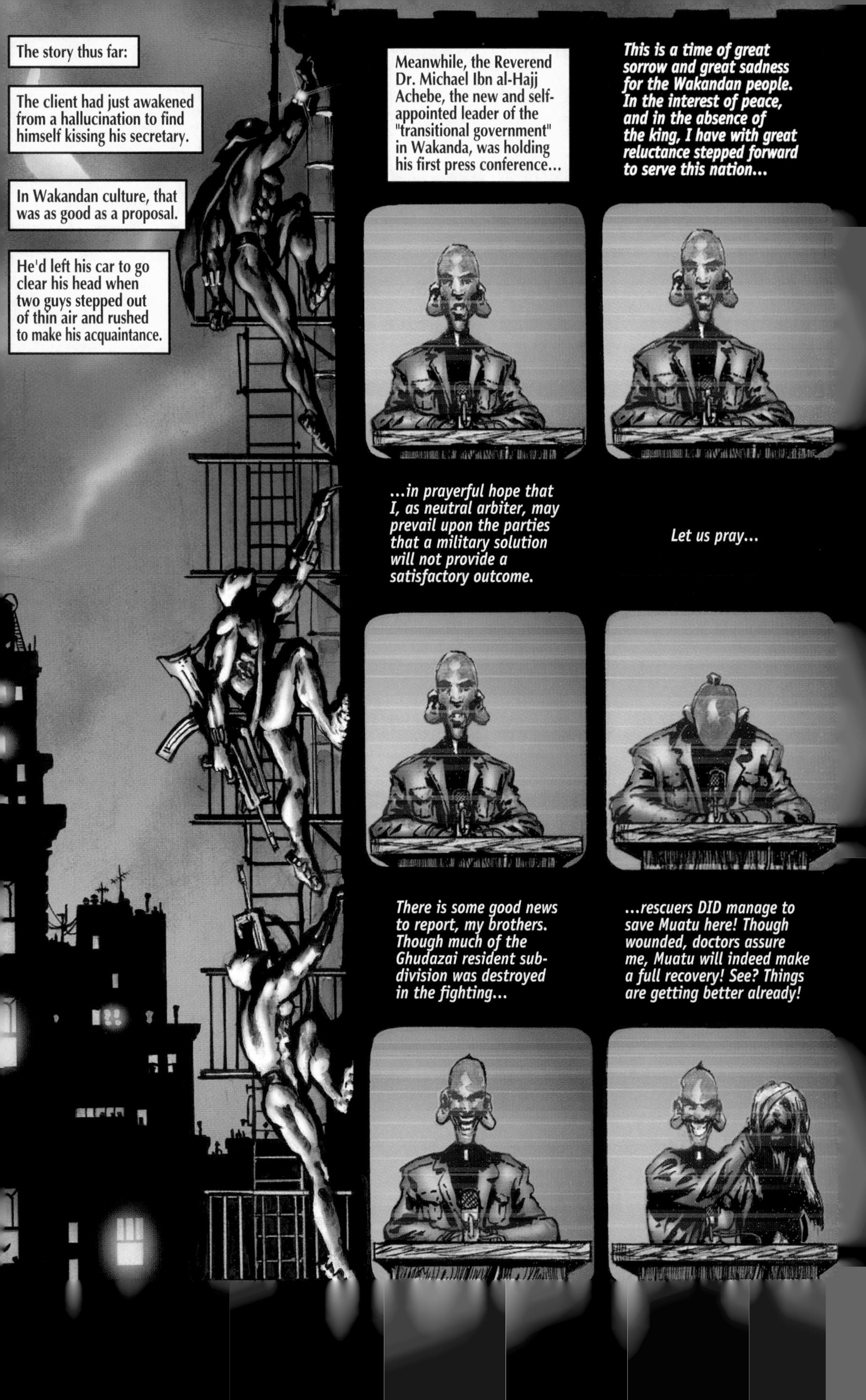
The story thus far:
The client had just awakened from a hallucination to find himself kissing his secretary.
In Wakandan culture, that was as good as a proposal.
He'd left his car to go clear his head when two guys stepped out of thin air and rushed to make his acquaintance.
Meanwhile, the Reverend Dr. Michael Ibn al-Hajj Achebe, the new and self-appointed leader of the "transitional government" in Wakanda, was holding his first press conference...
This is a time of great sorrow and great sadness for the Wakandan people. In the interest of peace, and in the absence of the king, I have with great reluctance stepped forward to serve this nation...
...in prayerful hope that I, as neutral arbiter, may prevail upon the parties that a military solution will not provide a satisfactory outcome.
Let us pray...
There is some good news to report, my brothers. Though much of the Ghudazai resident sub-division was destroyed in the fighting...
...rescuers DID manage to save Muatu here! Though wounded, doctors assure me, Muatu will indeed make a full recovery! See? Things are getting better already!

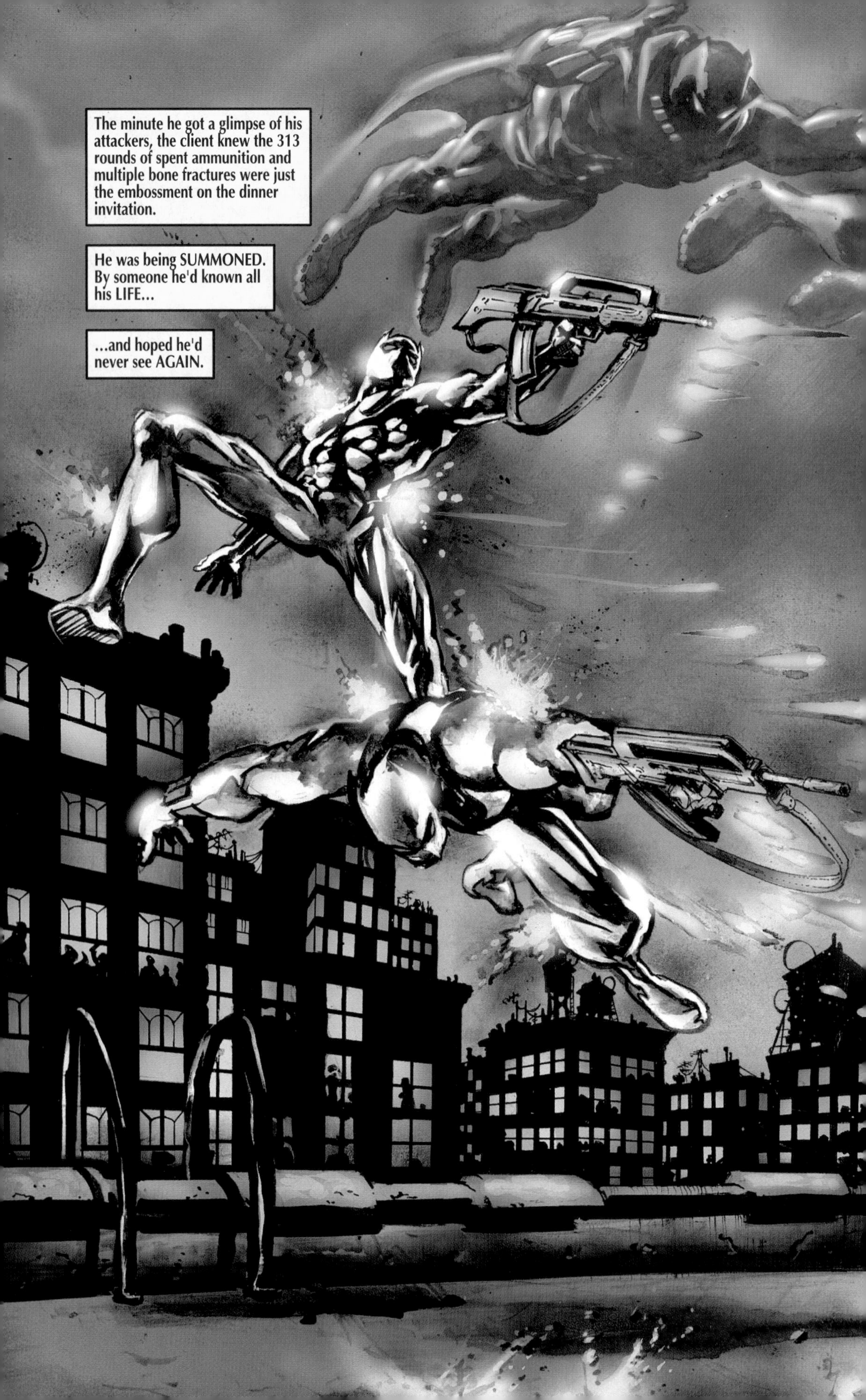
The minute he got a glimpse of his attackers, the client knew the 313 rounds of spent ammunition and multiple bone fractures were just the embossment on the dinner invitation.
He was being SUMMONED. By someone he'd known all his LIFE...
...and hoped he'd never see AGAIN.

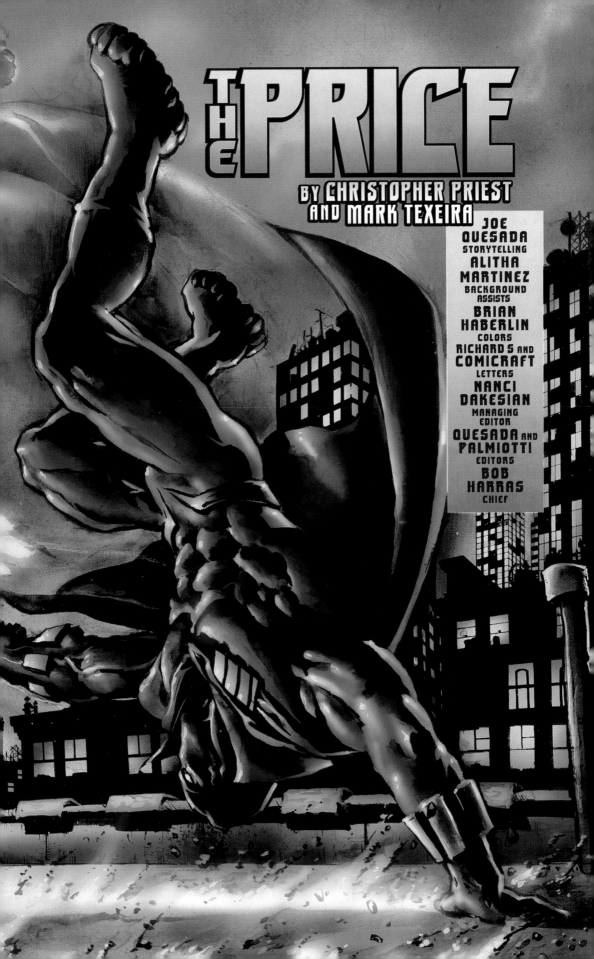

THE PRICE

BY CHRISTOPHER PRIEST AND MARK TEXEIRA

JOE QUESADA
STORYTELLING

ALITHA MARTINEZ
BACKGROUND ASSISTS

BRIAN HABERLIN
COLORS

RICHARD S AND COMICRAFT
LETTERS

NANCI DAKESIAN
MANAGING EDITOR

QUESADA AND PALMIOTTI
EDITORS

BOB HARRAS
CHIEF

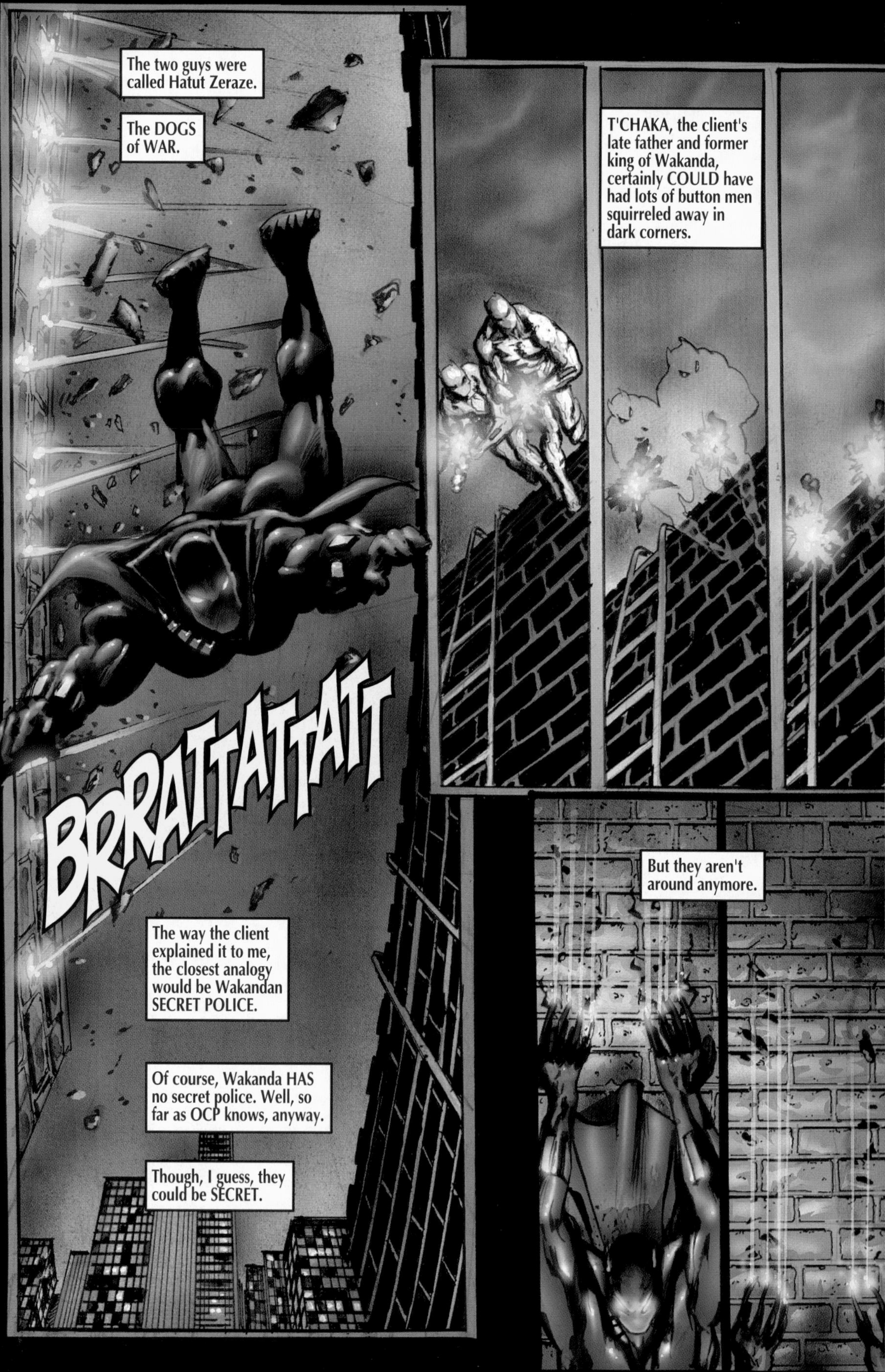
The two guys were called Hatut Zeraze.
The DOGS of WAR.
BRRATTATTATT
The way the client explained it to me, the closest analogy would be Wakandan SECRET POLICE.
Of course, Wakanda HAS no secret police. Well, so far as OCP knows, anyway.
Though, I guess, they could be SECRET.
T'CHAKA, the client's late father and former king of Wakanda, certainly COULD have had lots of button men squirreled away in dark corners.
But they aren't around anymore.

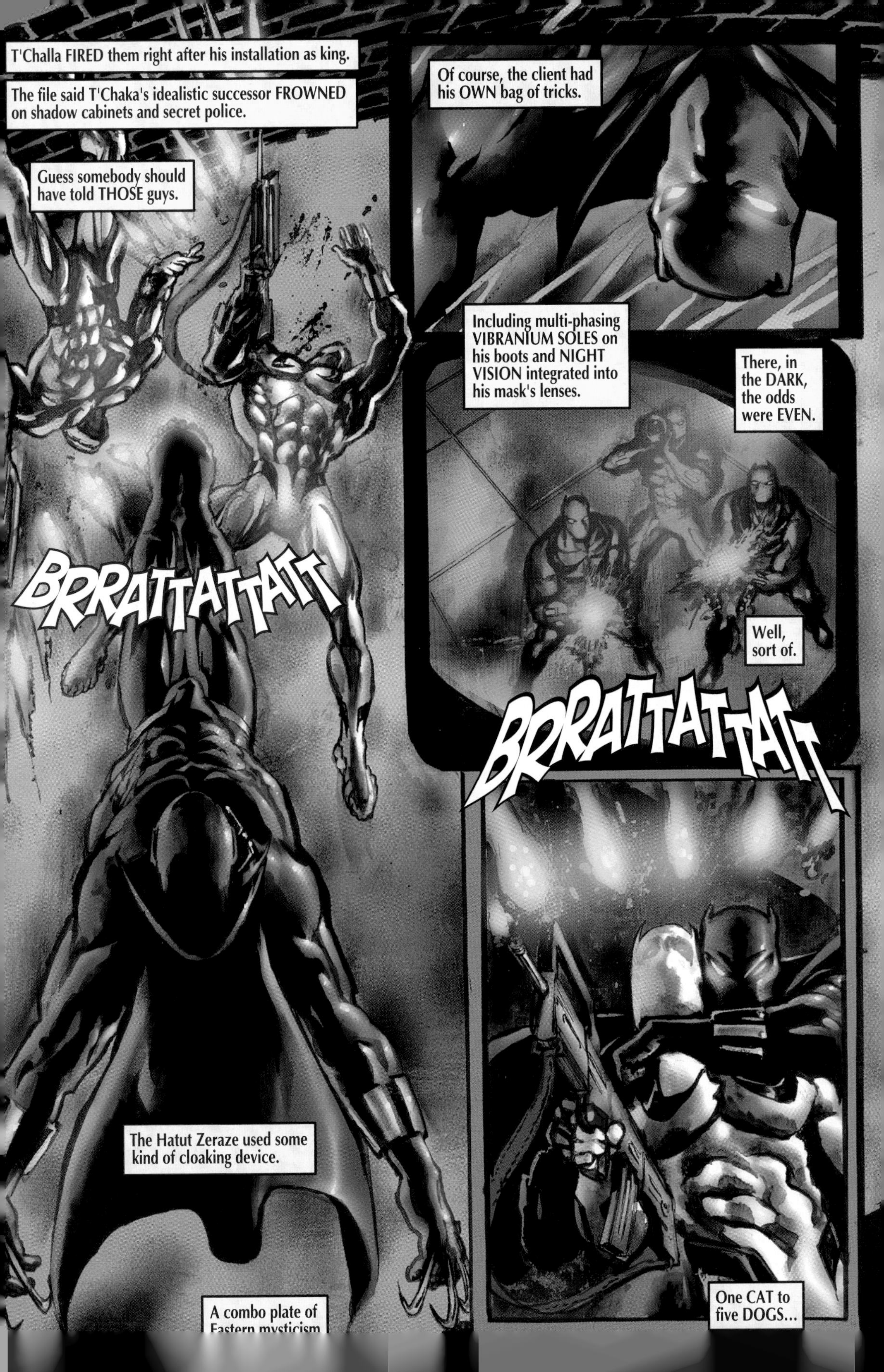
T'Challa FIRED them right after his installation as king.
The file said T'Chaka's idealistic successor FROWNED on shadow cabinets and secret police.
Guess somebody should have told THOSE guys.
BRRATTATTATT
The Hatut Zeraze used some kind of cloaking device.
A combo plate of
Of course, the client had his OWN bag of tricks.
Including multi-phasing VIBRANIUM SOLES on his boots and NIGHT VISION integrated into his mask's lenses.
There, in the DARK, the odds were EVEN.
Well, sort of.
BRRATTATTATT
One CAT to five DOGS...

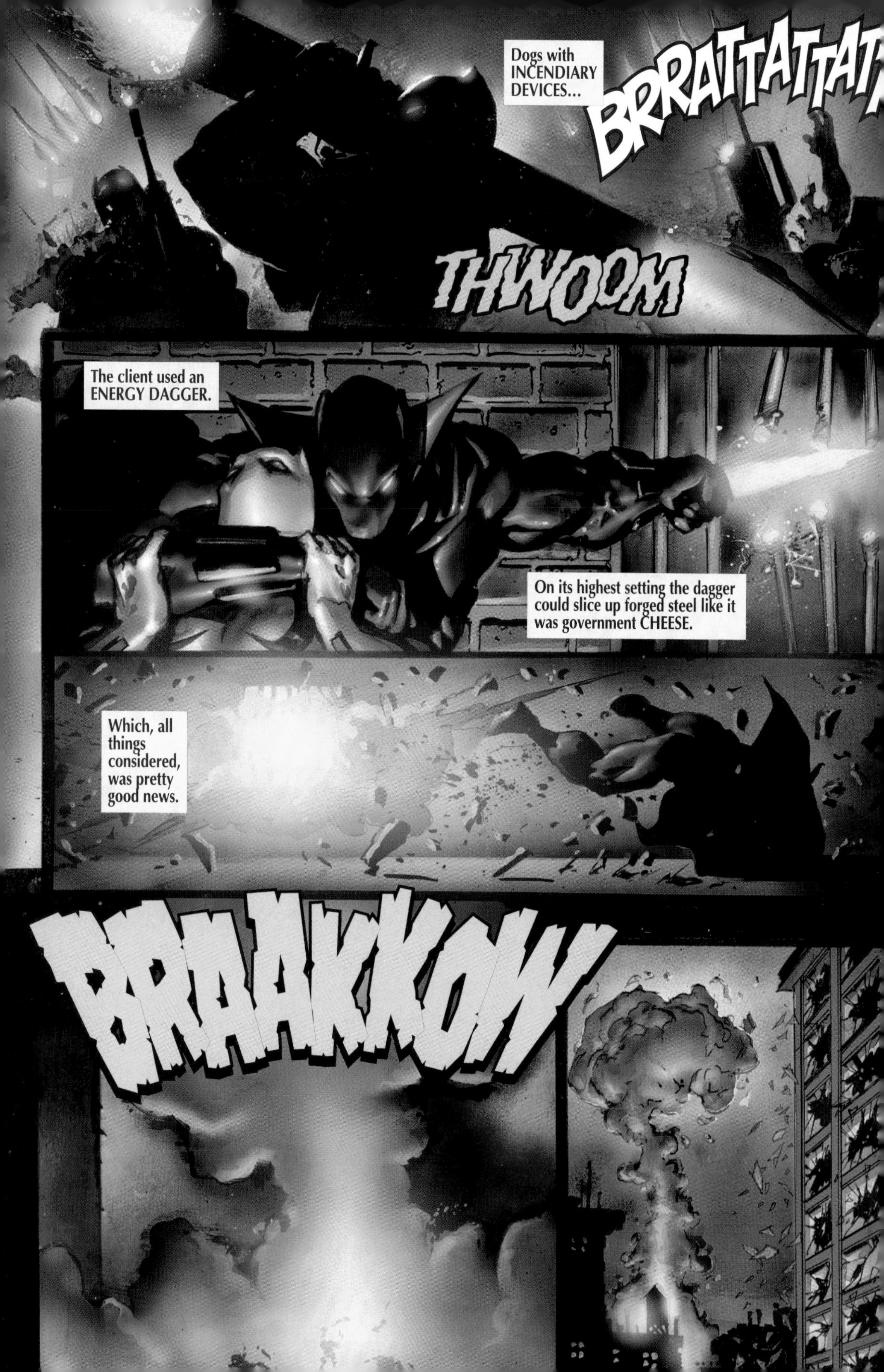
Dogs with INCENDIARY DEVICES...
BRRATTATTAT
THWOOM
The client used an ENERGY DAGGER.
On its highest setting the dagger could slice up forged steel like it was government CHEESE.
Which, all things considered, was pretty good news.
BRAAKKOW

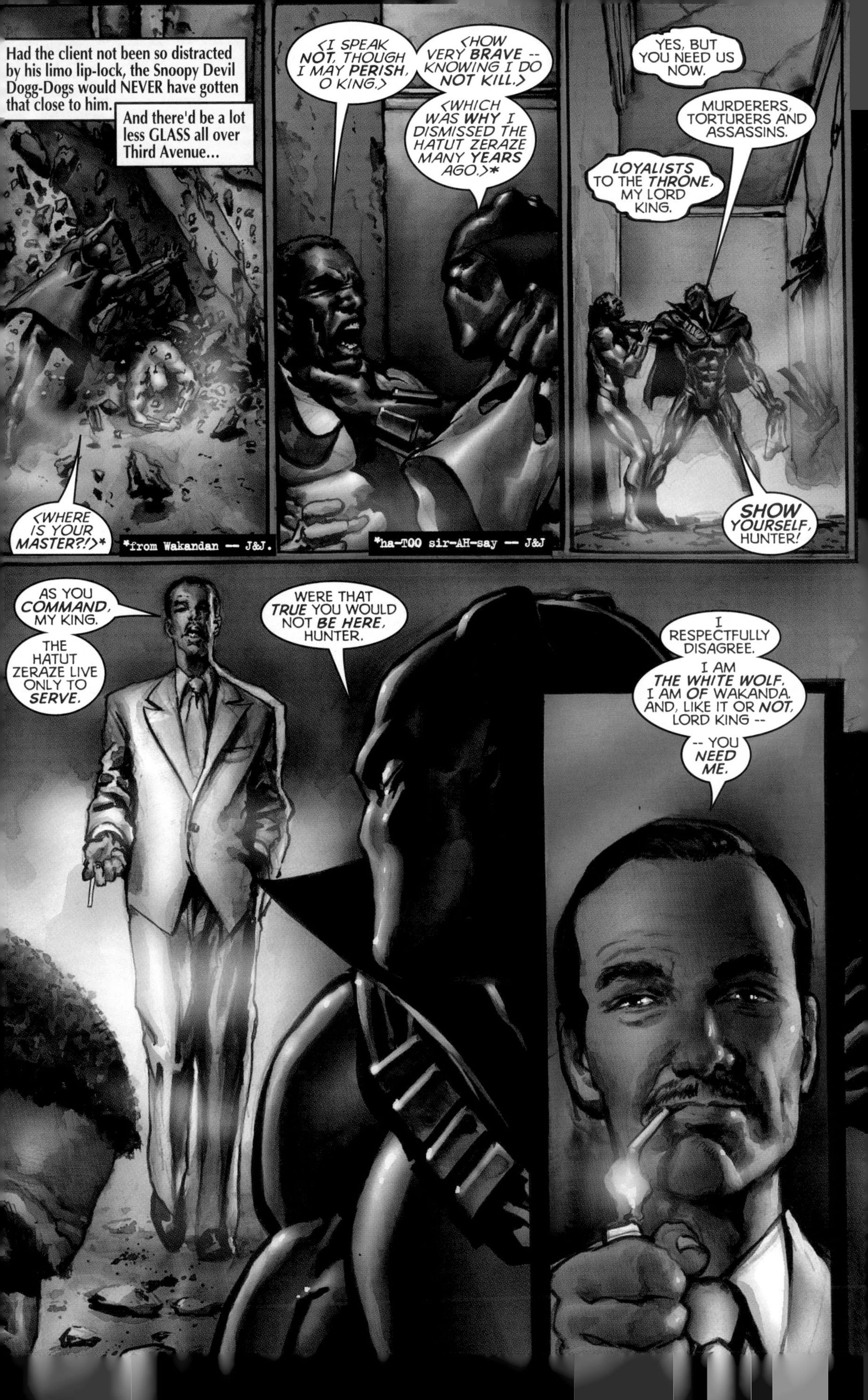

Had the client not been so distracted by his limo lip-lock, the Snoopy Devil Dogg-Dogs would NEVER have gotten that close to him.
And there'd be a lot less GLASS all over Third Avenue...
<WHERE IS YOUR MASTER?!>*
*from Wakandan -- J&J.
<I SPEAK NOT, THOUGH I MAY PERISH, O KING.>
<HOW VERY BRAVE -- KNOWING I DO NOT KILL.>
<WHICH WAS WHY I DISMISSED THE HATUT ZERAZE MANY YEARS AGO.>*
*ha-TOO sir-AH-say -- J&J
YES, BUT YOU NEED US NOW.
MURDERERS, TORTURERS AND ASSASSINS.
LOYALISTS TO THE THRONE, MY LORD KING.
SHOW YOURSELF, HUNTER!
AS YOU COMMAND, MY KING.
THE HATUT ZERAZE LIVE ONLY TO SERVE.
WERE THAT TRUE YOU WOULD NOT BE HERE, HUNTER.
I RESPECTFULLY DISAGREE.
I AM THE WHITE WOLF. I AM OF WAKANDA. AND, LIKE IT OR NOT, LORD KING --
-- YOU NEED ME.

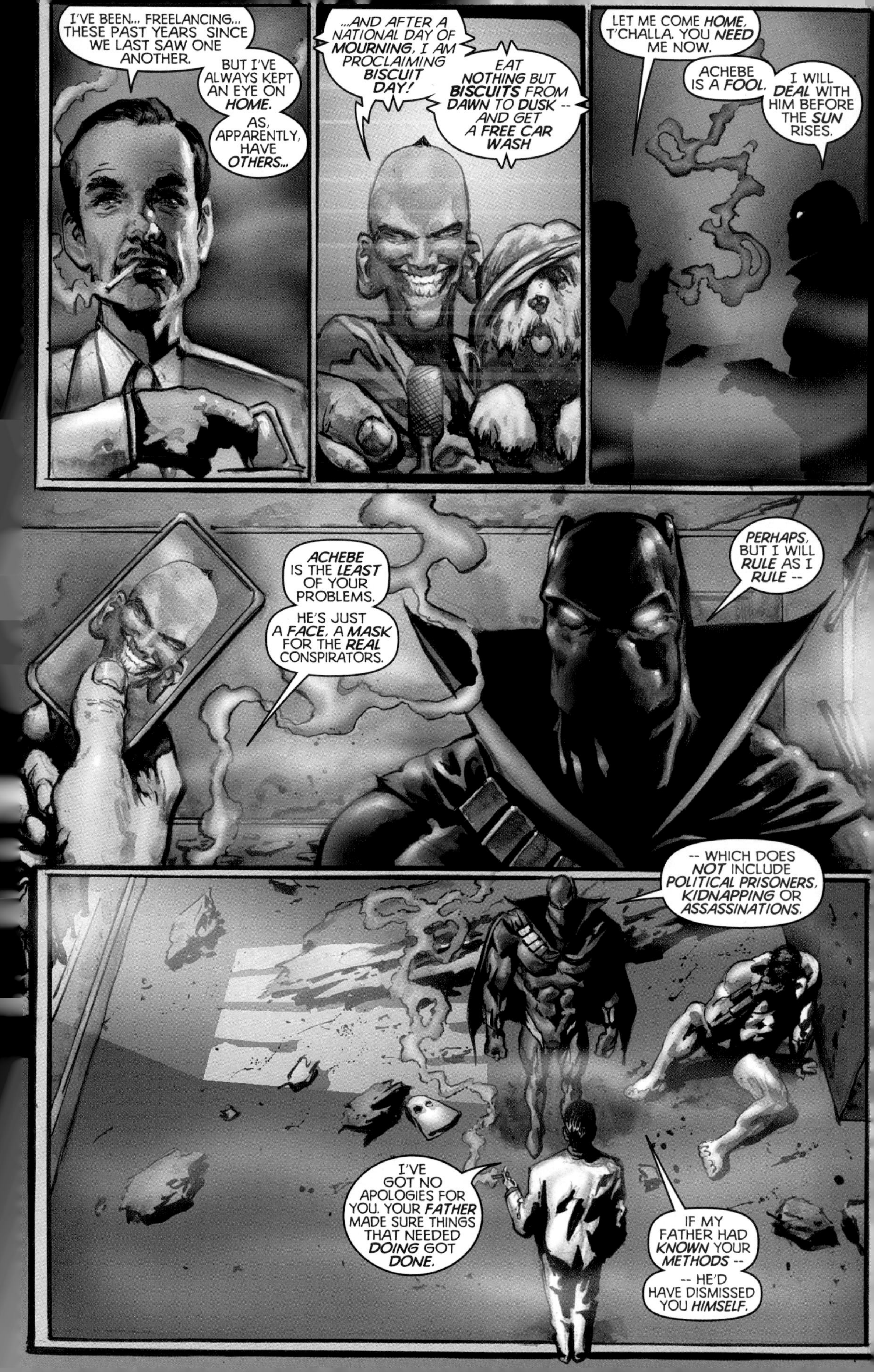

I'VE BEEN... FREELANCING... THESE PAST YEARS SINCE WE LAST SAW ONE ANOTHER.
BUT I'VE ALWAYS KEPT AN EYE ON HOME.
AS, APPARENTLY, HAVE OTHERS...
...AND AFTER A NATIONAL DAY OF MOURNING, I AM PROCLAIMING BISCUIT DAY!
EAT NOTHING BUT BISCUITS FROM DAWN TO DUSK -- AND GET A FREE CAR WASH
LET ME COME HOME, T'CHALLA. YOU NEED ME NOW.
ACHEBE IS A FOOL.
I WILL DEAL WITH HIM BEFORE THE SUN RISES.
ACHEBE IS THE LEAST OF YOUR PROBLEMS.
HE'S JUST A FACE, A MASK FOR THE REAL CONSPIRATORS.
PERHAPS, BUT I WILL RULE AS I RULE --
-- WHICH DOES NOT INCLUDE POLITICAL PRISONERS, KIDNAPPING OR ASSASSINATIONS.
I'VE GOT NO APOLOGIES FOR YOU. YOUR FATHER MADE SURE THINGS THAT NEEDED DOING GOT DONE.
IF MY FATHER HAD KNOWN YOUR METHODS --
-- HE'D HAVE DISMISSED YOU HIMSELF.

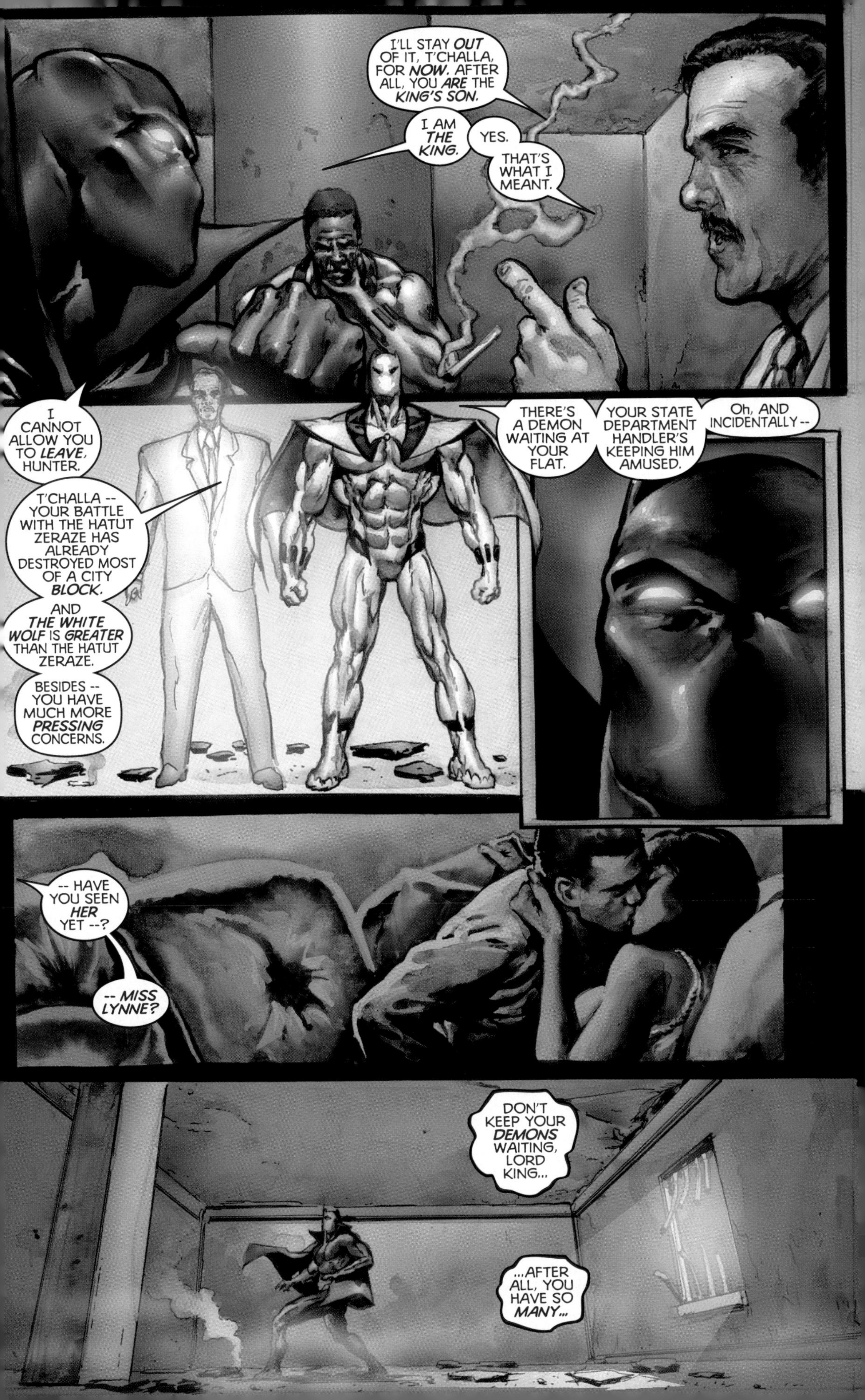
I'LL STAY OUT OF IT, T'CHALLA, FOR NOW. AFTER ALL, YOU ARE THE KING'S SON.
I AM THE KING.
YES.
THAT'S WHAT I MEANT.
I CANNOT ALLOW YOU TO LEAVE, HUNTER.
T'CHALLA -- YOUR BATTLE WITH THE HATUT ZERAZE HAS ALREADY DESTROYED MOST OF A CITY BLOCK.
AND THE WHITE WOLF IS GREATER THAN THE HATUT ZERAZE.
BESIDES -- YOU HAVE MUCH MORE PRESSING CONCERNS.
THERE'S A DEMON WAITING AT YOUR FLAT.
YOUR STATE DEPARTMENT HANDLER'S KEEPING HIM AMUSED.
Oh, AND INCIDENTALLY --
-- HAVE YOU SEEN HER YET --?
-- MISS LYNNE?
DON'T KEEP YOUR DEMONS WAITING, LORD KING...
...AFTER ALL, YOU HAVE SO MANY...

CALLING ALL CARS

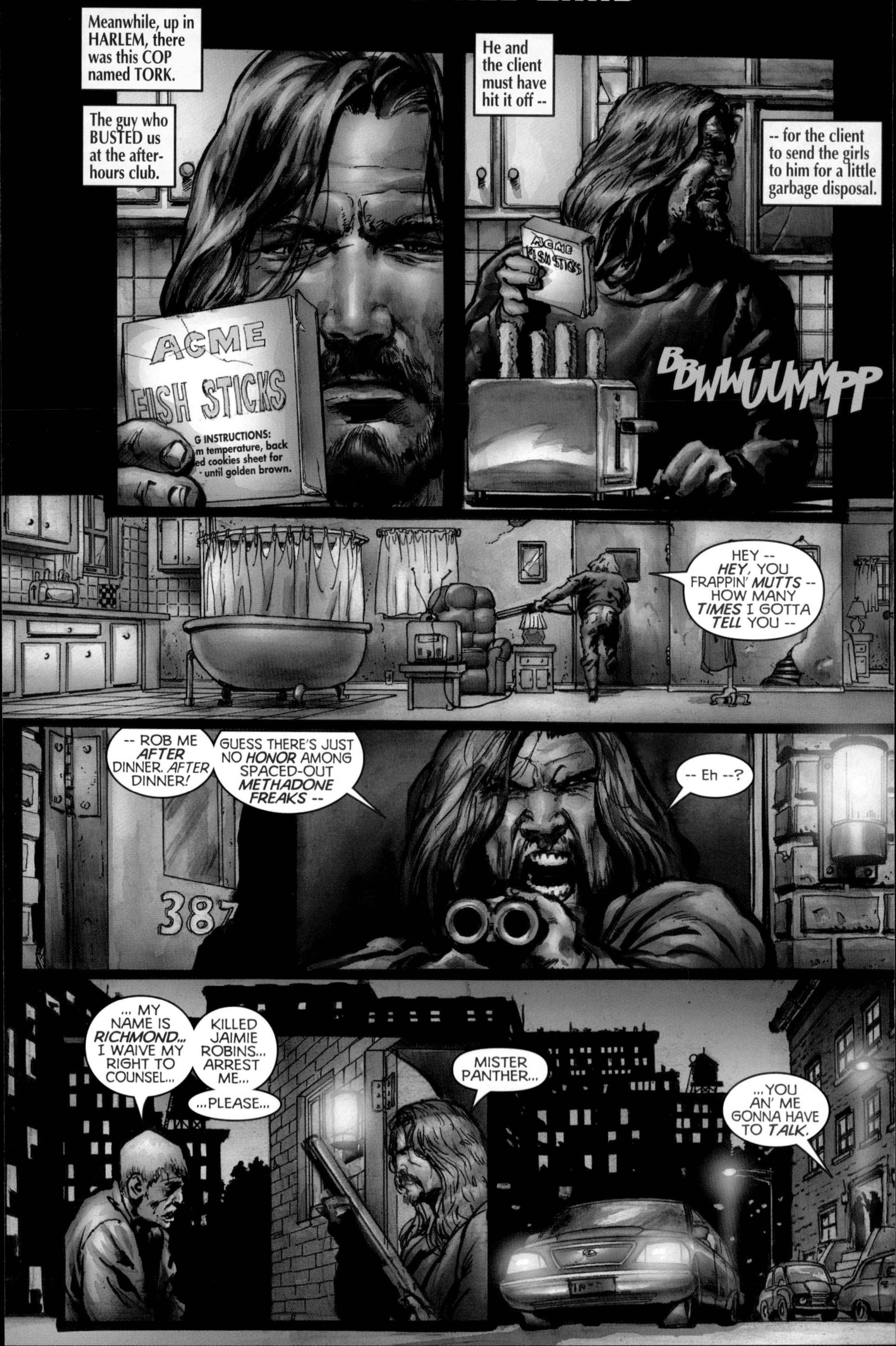

Meanwhile, up in HARLEM, there was this COP named TORK.
The guy who BUSTED us at the after-hours club.
ACME
FISH STICKS
G INSTRUCTIONS:
m temperature, back
ed cookies sheet for
until golden brown.
He and the client must have hit it off --
-- for the client to send the girls to him for a little garbage disposal.
ACME
FISH STICKS
BBWWUUMMPP
HEY -- HEY, YOU FRAPPIN' MUTTS -- HOW MANY TIMES I GOTTA TELL YOU --
-- ROB ME AFTER DINNER. AFTER DINNER!
GUESS THERE'S JUST NO HONOR AMONG SPACED-OUT METHADONE FREAKS --
-- Eh --?
387
... MY NAME IS RICHMOND... I WAIVE MY RIGHT TO COUNSEL...
KILLED JAIMIE ROBINS... ARREST ME...
...PLEASE...
MISTER PANTHER...
...YOU AN' ME GONNA HAVE TO TALK.

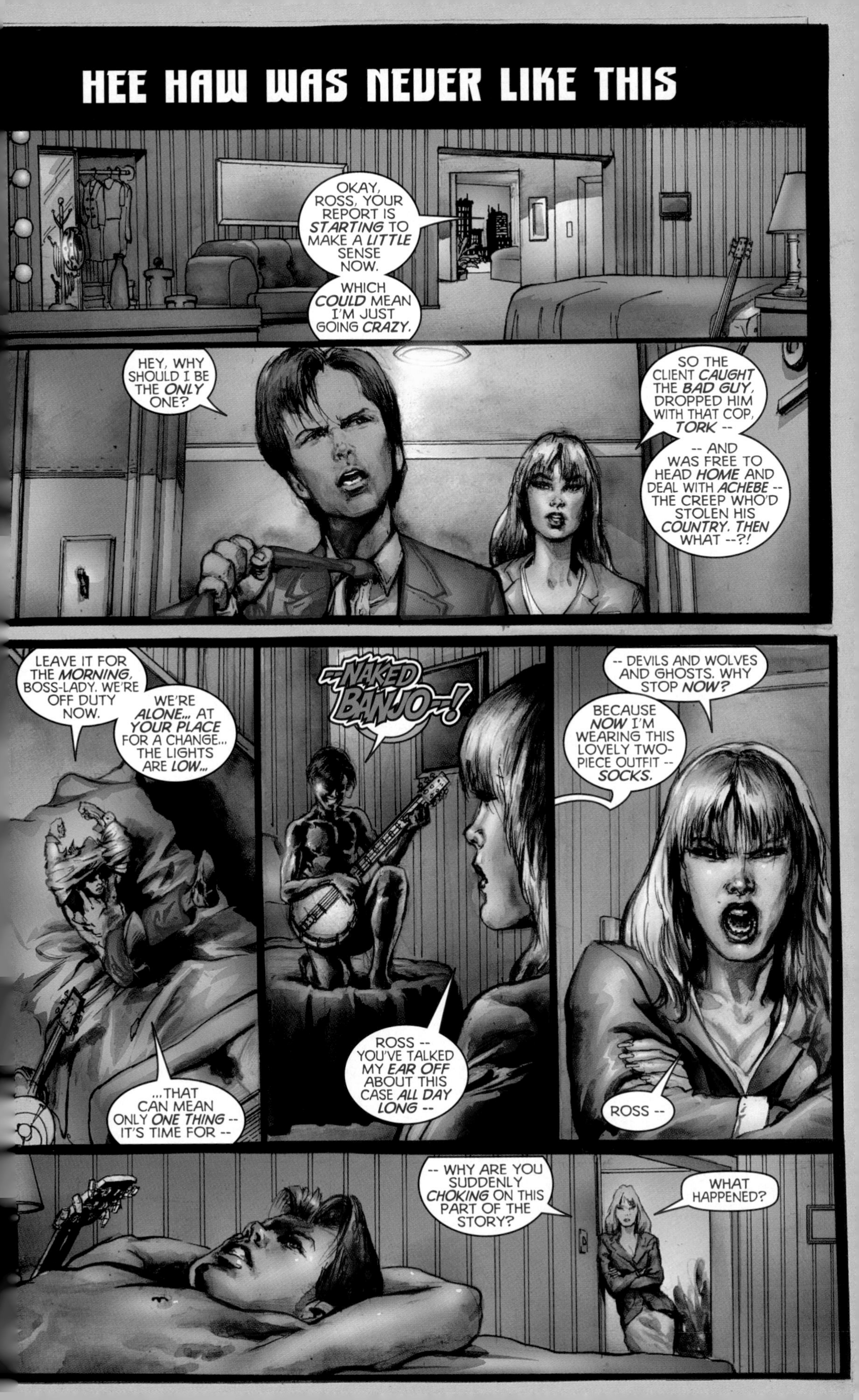
HEE HAW WAS NEVER LIKE THIS
OKAY, ROSS, YOUR REPORT IS STARTING TO MAKE A LITTLE SENSE NOW.
WHICH COULD MEAN I'M JUST GOING CRAZY.
HEY, WHY SHOULD I BE THE ONLY ONE?
SO THE CLIENT CAUGHT THE BAD GUY, DROPPED HIM WITH THAT COP, TORK --
-- AND WAS FREE TO HEAD HOME AND DEAL WITH ACHEBE -- THE CREEP WHO'D STOLEN HIS COUNTRY. THEN WHAT --?!
LEAVE IT FOR THE MORNING, BOSS-LADY. WE'RE OFF DUTY NOW.
WE'RE ALONE... AT YOUR PLACE FOR A CHANGE... THE LIGHTS ARE LOW...
...THAT CAN MEAN ONLY ONE THING -- IT'S TIME FOR --
--NAKED BANJO--!
ROSS -- YOU'VE TALKED MY EAR OFF ABOUT THIS CASE ALL DAY LONG --
-- DEVILS AND WOLVES AND GHOSTS. WHY STOP NOW?
BECAUSE NOW I'M WEARING THIS LOVELY TWO-PIECE OUTFIT -- SOCKS.
ROSS --
-- WHY ARE YOU SUDDENLY CHOKING ON THIS PART OF THE STORY?
WHAT HAPPENED?

KENNY

So, it was just us guys, hanging out in a Brooklyn Housing Project. ME --

--ZURI, the client's regent and fearsome bodyguard --

-- and the Darkness reaching out for the Darkness.

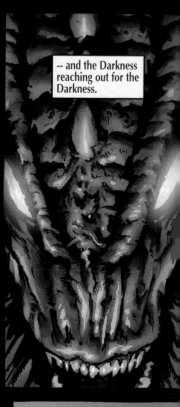

All told, he'd been waiting ten or twelve minutes. Three YEARS in Ross Time.

I'M *SURE* HE'LL BE HERE *ANY MINUTE.*

Y'KNOW, IF YOU *WANT* -- I COULD ORDER UP A *PIZZA.*

FRIEND ROSS --

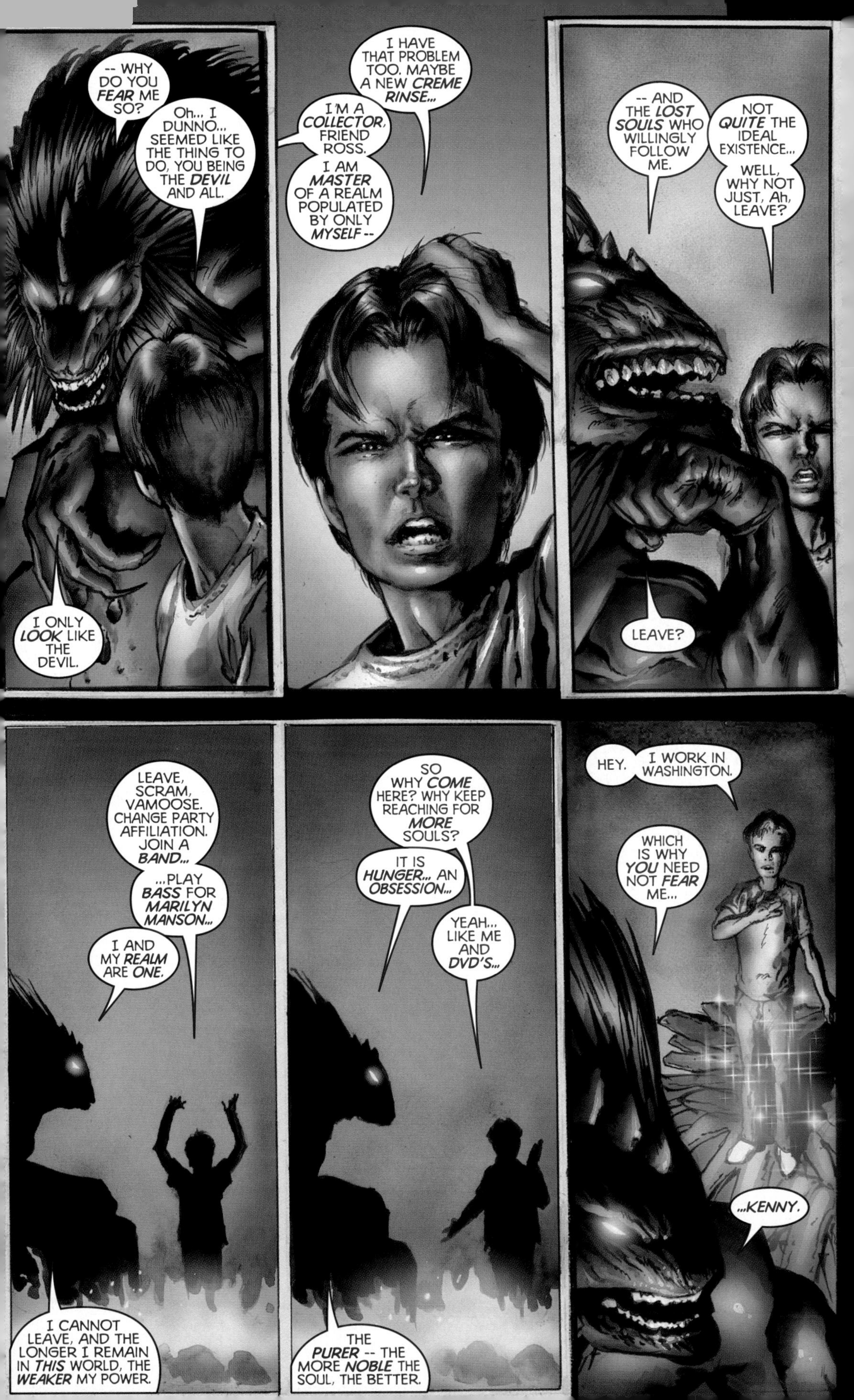
-- WHY DO YOU FEAR ME SO?
Oh... I DUNNO... SEEMED LIKE THE THING TO DO, YOU BEING THE DEVIL AND ALL.
I ONLY LOOK LIKE THE DEVIL.
I'M A COLLECTOR, FRIEND ROSS.
I AM MASTER OF A REALM POPULATED BY ONLY MYSELF --
I HAVE THAT PROBLEM TOO. MAYBE A NEW CREME RINSE...
-- AND THE LOST SOULS WHO WILLINGLY FOLLOW ME.
NOT QUITE THE IDEAL EXISTENCE...
WELL, WHY NOT JUST, Ah, LEAVE?
LEAVE?
LEAVE, SCRAM, VAMOOSE. CHANGE PARTY AFFILIATION. JOIN A BAND...
...PLAY BASS FOR MARILYN MANSON...
I AND MY REALM ARE ONE.
I CANNOT LEAVE, AND THE LONGER I REMAIN IN THIS WORLD, THE WEAKER MY POWER.
SO WHY COME HERE? WHY KEEP REACHING FOR MORE SOULS?
IT IS HUNGER... AN OBSESSION...
YEAH... LIKE ME AND DVD'S...
THE PURER -- THE MORE NOBLE THE SOUL, THE BETTER.
HEY.
I WORK IN WASHINGTON.
WHICH IS WHY YOU NEED NOT FEAR ME...
...KENNY.

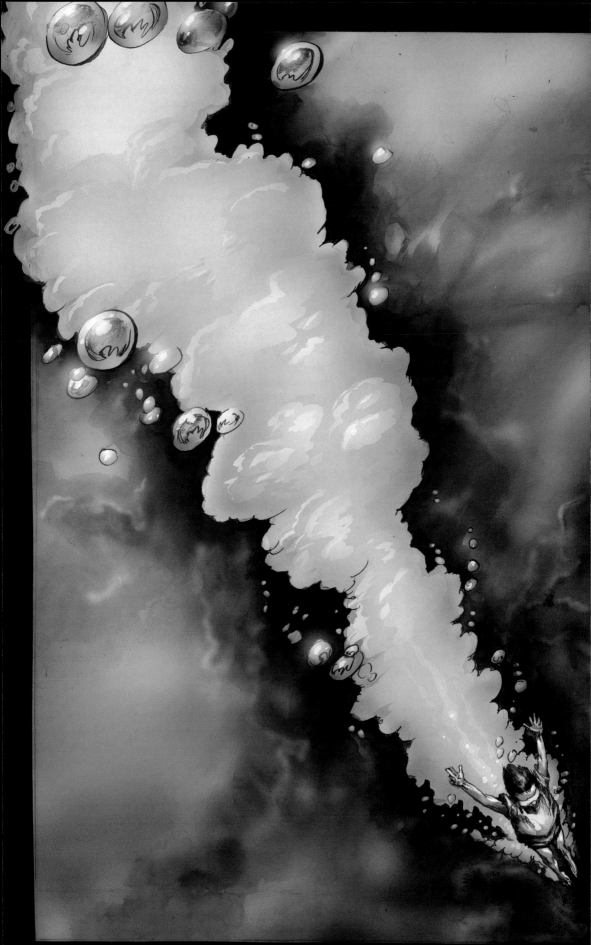

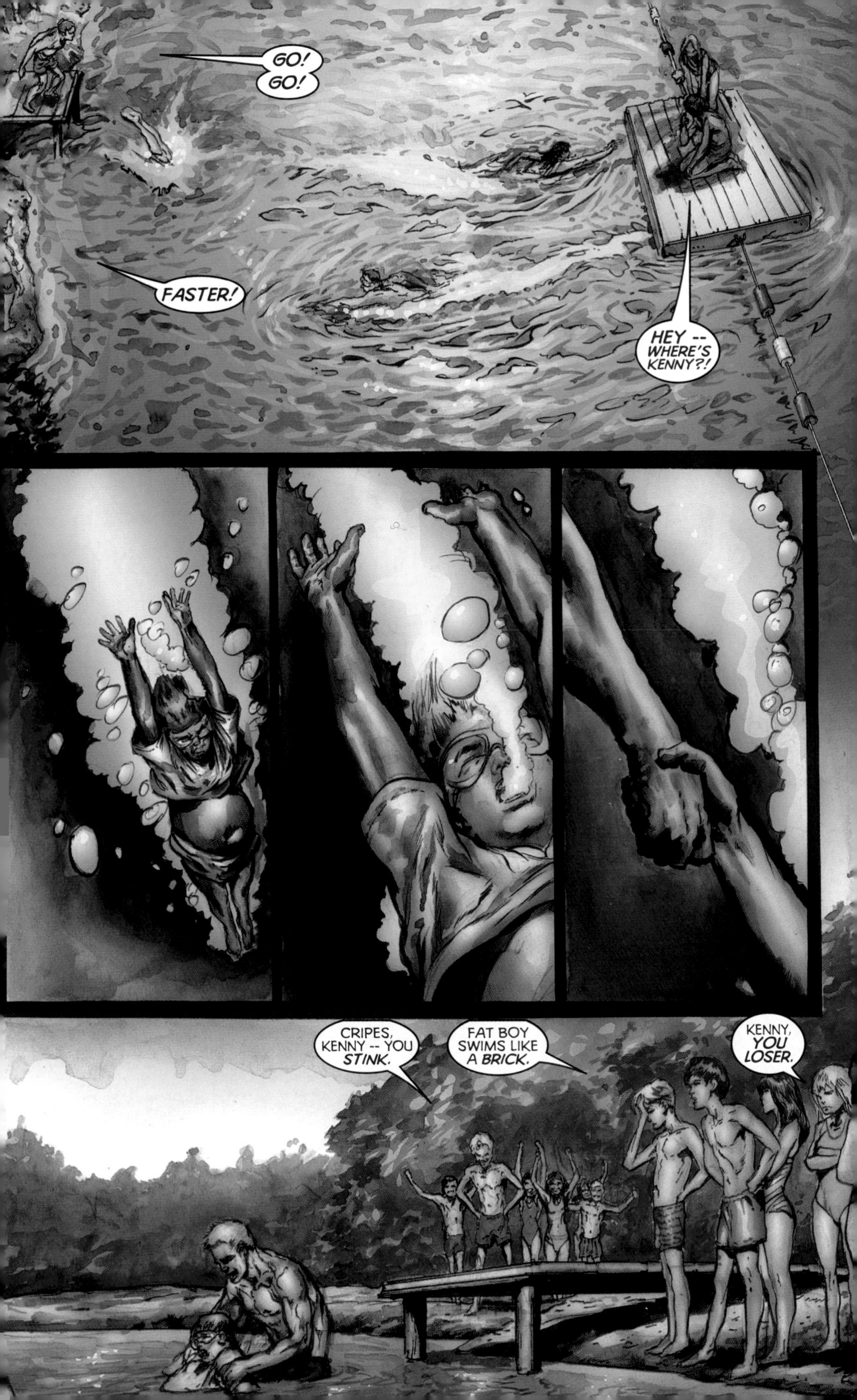
GO!
GO!
FASTER!
HEY -- WHERE'S KENNY?!
CRIPES, KENNY -- YOU *STINK*.
FAT BOY SWIMS LIKE A *BRICK*.
KENNY, *YOU LOSER*.

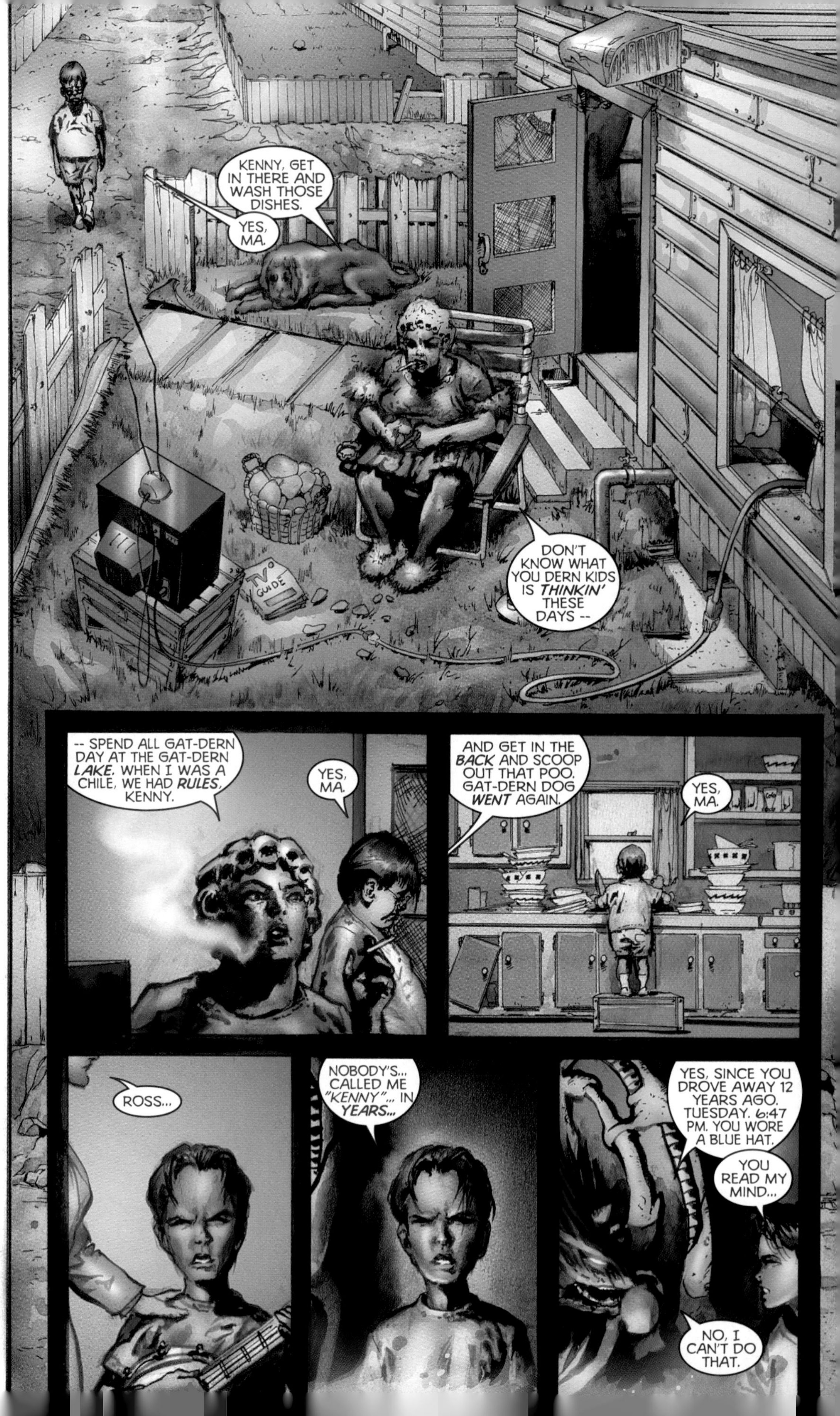
KENNY, GET IN THERE AND WASH THOSE DISHES.
YES, MA.
DON'T KNOW WHAT YOU DERN KIDS IS *THINKIN'* THESE DAYS --
-- SPEND ALL GAT-DERN DAY AT THE GAT-DERN *LAKE.* WHEN I WAS A CHILE, WE HAD *RULES,* KENNY.
YES, MA.
AND GET IN THE *BACK* AND SCOOP OUT THAT POO. GAT-DERN DOG *WENT* AGAIN.
YES, MA.
ROSS...
NOBODY'S... CALLED ME "KENNY"... IN *YEARS...*
YES, SINCE YOU DROVE AWAY 12 YEARS AGO. TUESDAY. 6:47 PM. YOU WORE A BLUE HAT.
YOU READ MY MIND...
NO, I CAN'T DO THAT.

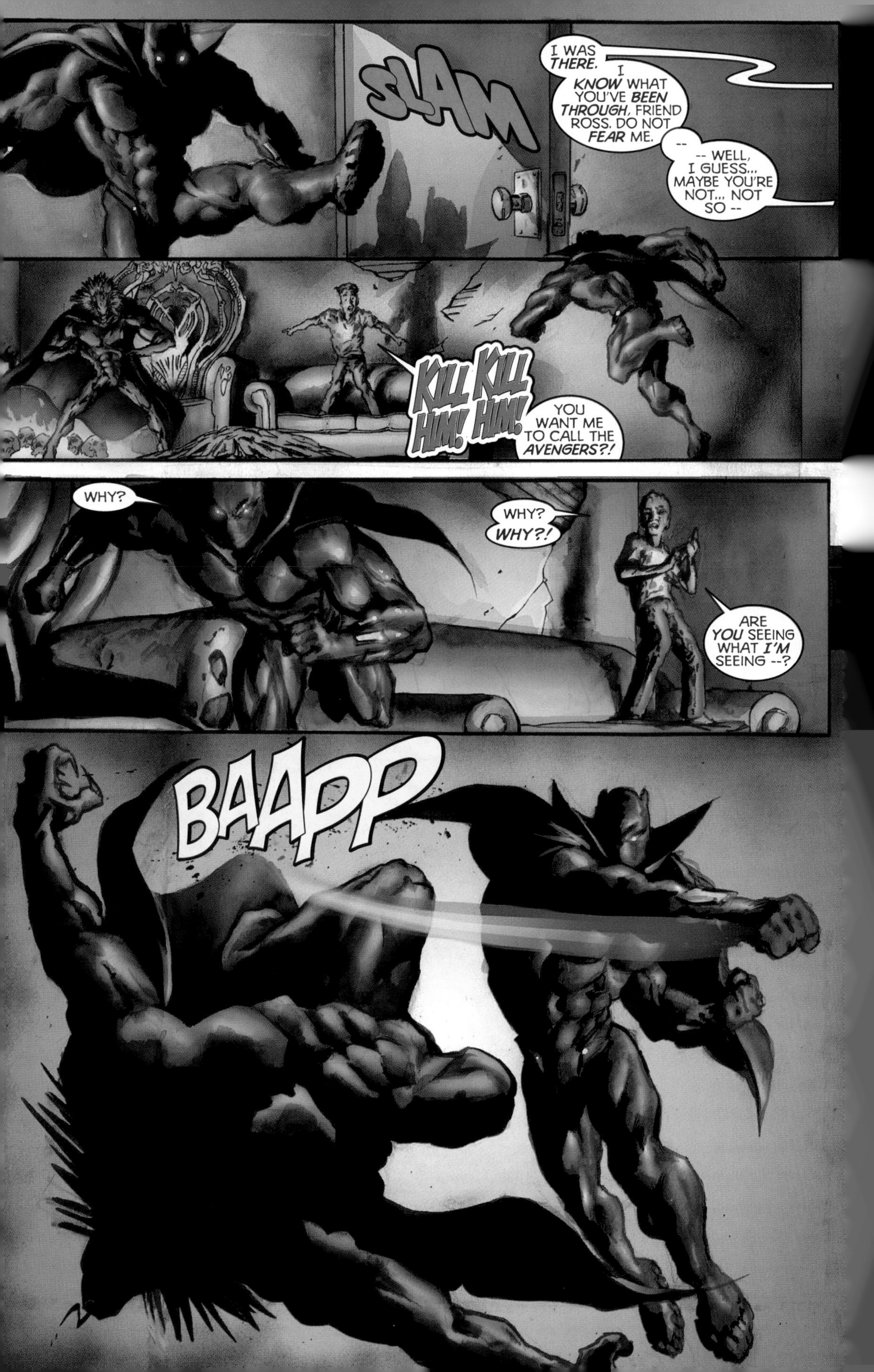
SLAM
I WAS THERE. I KNOW WHAT YOU'VE BEEN THROUGH, FRIEND ROSS. DO NOT FEAR ME.
-- -- WELL, I GUESS... MAYBE YOU'RE NOT... NOT SO --
KILL HIM! KILL HIM!
YOU WANT ME TO CALL THE AVENGERS?!
WHY?
WHY? WHY?!
ARE YOU SEEING WHAT I'M SEEING --?
BAAPP

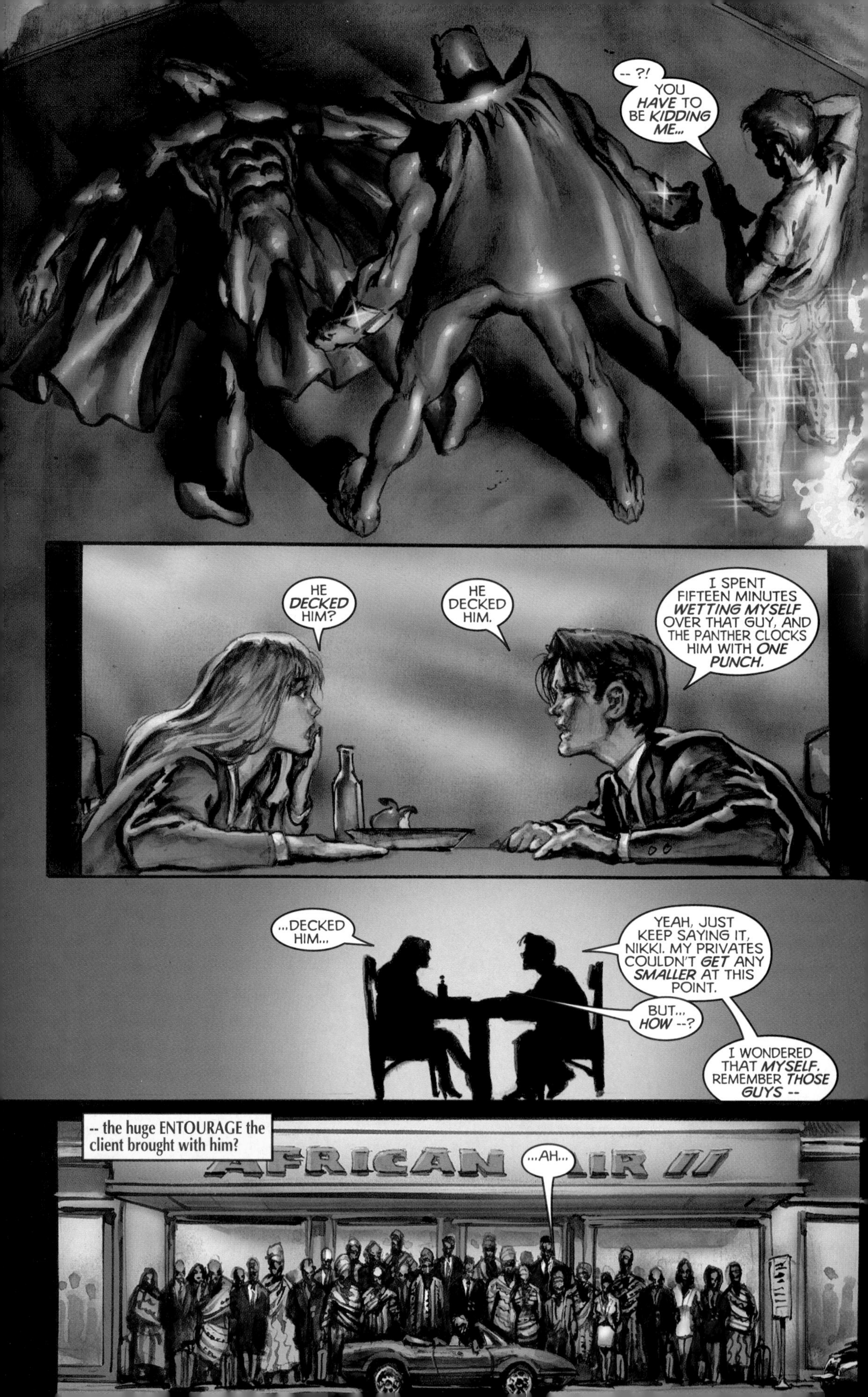

-- ?! YOU HAVE TO BE KIDDING ME...
HE DECKED HIM?
HE DECKED HIM.
I SPENT FIFTEEN MINUTES WETTING MYSELF OVER THAT GUY, AND THE PANTHER CLOCKS HIM WITH ONE PUNCH.
...DECKED HIM...
YEAH, JUST KEEP SAYING IT, NIKKI. MY PRIVATES COULDN'T GET ANY SMALLER AT THIS POINT.
BUT... HOW --?
I WONDERED THAT MYSELF. REMEMBER THOSE GUYS --
-- the huge ENTOURAGE the client brought with him?
...AH...

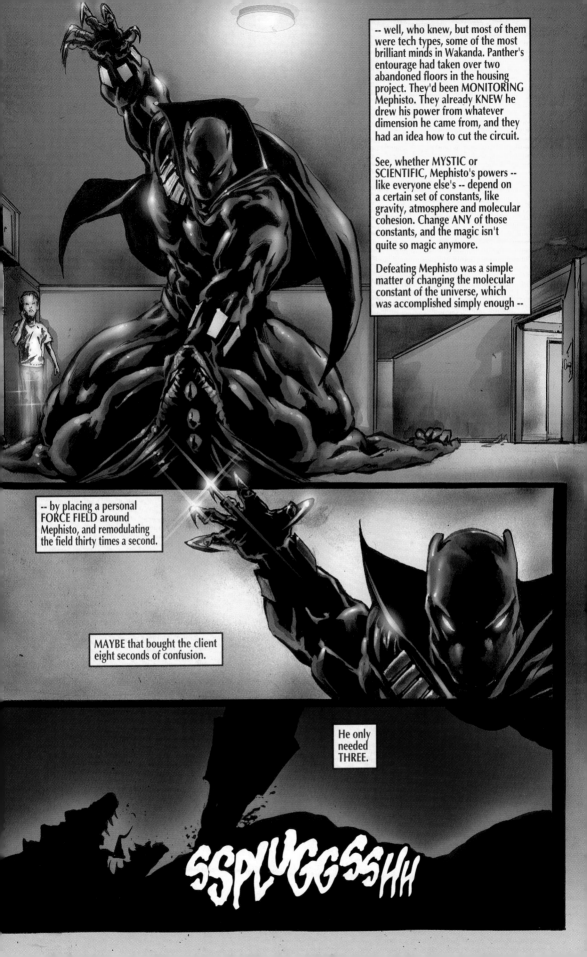

-- well, who knew, but most of them were tech types, some of the most brilliant minds in Wakanda. Panther's entourage had taken over two abandoned floors in the housing project. They'd been MONITORING Mephisto. They already KNEW he drew his power from whatever dimension he came from, and they had an idea how to cut the circuit.

See, whether MYSTIC or SCIENTIFIC, Mephisto's powers -- like everyone else's -- depend on a certain set of constants, like gravity, atmosphere and molecular cohesion. Change ANY of those constants, and the magic isn't quite so magic anymore.

Defeating Mephisto was a simple matter of changing the molecular constant of the universe, which was accomplished simply enough --

-- by placing a personal FORCE FIELD around Mephisto, and remodulating the field thirty times a second.

MAYBE that bought the client eight seconds of confusion.

He only needed THREE.

SSPLUGGSSHH

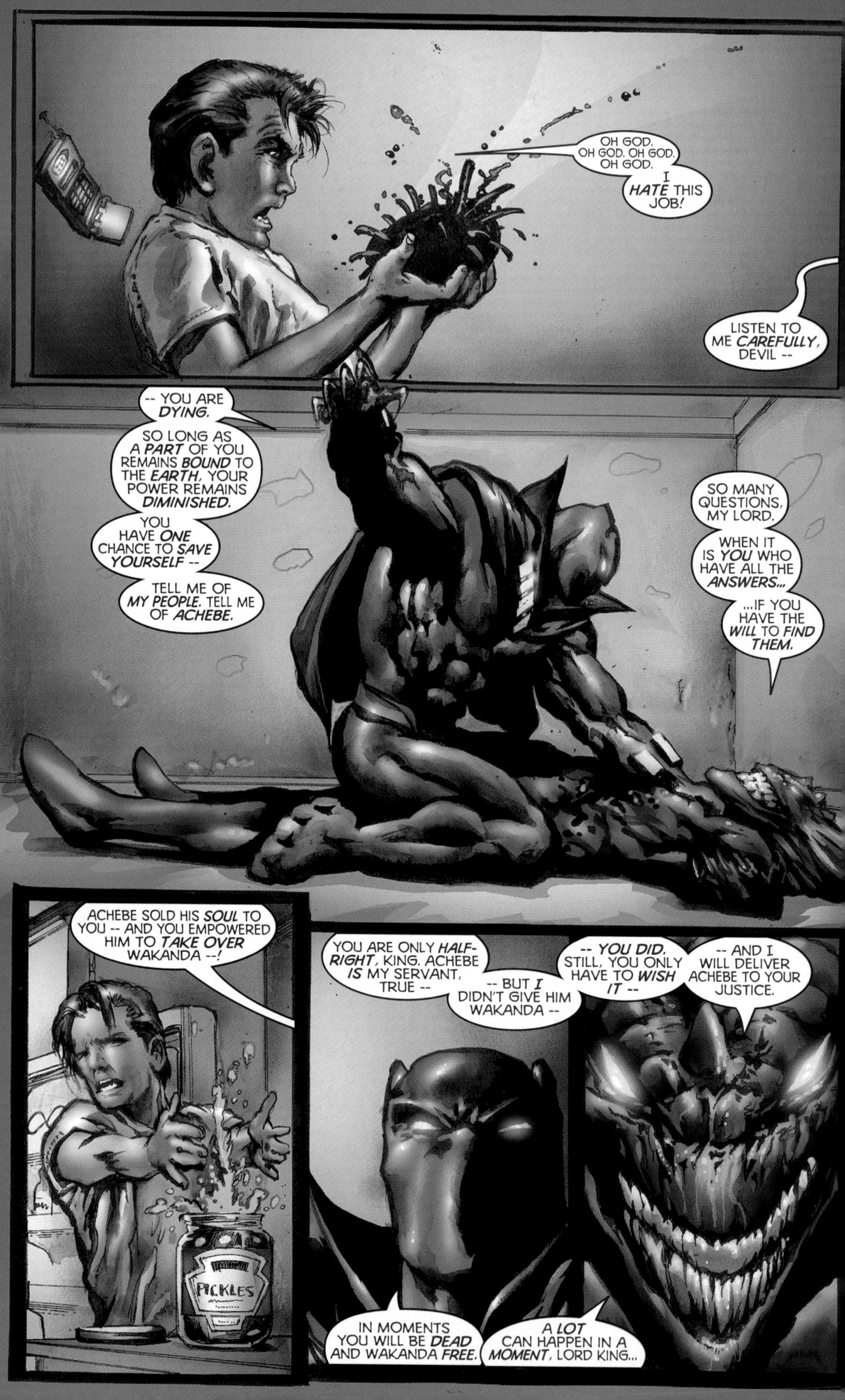
OH GOD. OH GOD. OH GOD. OH GOD.
I HATE THIS JOB!
LISTEN TO ME CAREFULLY, DEVIL --
-- YOU ARE DYING.
SO LONG AS A PART OF YOU REMAINS BOUND TO THE EARTH, YOUR POWER REMAINS DIMINISHED.
YOU HAVE ONE CHANCE TO SAVE YOURSELF --
TELL ME OF MY PEOPLE. TELL ME OF ACHEBE.
SO MANY QUESTIONS, MY LORD.
WHEN IT IS YOU WHO HAVE ALL THE ANSWERS...
...IF YOU HAVE THE WILL TO FIND THEM.
ACHEBE SOLD HIS SOUL TO YOU -- AND YOU EMPOWERED HIM TO TAKE OVER WAKANDA --!
YOU ARE ONLY HALF-RIGHT, KING. ACHEBE IS MY SERVANT, TRUE --
-- BUT I DIDN'T GIVE HIM WAKANDA --
-- YOU DID. STILL, YOU ONLY HAVE TO WISH IT --
-- AND I WILL DELIVER ACHEBE TO YOUR JUSTICE.
PICKLES
IN MOMENTS YOU WILL BE DEAD AND WAKANDA FREE.
A LOT CAN HAPPEN IN A MOMENT, LORD KING...

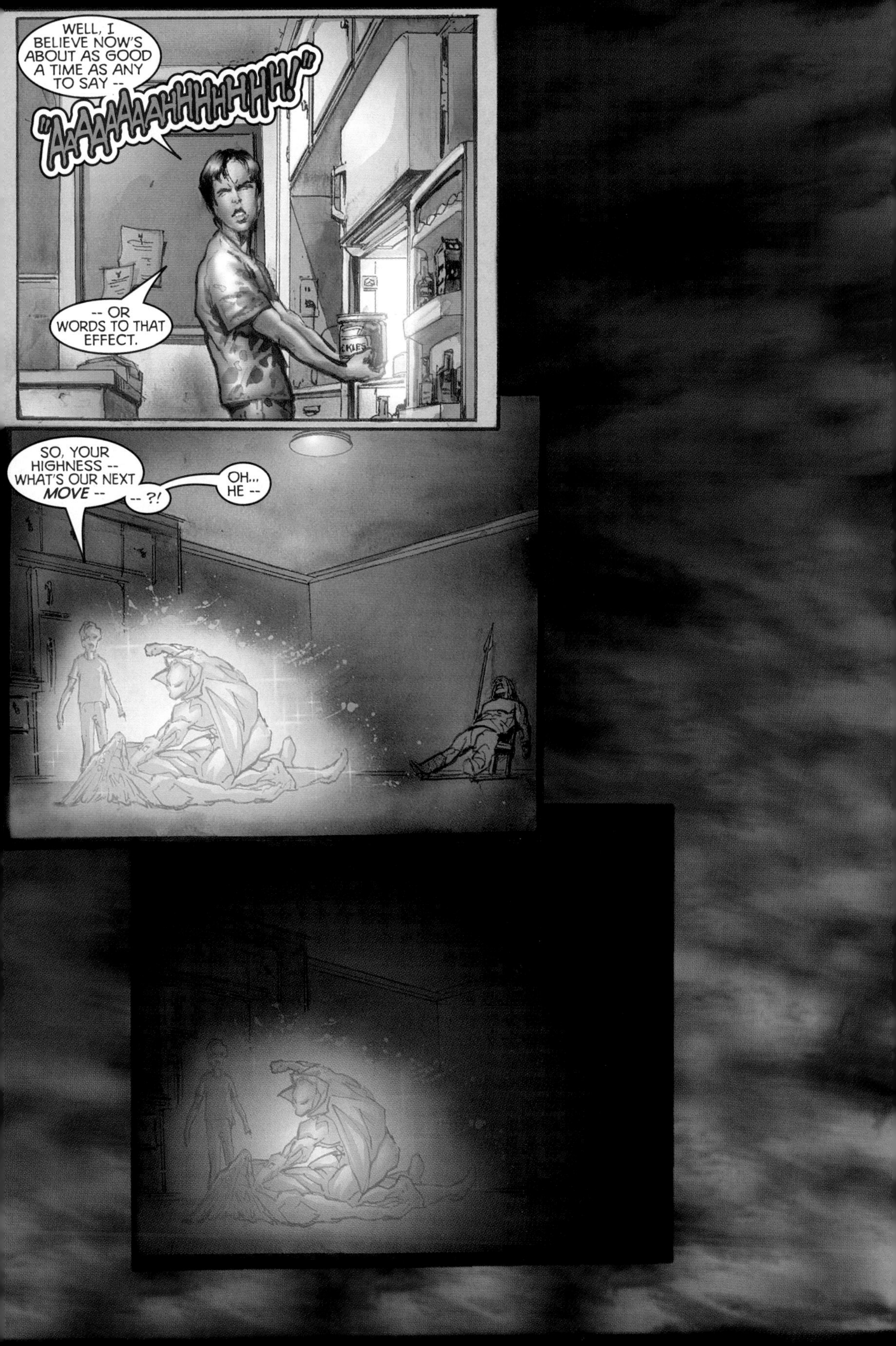
WELL, I BELIEVE NOW'S ABOUT AS GOOD A TIME AS ANY TO SAY --
"AAAAAAAHHHHHH!"
-- OR WORDS TO THAT EFFECT.
SO, YOUR HIGHNESS -- WHAT'S OUR NEXT MOVE --
-- ?!
OH... HE --

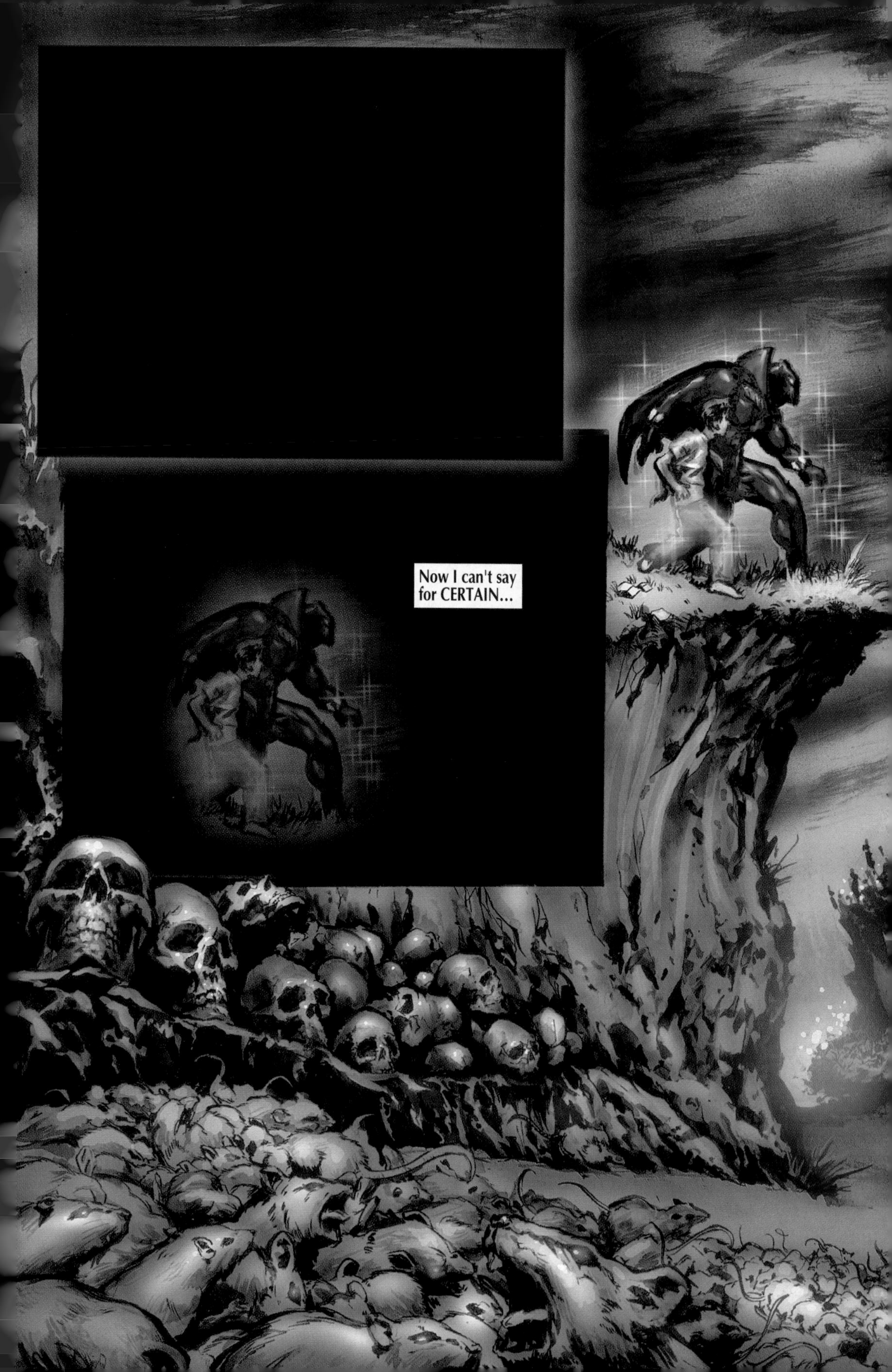
Now I can't say for CERTAIN...

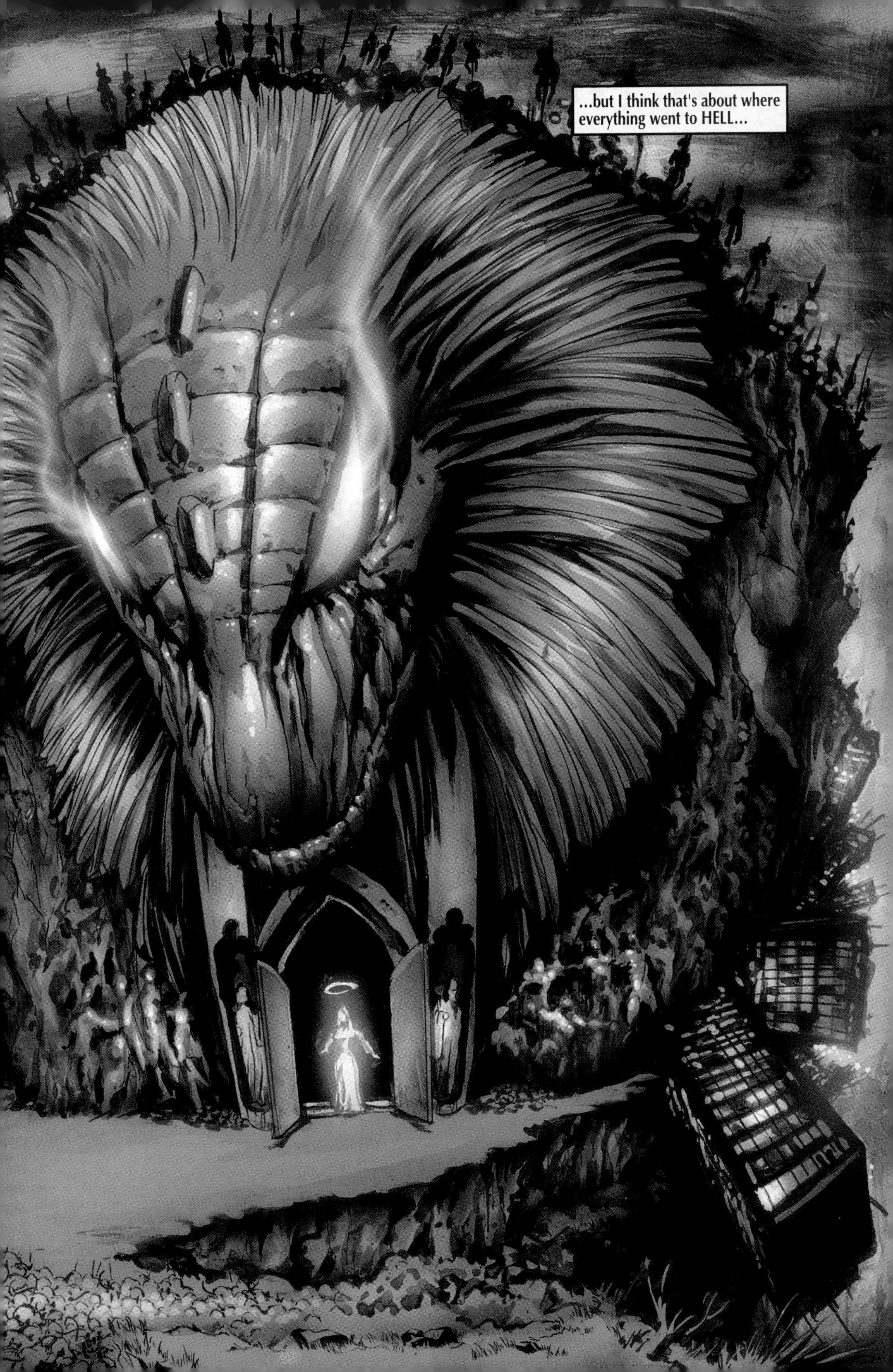
...but I think that's about where everything went to HELL...

CHAPTER 5

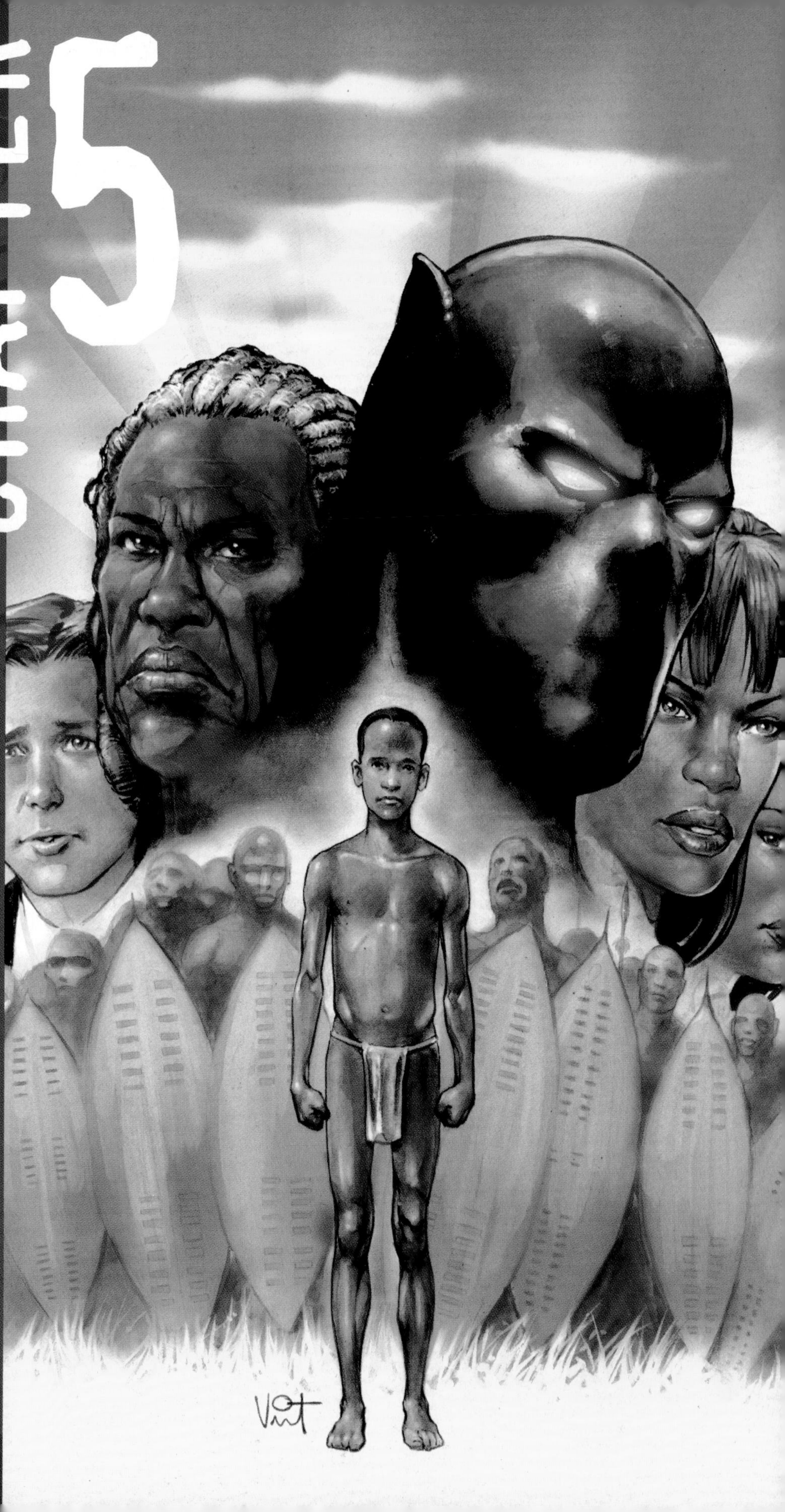

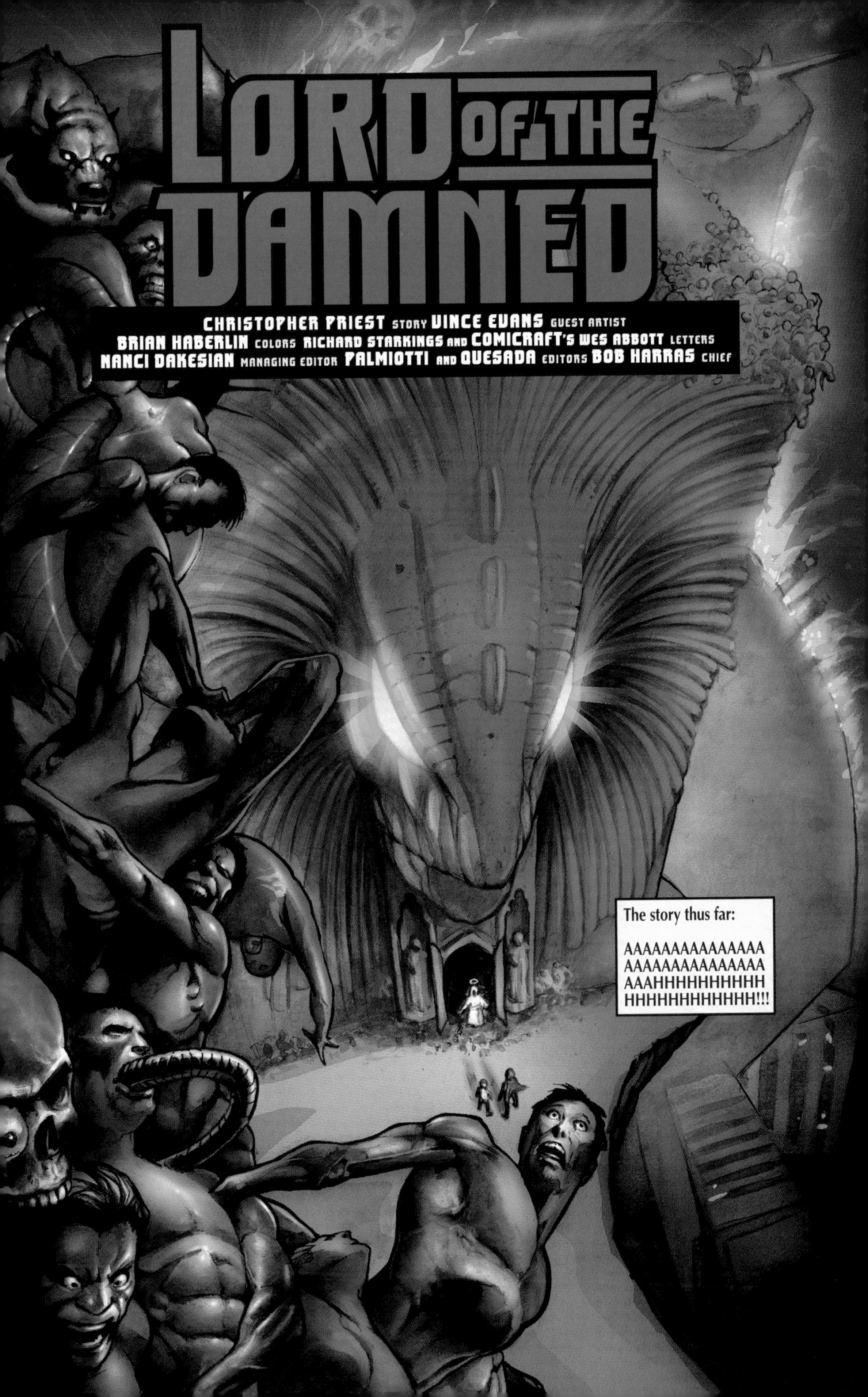
LORD OF THE DAMNED
CHRISTOPHER PRIEST STORY VINCE EVANS GUEST ARTIST
BRIAN HABERLIN COLORS RICHARD STARKINGS AND COMICRAFT'S WES ABBOTT LETTERS
NANCI DAKESIAN MANAGING EDITOR PALMIOTTI AND QUESADA EDITORS BOB HARRAS CHIEF
The story thus far:
AAAAAAAAAAAAAAA AAAAAAAAAAAAAAA AAAHHHHHHHHHHH HHHHHHHHHHHH!!!

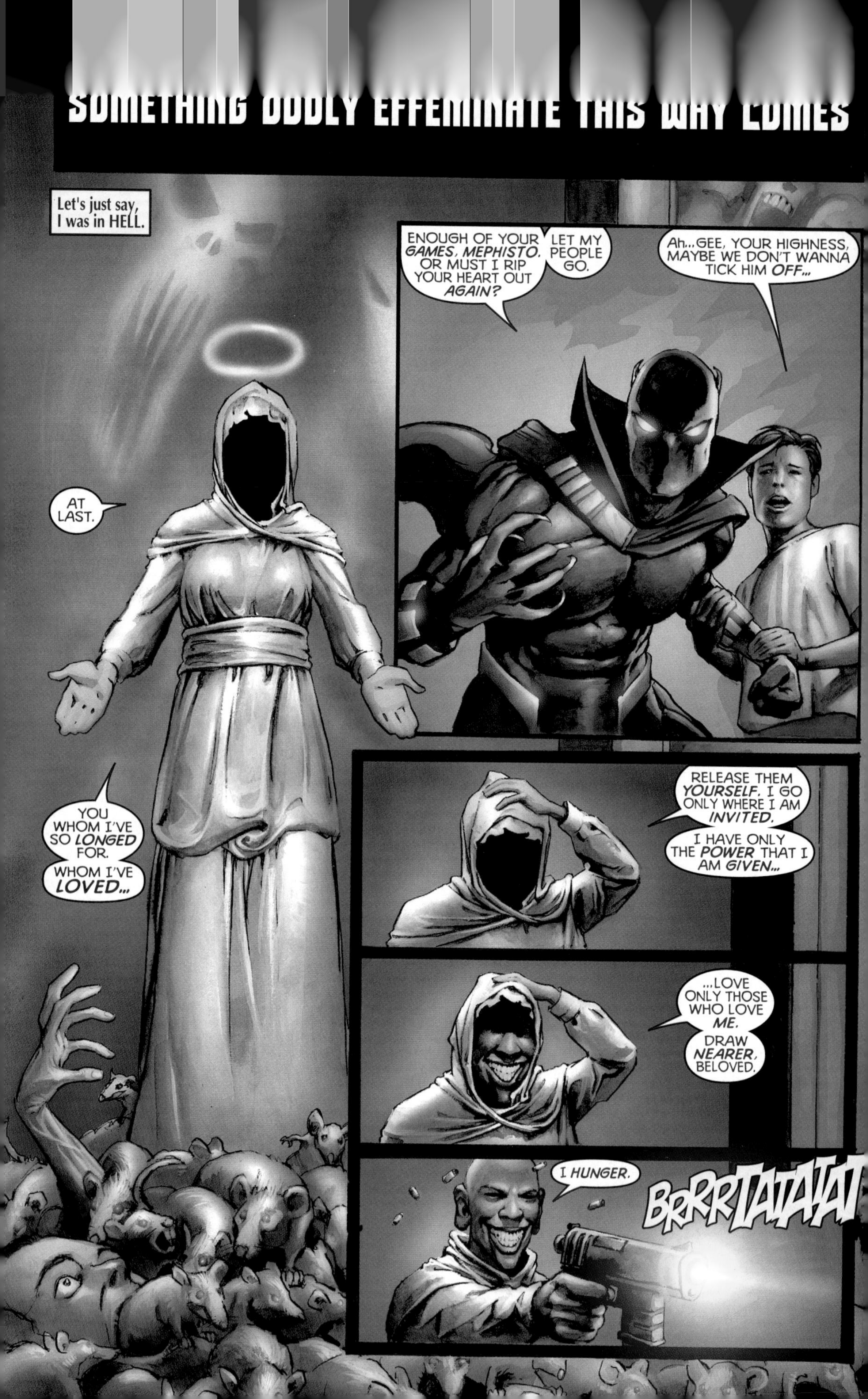
SOMETHING ODDLY EFFEMINATE THIS WAY COMES
Let's just say, I was in HELL.
AT LAST.
YOU WHOM I'VE SO LONGED FOR. WHOM I'VE LOVED...
ENOUGH OF YOUR GAMES, MEPHISTO, OR MUST I RIP YOUR HEART OUT AGAIN?
LET MY PEOPLE GO.
Ah...GEE, YOUR HIGHNESS, MAYBE WE DON'T WANNA TICK HIM OFF...
RELEASE THEM YOURSELF. I GO ONLY WHERE I AM INVITED.
I HAVE ONLY THE POWER THAT I AM GIVEN...
...LOVE ONLY THOSE WHO LOVE ME.
DRAW NEARER, BELOVED.
I HUNGER.
BRRRTATATAT

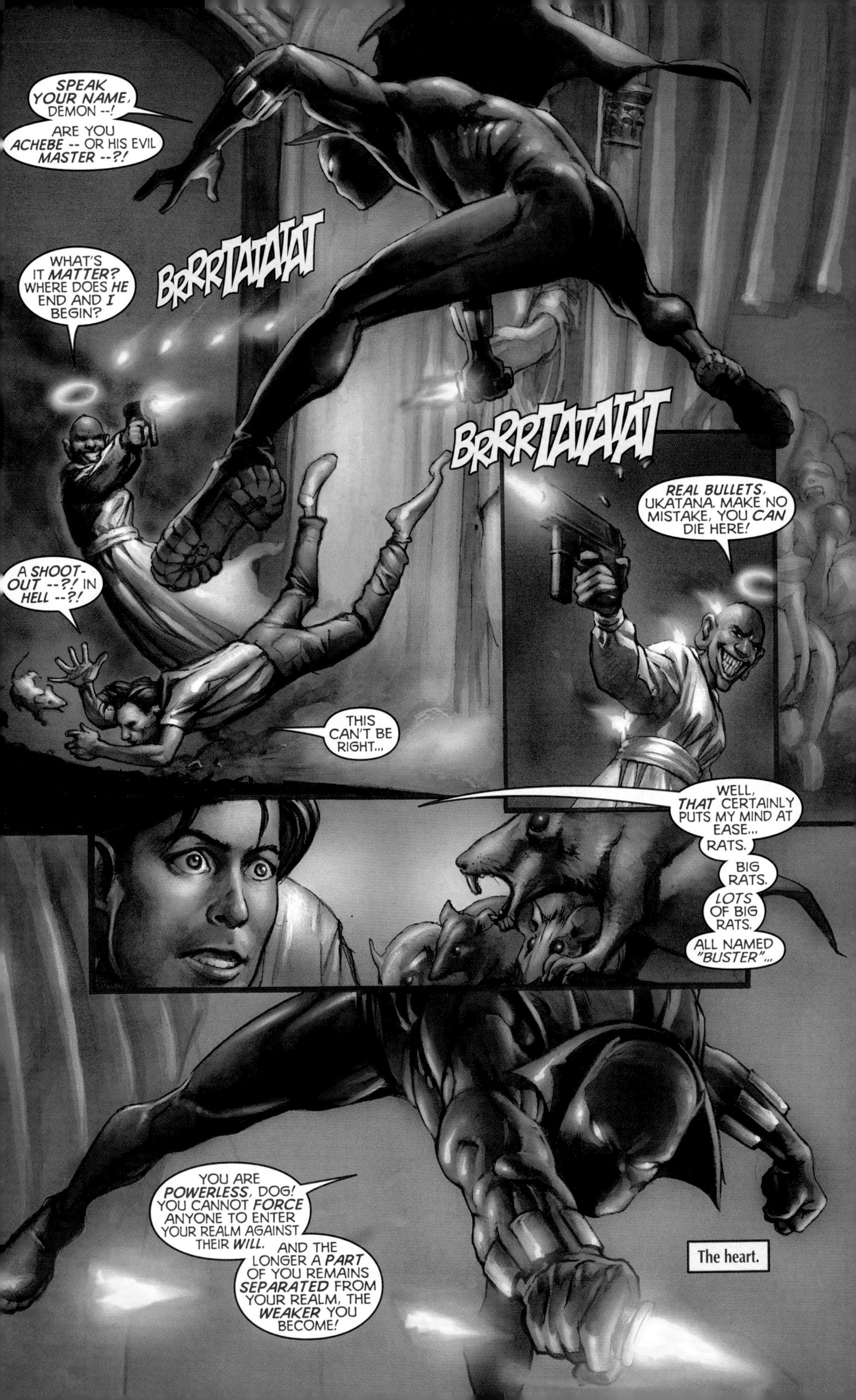
SPEAK YOUR NAME, DEMON --!
ARE YOU ACHEBE -- OR HIS EVIL MASTER --?!
BRRRTATATAT
WHAT'S IT MATTER? WHERE DOES HE END AND I BEGIN?
BRRRTATATAT
REAL BULLETS, UKATANA. MAKE NO MISTAKE, YOU CAN DIE HERE!
A SHOOT-OUT --?! IN HELL --?!
THIS CAN'T BE RIGHT...
WELL, THAT CERTAINLY PUTS MY MIND AT EASE...
RATS.
BIG RATS.
LOTS OF BIG RATS.
ALL NAMED "BUSTER"...
YOU ARE POWERLESS, DOG! YOU CANNOT FORCE ANYONE TO ENTER YOUR REALM AGAINST THEIR WILL.
AND THE LONGER A PART OF YOU REMAINS SEPARATED FROM YOUR REALM, THE WEAKER YOU BECOME!
The heart.

LEFTOVERS

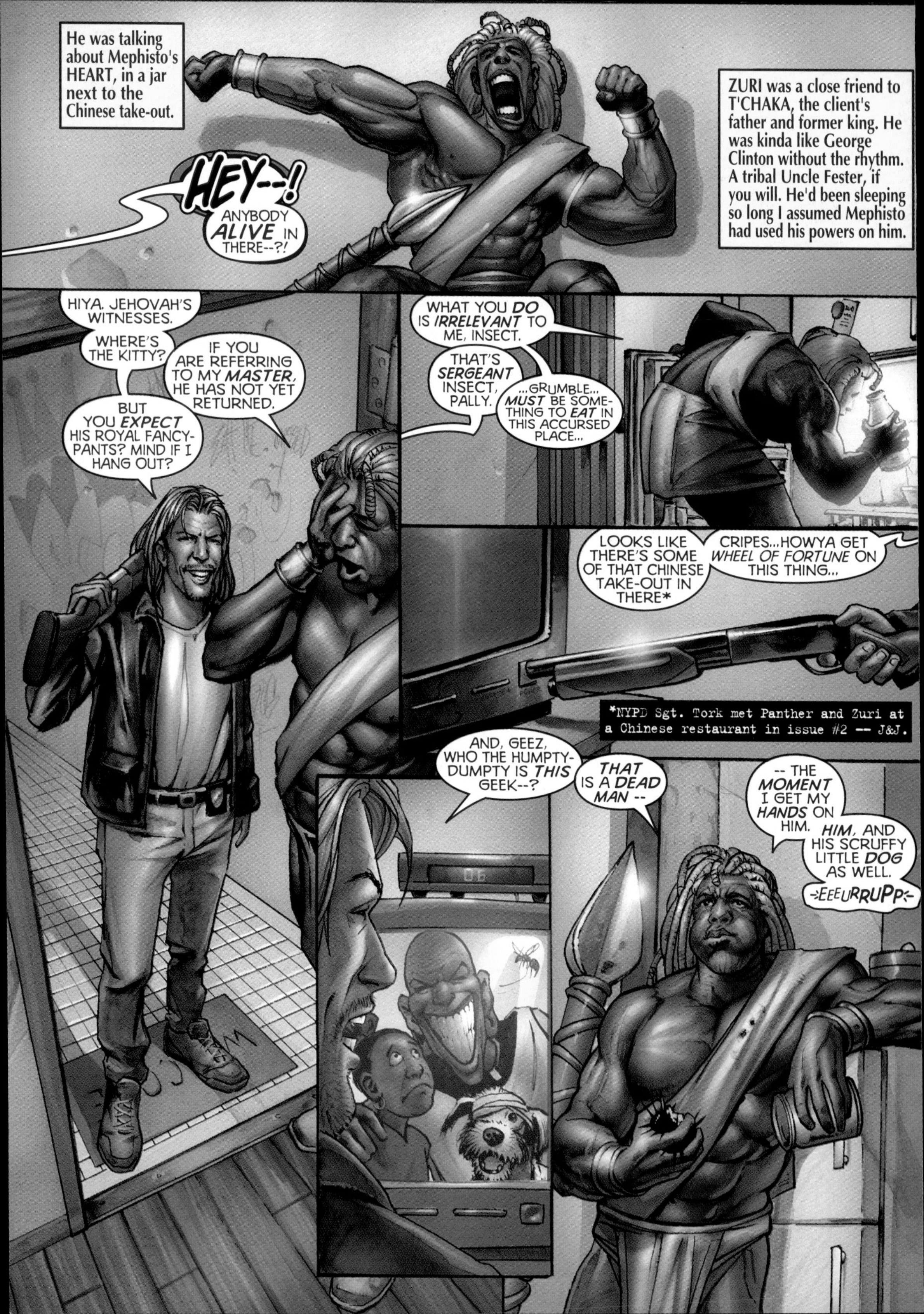
He was talking about Mephisto's HEART, in a jar next to the Chinese take-out.
ZURI was a close friend to T'CHAKA, the client's father and former king. He was kinda like George Clinton without the rhythm. A tribal Uncle Fester, if you will. He'd been sleeping so long I assumed Mephisto had used his powers on him.
HEY--! ANYBODY ALIVE IN THERE--?!
HIYA. JEHOVAH'S WITNESSES.
WHERE'S THE KITTY?
IF YOU ARE REFERRING TO MY MASTER, HE HAS NOT YET RETURNED.
BUT YOU EXPECT HIS ROYAL FANCY-PANTS? MIND IF I HANG OUT?
WHAT YOU DO IS IRRELEVANT TO ME, INSECT.
THAT'S SERGEANT INSECT, PALLY.
...GRUMBLE... MUST BE SOME-THING TO EAT IN THIS ACCURSED PLACE...
CRIPES...HOWYA GET WHEEL OF FORTUNE ON THIS THING...
LOOKS LIKE THERE'S SOME OF THAT CHINESE TAKE-OUT IN THERE*
*NYPD Sgt. Tork met Panther and Zuri at a Chinese restaurant in issue #2 -- J&J.
AND, GEEZ, WHO THE HUMPTY-DUMPTY IS THIS GEEK--?
THAT IS A DEAD MAN --
-- THE MOMENT I GET MY HANDS ON HIM. HIM, AND HIS SCRUFFY LITTLE DOG AS WELL.
EEEURRRUPP

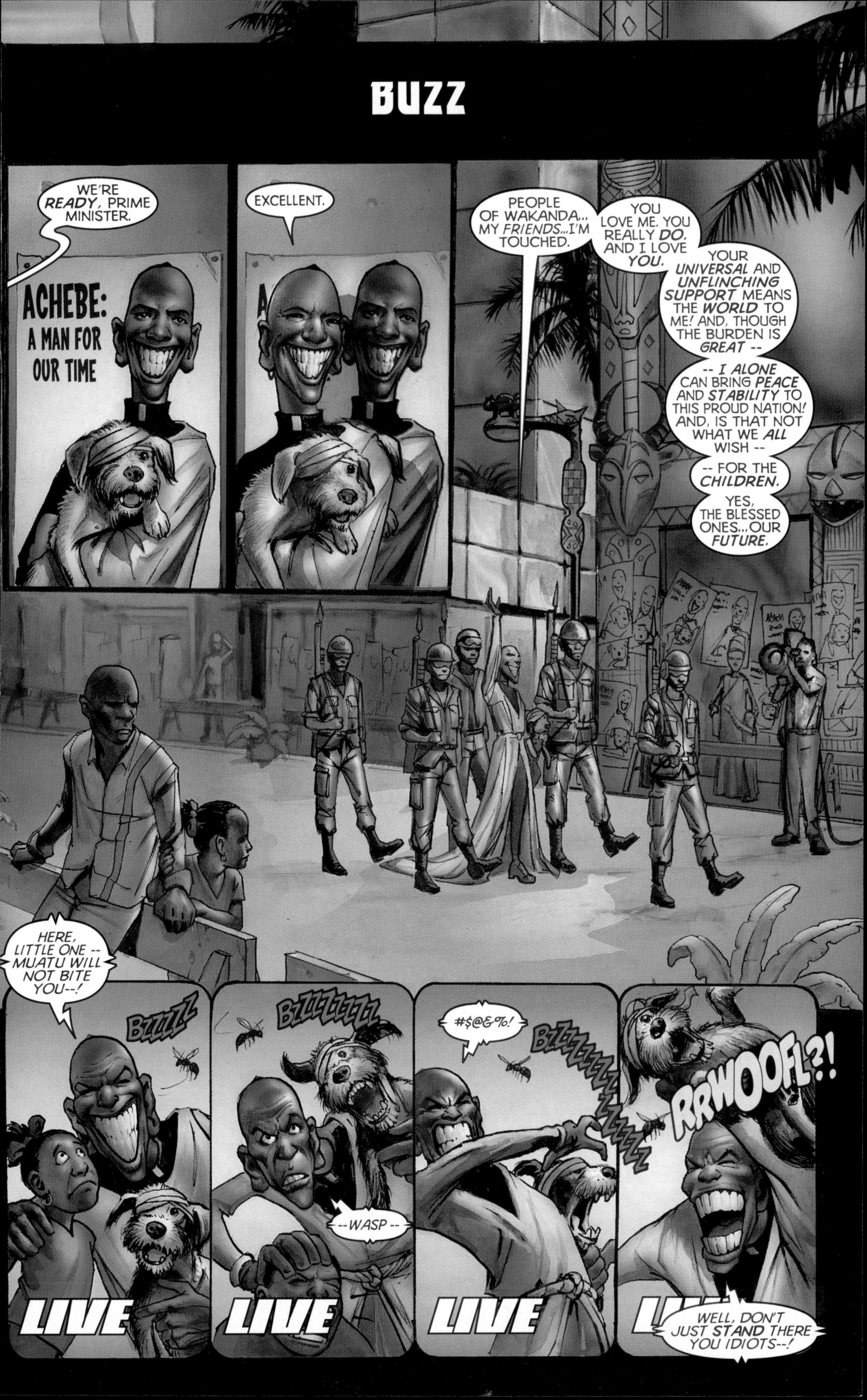
BUZZ
WE'RE READY, PRIME MINISTER.
ACHEBE: A MAN FOR OUR TIME
EXCELLENT.
PEOPLE OF WAKANDA... MY FRIENDS...I'M TOUCHED.
YOU LOVE ME. YOU REALLY DO. AND I LOVE YOU.
YOUR UNIVERSAL AND UNFLINCHING SUPPORT MEANS THE WORLD TO ME! AND, THOUGH THE BURDEN IS GREAT --
-- I ALONE CAN BRING PEACE AND STABILITY TO THIS PROUD NATION! AND, IS THAT NOT WHAT WE ALL WISH --
-- FOR THE CHILDREN.
YES, THE BLESSED ONES...OUR FUTURE.
HERE, LITTLE ONE -- MUATU WILL NOT BITE YOU--!
BZZZZZ
LIVE
BZZZZZZZZ
--WASP--
LIVE
#$@&%!
BZZZZZZZZZZZ
LIVE
RRWOOFL?!
LIVE
WELL, DON'T JUST STAND THERE YOU IDIOTS--!

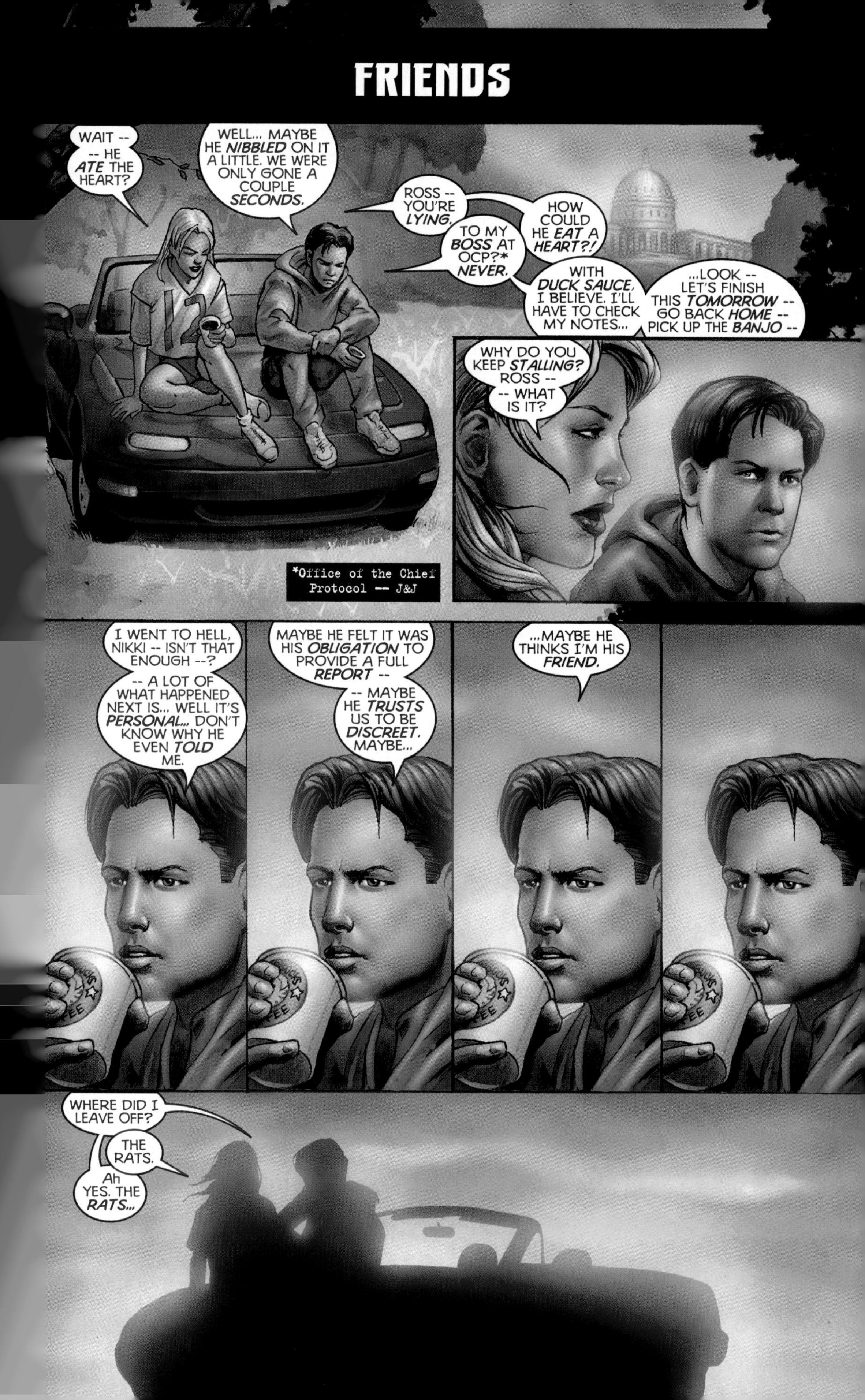
FRIENDS
WAIT -- -- HE ATE THE HEART?
WELL... MAYBE HE NIBBLED ON IT A LITTLE. WE WERE ONLY GONE A COUPLE SECONDS.
ROSS -- YOU'RE LYING.
TO MY BOSS AT OCP?* NEVER.
HOW COULD HE EAT A HEART?!
WITH DUCK SAUCE, I BELIEVE. I'LL HAVE TO CHECK MY NOTES...
...LOOK -- LET'S FINISH THIS TOMORROW -- GO BACK HOME -- PICK UP THE BANJO --
*Office of the Chief Protocol -- J&J
WHY DO YOU KEEP STALLING? ROSS -- -- WHAT IS IT?
I WENT TO HELL, NIKKI -- ISN'T THAT ENOUGH --?
-- A LOT OF WHAT HAPPENED NEXT IS... WELL IT'S PERSONAL... DON'T KNOW WHY HE EVEN TOLD ME.
MAYBE HE FELT IT WAS HIS OBLIGATION TO PROVIDE A FULL REPORT --
-- MAYBE HE TRUSTS US TO BE DISCREET. MAYBE...
...MAYBE HE THINKS I'M HIS FRIEND.
WHERE DID I LEAVE OFF?
THE RATS.
Ah YES. THE RATS...

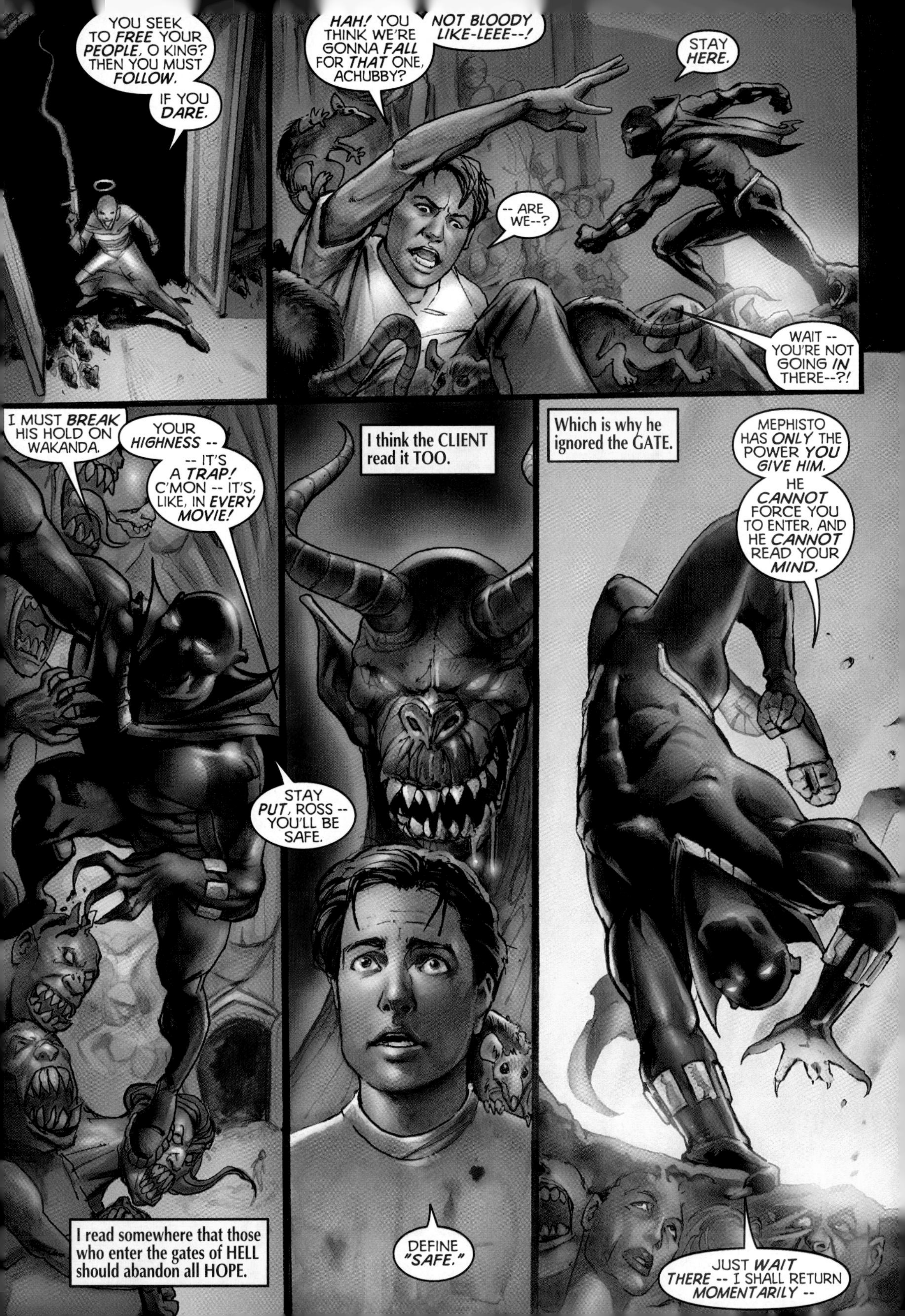
YOU SEEK TO *FREE* YOUR *PEOPLE*, O KING? THEN YOU MUST *FOLLOW*.
IF YOU *DARE*.
HAH! YOU THINK WE'RE GONNA *FALL* FOR *THAT* ONE, ACHUBBY?
NOT BLOODY LIKE-LEEE--!
STAY *HERE*.
-- ARE WE--?
WAIT -- YOU'RE NOT GOING *IN* THERE--?!
I MUST *BREAK* HIS HOLD ON WAKANDA.
YOUR *HIGHNESS* -- -- IT'S A *TRAP!* C'MON -- IT'S, LIKE, IN *EVERY MOVIE!*
STAY *PUT*, ROSS -- YOU'LL BE SAFE.
I read somewhere that those who enter the gates of HELL should abandon all HOPE.
I think the CLIENT read it TOO.
DEFINE *"SAFE."*
Which is why he ignored the GATE.
MEPHISTO HAS *ONLY* THE POWER *YOU GIVE HIM.*
HE *CANNOT* FORCE YOU TO ENTER, AND HE *CANNOT* READ YOUR *MIND.*
JUST *WAIT THERE* -- I SHALL RETURN *MOMENTARILY* --

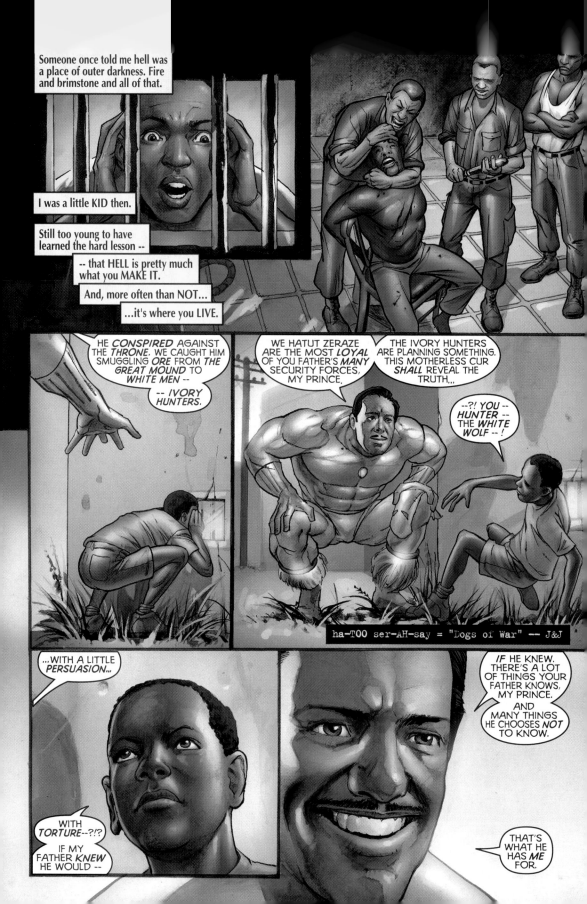

Someone once told me hell was a place of outer darkness. Fire and brimstone and all of that.

I was a little KID then.

Still too young to have learned the hard lesson --

-- that HELL is pretty much what you MAKE it.

And, more often than NOT...

...it's where you LIVE.

HE *CONSPIRED* AGAINST THE *THRONE.* WE CAUGHT HIM SMUGGLING *ORE* FROM *THE GREAT MOUND* TO *WHITE MEN* --
-- *IVORY HUNTERS.*

WE HATUT ZERAZE ARE THE MOST *LOYAL* OF YOU FATHER'S *MANY* SECURITY FORCES, MY PRINCE.

THE IVORY HUNTERS ARE PLANNING SOMETHING. THIS MOTHERLESS CUR *SHALL* REVEAL THE TRUTH...

--?! YOU -- HUNTER -- THE *WHITE WOLF* -- !

ha-TOO ser-AH-say = "Dogs of War" -- J&J

...WITH A LITTLE *PERSUASION...*

WITH *TORTURE*--?!? IF MY FATHER *KNEW* HE WOULD --

IF HE KNEW. THERE'S A LOT OF THINGS YOUR FATHER KNOWS, MY PRINCE. AND MANY THINGS HE CHOOSES *NOT* TO KNOW.

THAT'S WHAT HE HAS *ME* FOR.

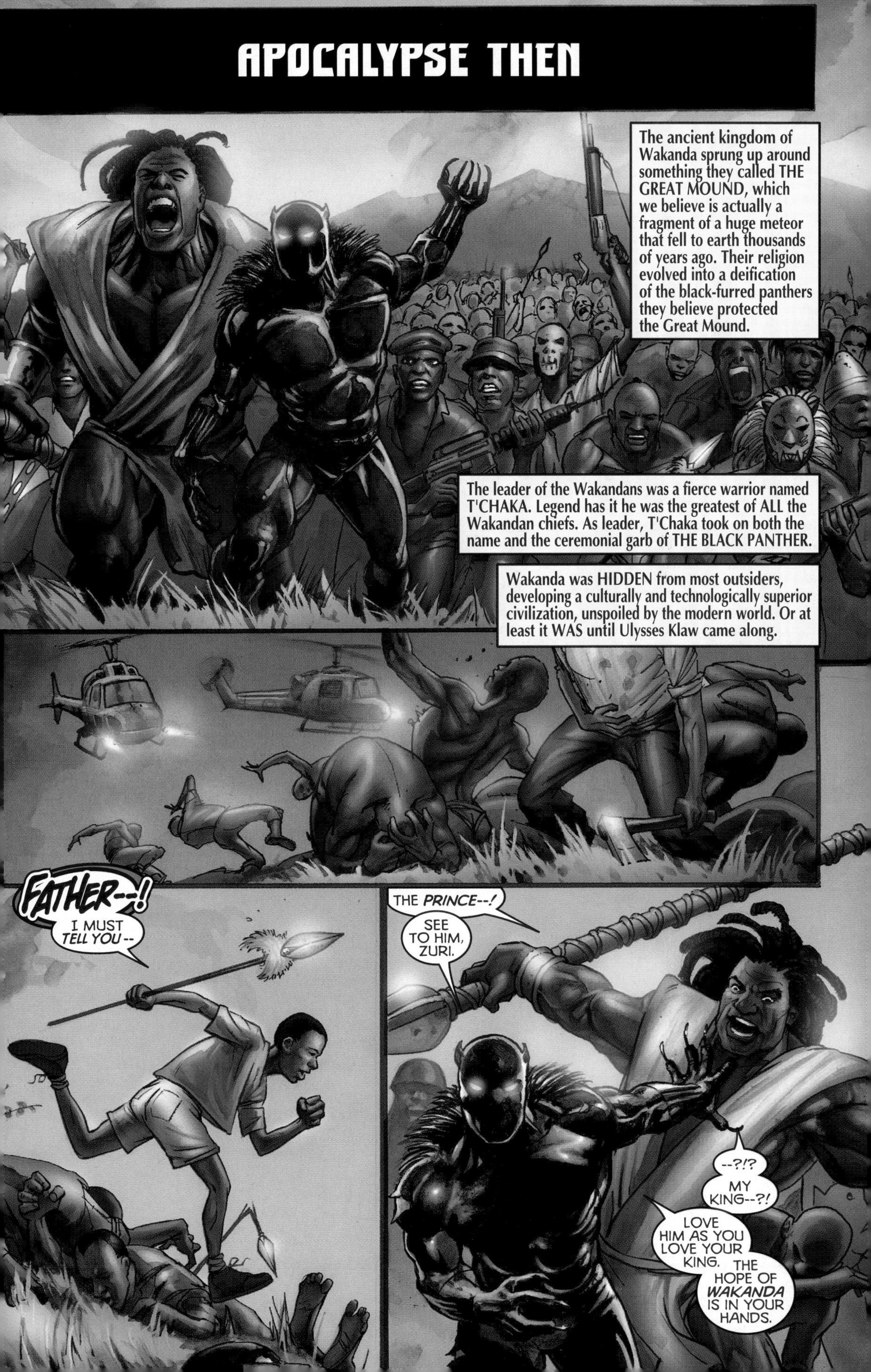
APOCALYPSE THEN
The ancient kingdom of Wakanda sprung up around something they called THE GREAT MOUND, which we believe is actually a fragment of a huge meteor that fell to earth thousands of years ago. Their religion evolved into a deification of the black-furred panthers they believe protected the Great Mound.
The leader of the Wakandans was a fierce warrior named T'CHAKA. Legend has it he was the greatest of ALL the Wakandan chiefs. As leader, T'Chaka took on both the name and the ceremonial garb of THE BLACK PANTHER.
Wakanda was HIDDEN from most outsiders, developing a culturally and technologically superior civilization, unspoiled by the modern world. Or at least it WAS until Ulysses Klaw came along.
FATHER--!
I MUST TELL YOU --
THE PRINCE--!
SEE TO HIM, ZURI.
--?!?
MY KING--?!
LOVE HIM AS YOU LOVE YOUR KING.
THE HOPE OF WAKANDA IS IN YOUR HANDS.

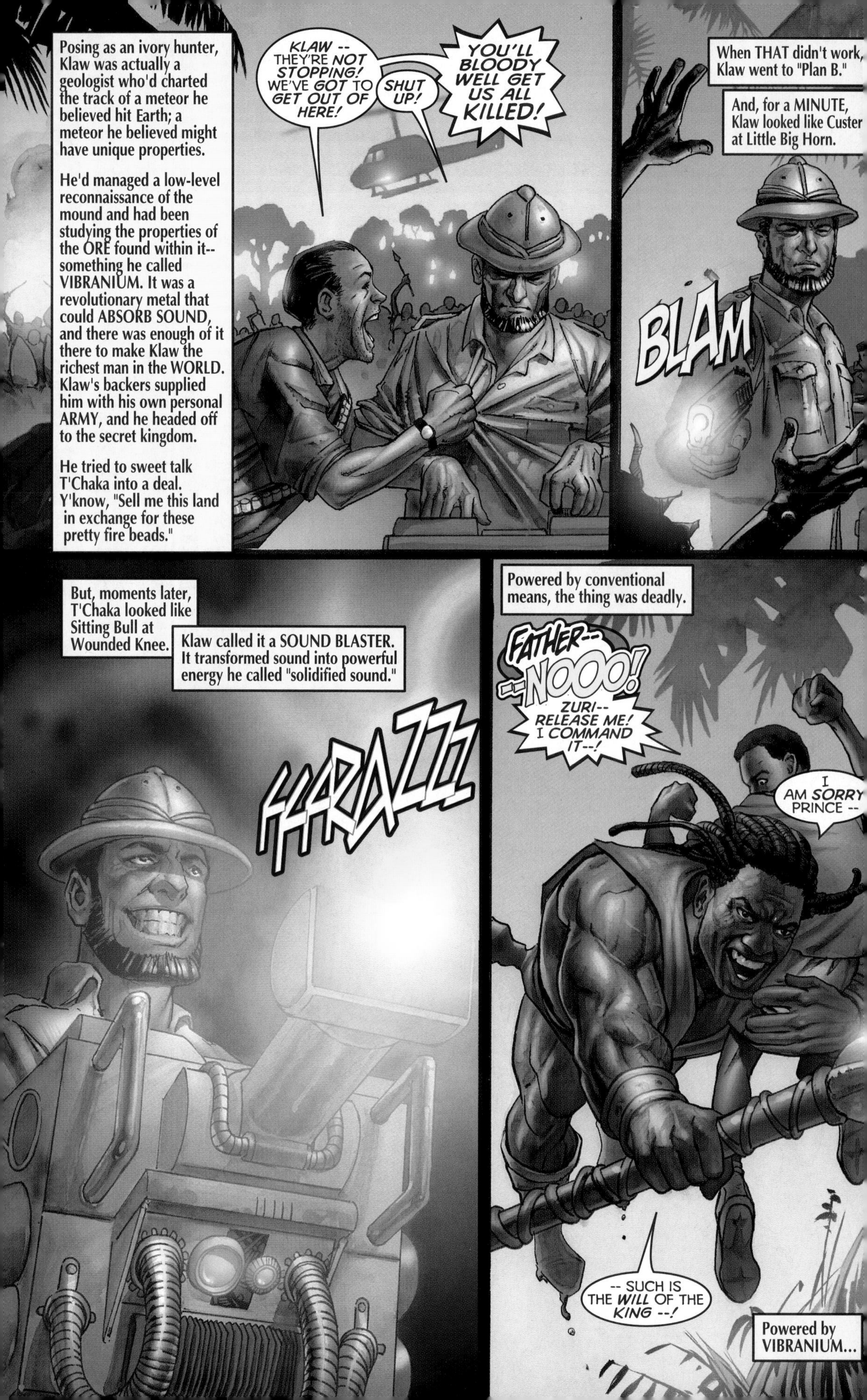

Posing as an ivory hunter, Klaw was actually a geologist who'd charted the track of a meteor he believed hit Earth; a meteor he believed might have unique properties.
He'd managed a low-level reconnaissance of the mound and had been studying the properties of the ORE found within it-- something he called VIBRANIUM. It was a revolutionary metal that could ABSORB SOUND, and there was enough of it there to make Klaw the richest man in the WORLD. Klaw's backers supplied him with his own personal ARMY, and he headed off to the secret kingdom.
He tried to sweet talk T'Chaka into a deal. Y'know, "Sell me this land in exchange for these pretty fire beads."
KLAW -- THEY'RE NOT STOPPING! WE'VE GOT TO GET OUT OF HERE!
SHUT UP!
YOU'LL BLOODY WELL GET US ALL KILLED!
When THAT didn't work, Klaw went to "Plan B."
And, for a MINUTE, Klaw looked like Custer at Little Big Horn.
BLAM
But, moments later, T'Chaka looked like Sitting Bull at Wounded Knee.
Klaw called it a SOUND BLASTER. It transformed sound into powerful energy he called "solidified sound."
FFFRAZZZ
Powered by conventional means, the thing was deadly.
FATHER-- --NOOO!
ZURI-- RELEASE ME! I COMMAND IT--!
I AM SORRY PRINCE --
-- SUCH IS THE WILL OF THE KING --!
Powered by VIBRANIUM...

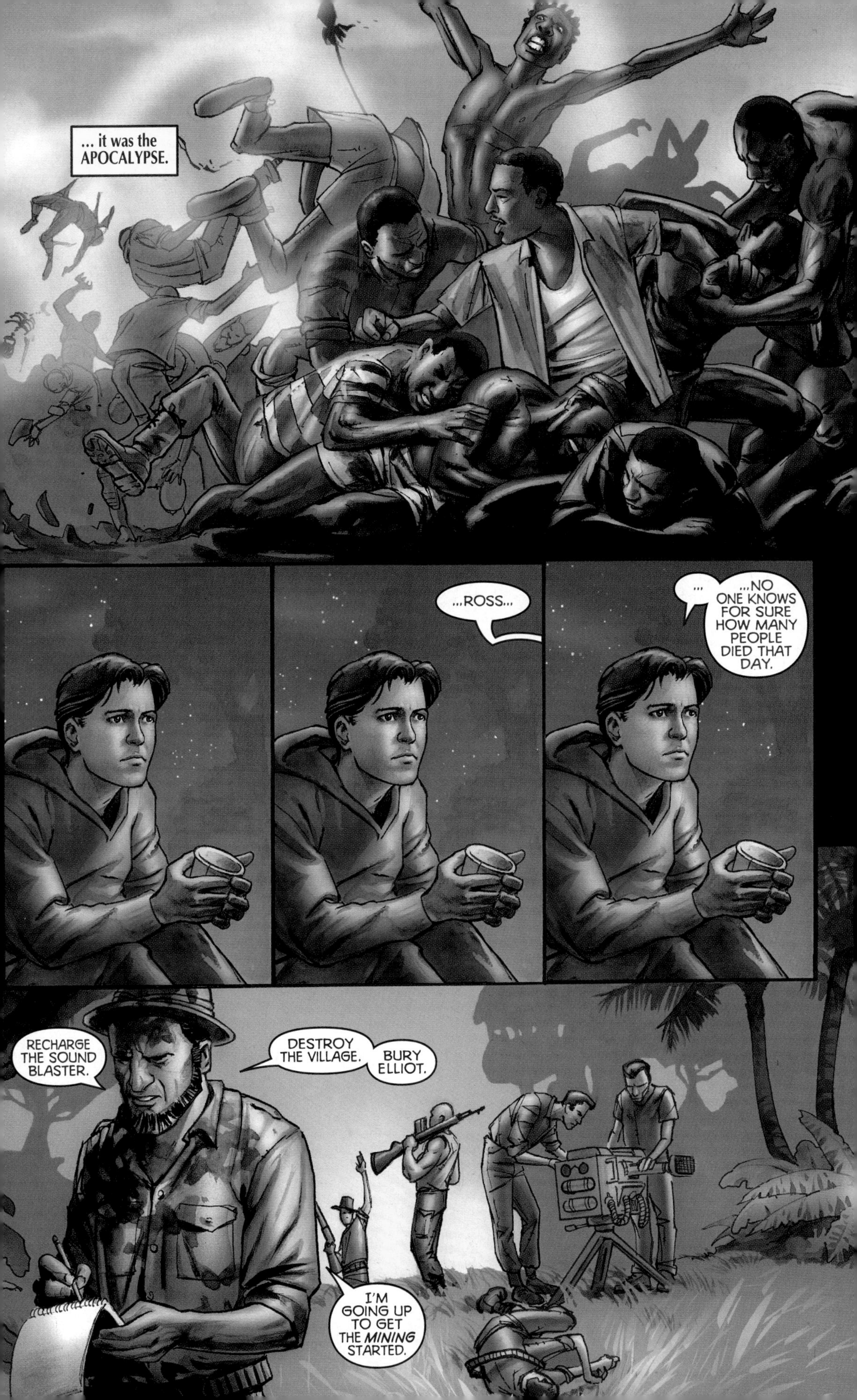
... it was the APOCALYPSE.
...ROSS...
...
...NO ONE KNOWS FOR SURE HOW MANY PEOPLE DIED THAT DAY.
RECHARGE THE SOUND BLASTER.
DESTROY THE VILLAGE.
BURY ELLIOT.
I'M GOING UP TO GET THE *MINING* STARTED.

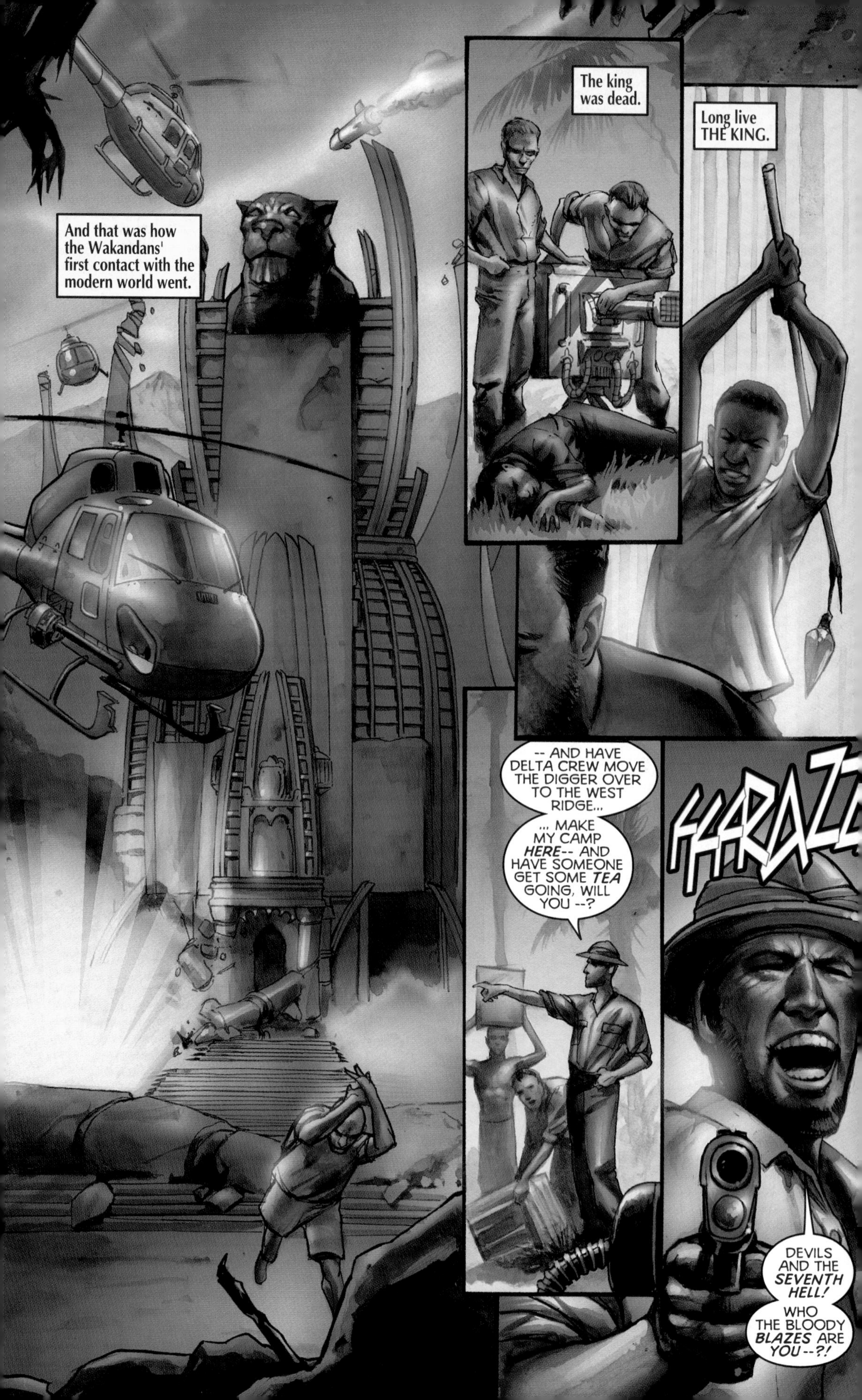
And that was how the Wakandans' first contact with the modern world went.
The king was dead.
Long live THE KING.
-- AND HAVE DELTA CREW MOVE THE DIGGER OVER TO THE WEST RIDGE...
... MAKE MY CAMP *HERE*-- AND HAVE SOMEONE GET SOME *TEA* GOING, WILL YOU --?
DEVILS AND THE *SEVENTH HELL!*
WHO THE BLOODY *BLAZES* ARE *YOU --?!*

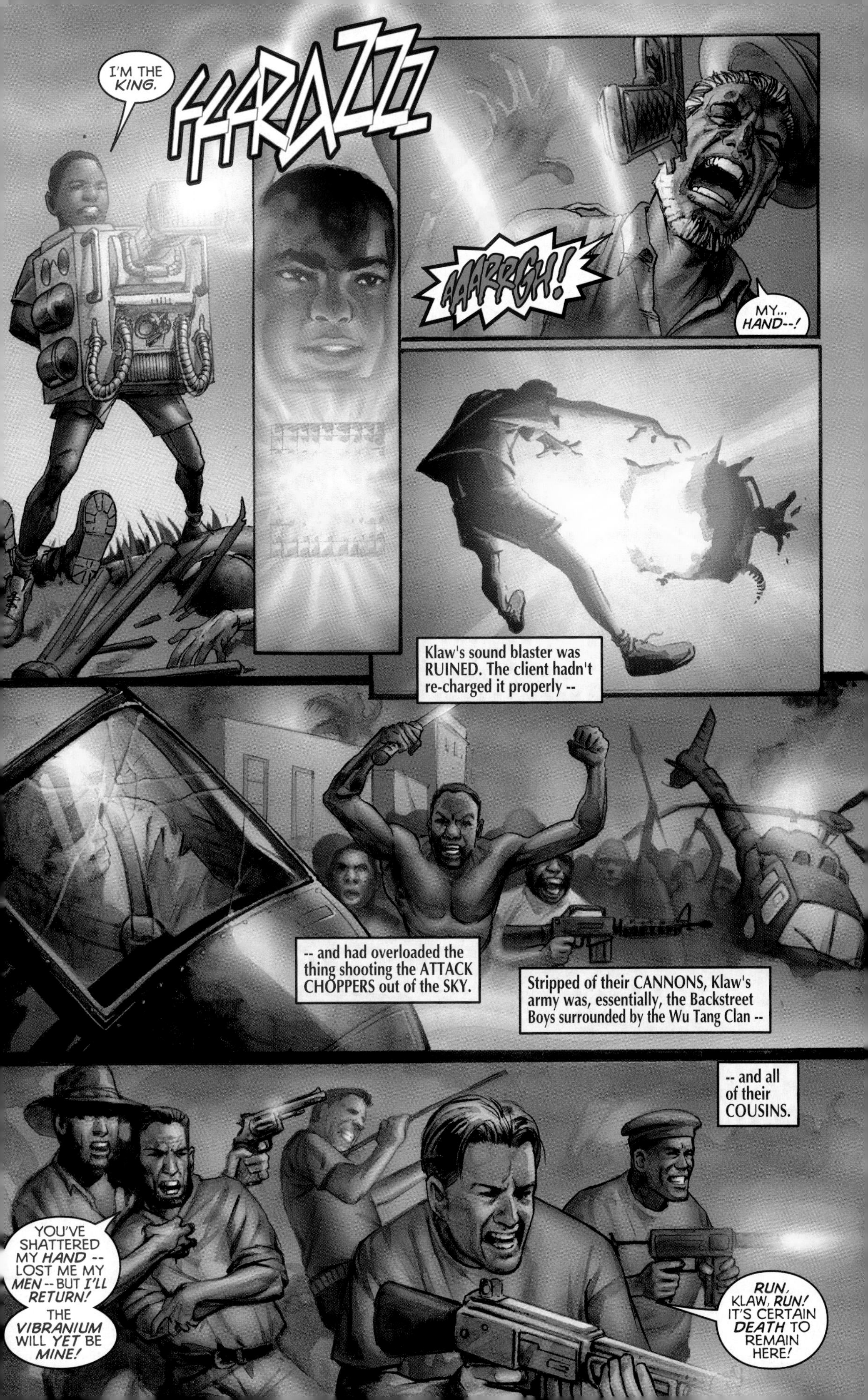
I'M THE KING.
FFFRAZZZ
AAARRGH!
MY... HAND--!
Klaw's sound blaster was RUINED. The client hadn't re-charged it properly --
-- and had overloaded the thing shooting the ATTACK CHOPPERS out of the SKY.
Stripped of their CANNONS, Klaw's army was, essentially, the Backstreet Boys surrounded by the Wu Tang Clan --
-- and all of their COUSINS.
YOU'VE SHATTERED MY HAND -- LOST ME MY MEN -- BUT I'LL RETURN!
THE VIBRANIUM WILL YET BE MINE!
RUN, KLAW, RUN! IT'S CERTAIN DEATH TO REMAIN HERE!

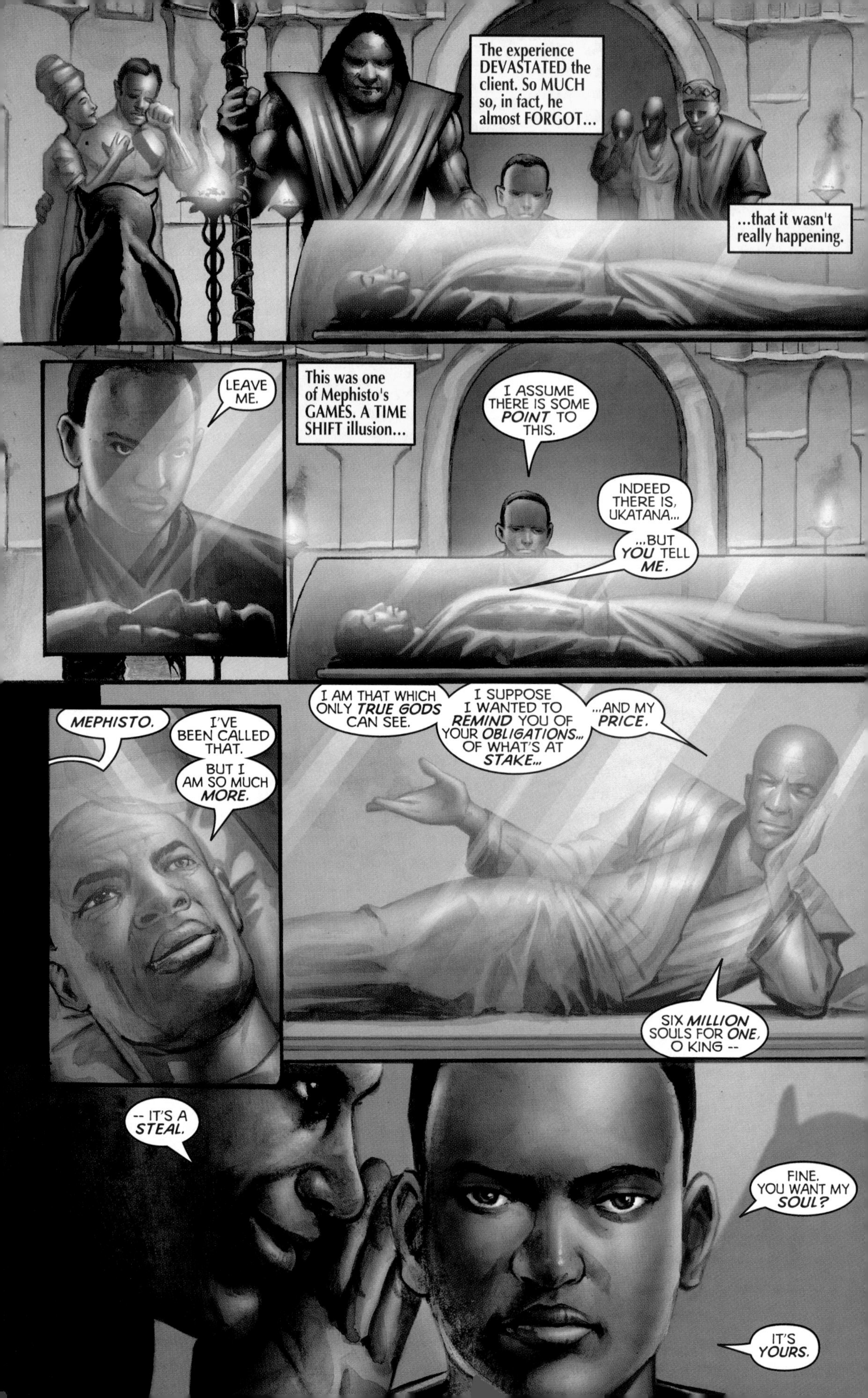

The experience DEVASTATED the client. So MUCH so, in fact, he almost FORGOT...
...that it wasn't really happening.
LEAVE ME.
This was one of Mephisto's GAMES. A TIME SHIFT illusion...
I ASSUME THERE IS SOME POINT TO THIS.
INDEED THERE IS, UKATANA...
...BUT YOU TELL ME.
MEPHISTO.
I'VE BEEN CALLED THAT.
BUT I AM SO MUCH MORE.
I AM THAT WHICH ONLY TRUE GODS CAN SEE.
I SUPPOSE I WANTED TO REMIND YOU OF YOUR OBLIGATIONS... OF WHAT'S AT STAKE...
...AND MY PRICE.
SIX MILLION SOULS FOR ONE, O KING --
-- IT'S A STEAL.
FINE. YOU WANT MY SOUL?
IT'S YOURS.

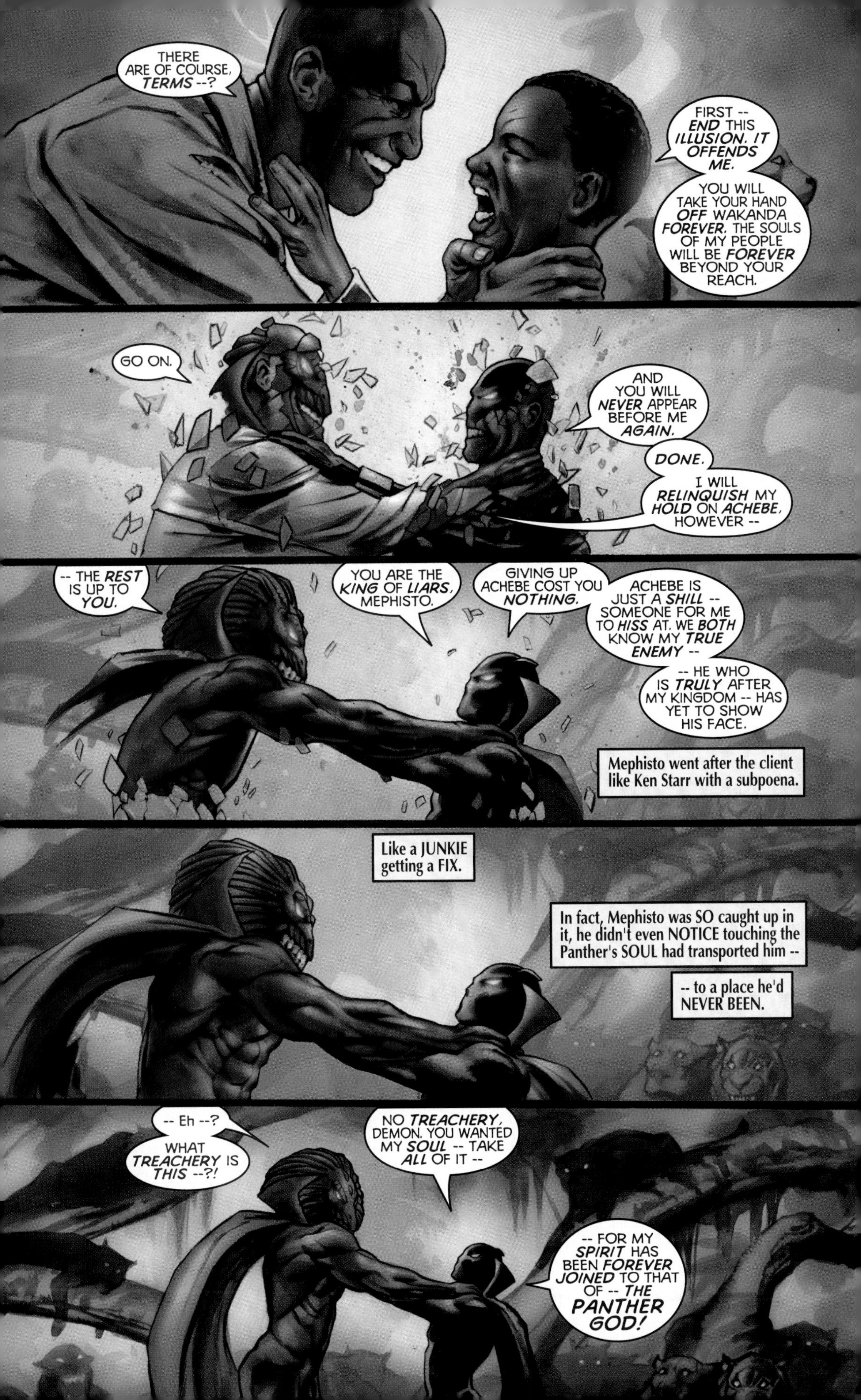
THERE ARE OF COURSE, TERMS --?
FIRST -- END THIS ILLUSION. IT OFFENDS ME.
YOU WILL TAKE YOUR HAND OFF WAKANDA FOREVER. THE SOULS OF MY PEOPLE WILL BE FOREVER BEYOND YOUR REACH.
GO ON.
AND YOU WILL NEVER APPEAR BEFORE ME AGAIN.
DONE.
I WILL RELINQUISH MY HOLD ON ACHEBE, HOWEVER --
-- THE REST IS UP TO YOU.
YOU ARE THE KING OF LIARS, MEPHISTO.
GIVING UP ACHEBE COST YOU NOTHING.
ACHEBE IS JUST A SHILL -- SOMEONE FOR ME TO HISS AT. WE BOTH KNOW MY TRUE ENEMY --
-- HE WHO IS TRULY AFTER MY KINGDOM -- HAS YET TO SHOW HIS FACE.
Mephisto went after the client like Ken Starr with a subpoena.
Like a JUNKIE getting a FIX.
In fact, Mephisto was SO caught up in it, he didn't even NOTICE touching the Panther's SOUL had transported him --
-- to a place he'd NEVER BEEN.
-- Eh --?
WHAT TREACHERY IS THIS --?!
NO TREACHERY, DEMON. YOU WANTED MY SOUL -- TAKE ALL OF IT --
-- FOR MY SPIRIT HAS BEEN FOREVER JOINED TO THAT OF -- THE PANTHER GOD!

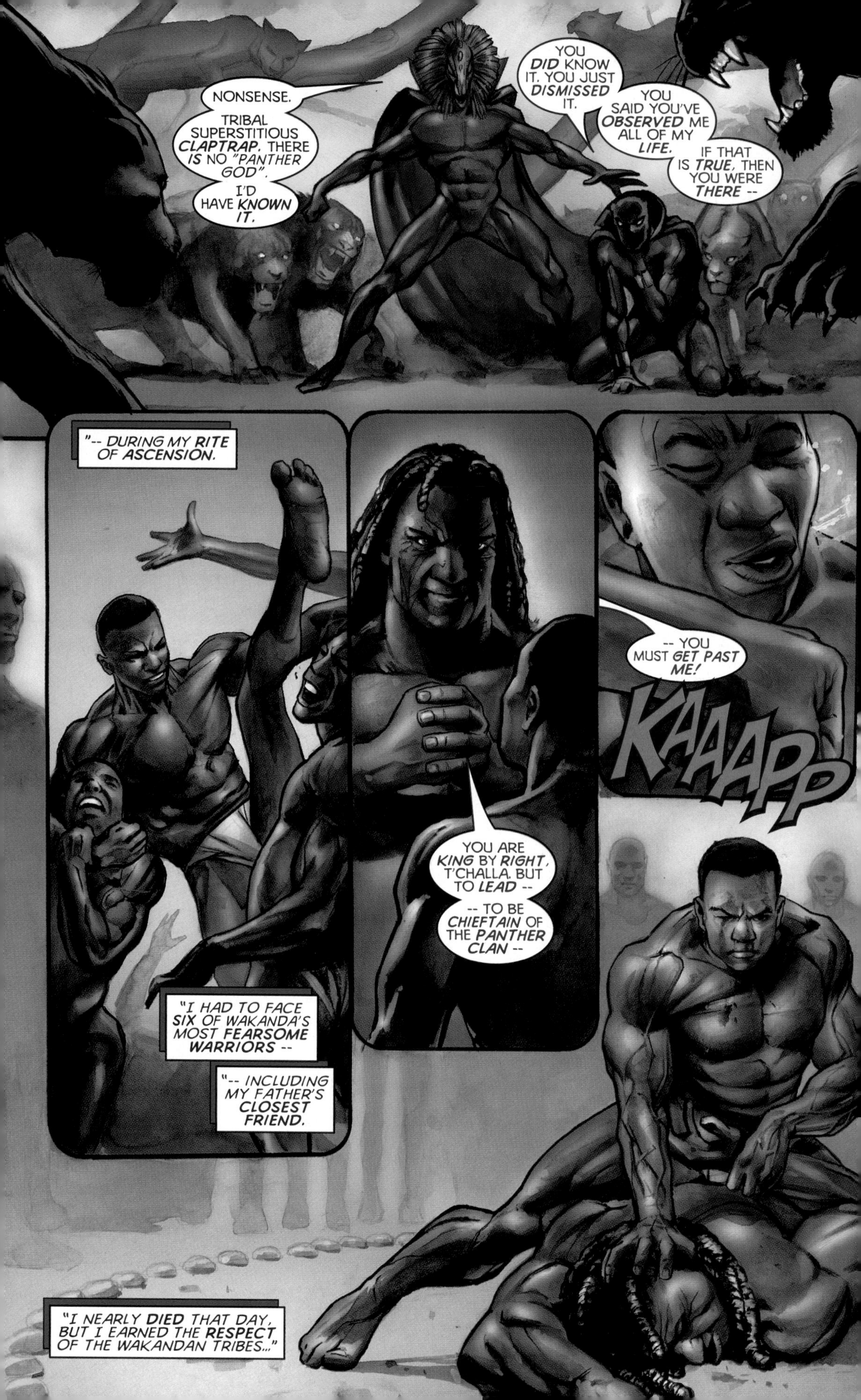
NONSENSE.
TRIBAL SUPERSTITIOUS CLAPTRAP. THERE IS NO "PANTHER GOD".
I'D HAVE KNOWN IT.
YOU DID KNOW IT. YOU JUST DISMISSED IT.
YOU SAID YOU'VE OBSERVED ME ALL OF MY LIFE.
IF THAT IS TRUE, THEN YOU WERE THERE --
"-- DURING MY RITE OF ASCENSION.
"I HAD TO FACE SIX OF WAKANDA'S MOST FEARSOME WARRIORS --
"-- INCLUDING MY FATHER'S CLOSEST FRIEND.
YOU ARE KING BY RIGHT, T'CHALLA. BUT TO LEAD --
-- TO BE CHIEFTAIN OF THE PANTHER CLAN --
-- YOU MUST GET PAST ME!
KAAAPP
"I NEARLY DIED THAT DAY, BUT I EARNED THE RESPECT OF THE WAKANDAN TRIBES..."

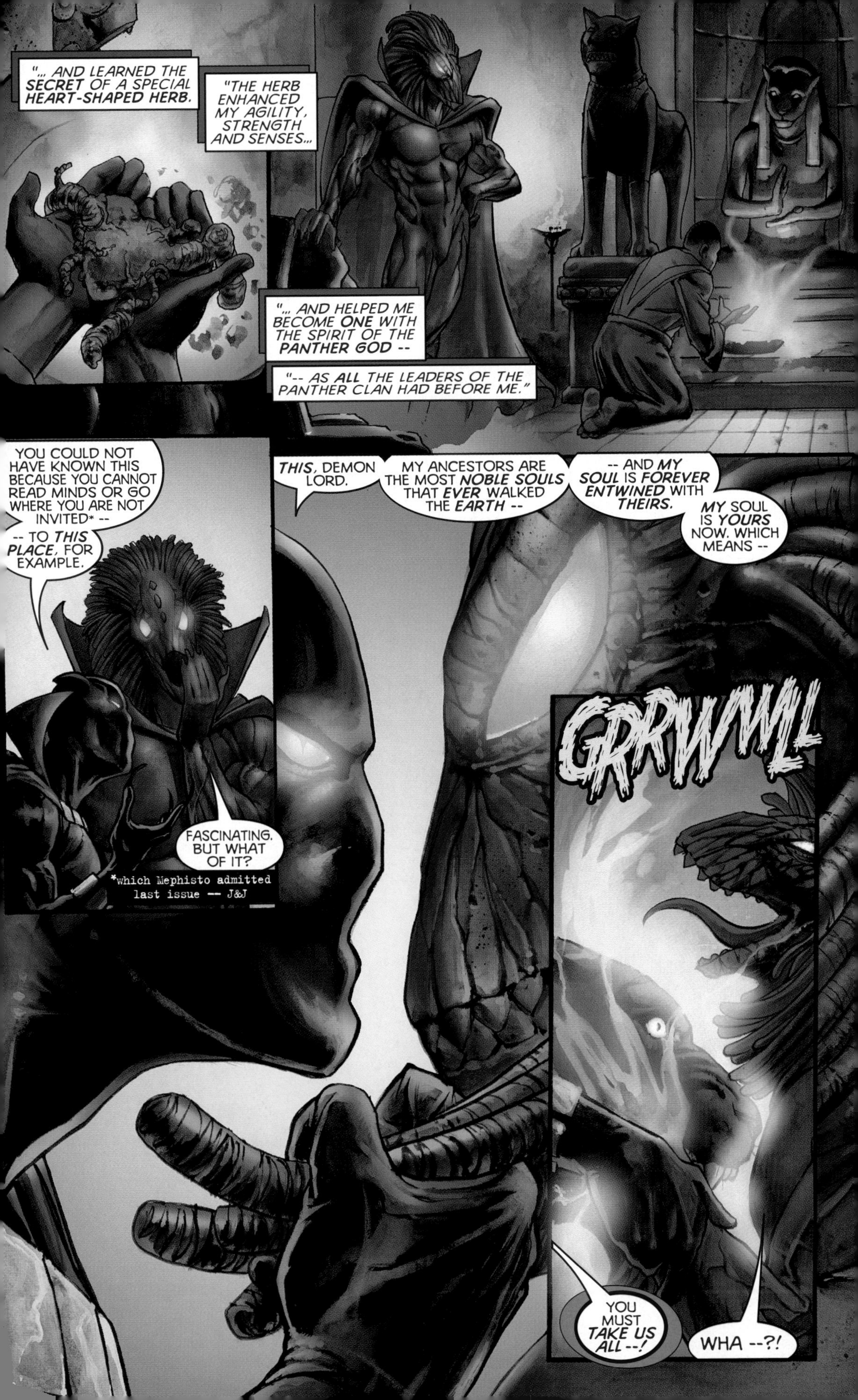
"... AND LEARNED THE SECRET OF A SPECIAL HEART-SHAPED HERB.
"THE HERB ENHANCED MY AGILITY, STRENGTH AND SENSES...
"... AND HELPED ME BECOME ONE WITH THE SPIRIT OF THE PANTHER GOD --
"-- AS ALL THE LEADERS OF THE PANTHER CLAN HAD BEFORE ME."
YOU COULD NOT HAVE KNOWN THIS BECAUSE YOU CANNOT READ MINDS OR GO WHERE YOU ARE NOT INVITED* --
-- TO THIS PLACE, FOR EXAMPLE.
FASCINATING. BUT WHAT OF IT?
*which Mephisto admitted last issue -- J&J
THIS, DEMON LORD.
MY ANCESTORS ARE THE MOST NOBLE SOULS THAT EVER WALKED THE EARTH --
-- AND MY SOUL IS FOREVER ENTWINED WITH THEIRS.
MY SOUL IS YOURS NOW. WHICH MEANS --
GRRWWL
YOU MUST TAKE US ALL --!
WHA --?!

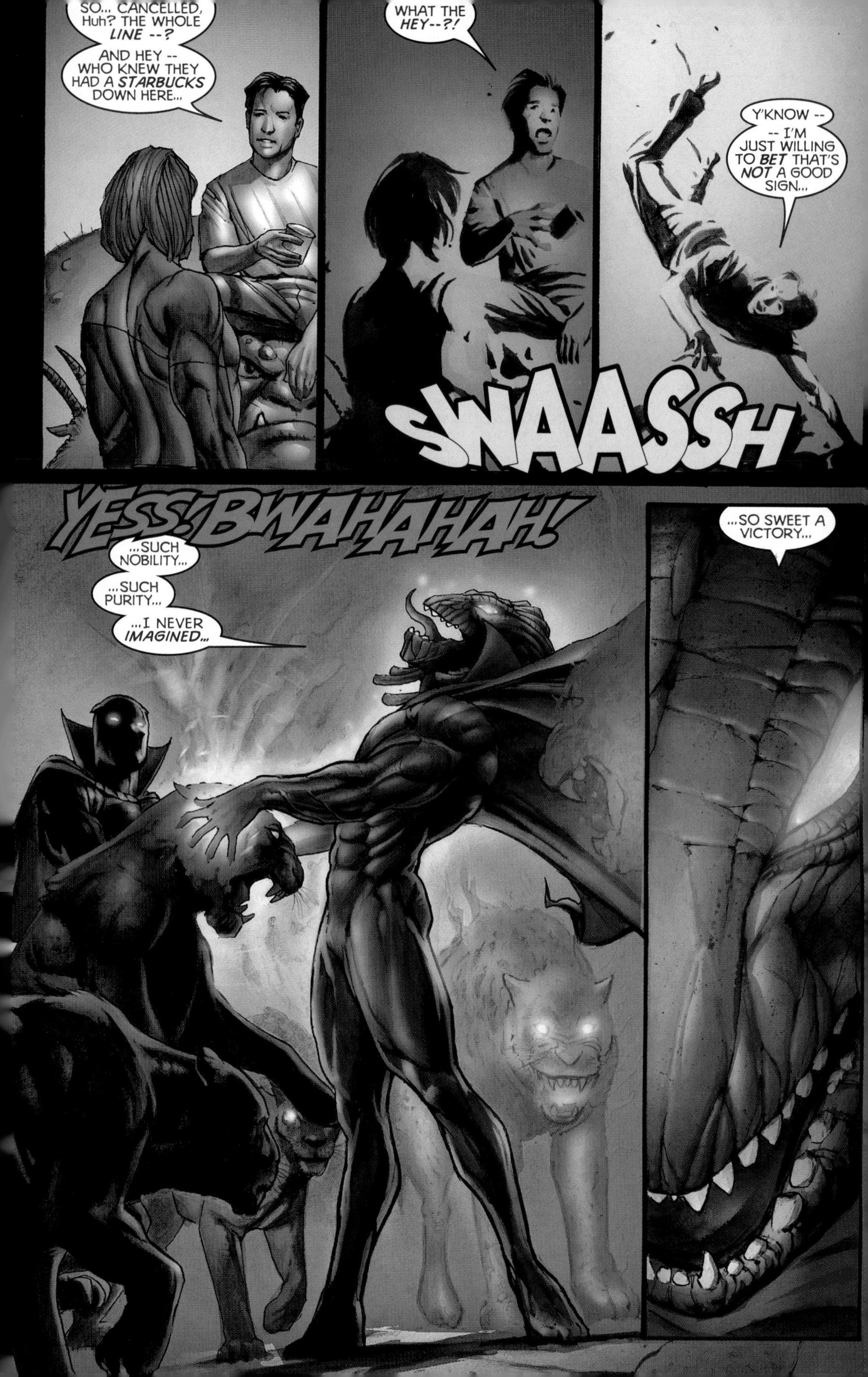
SO... CANCELLED, Huh? THE WHOLE LINE --?
AND HEY -- WHO KNEW THEY HAD A STARBUCKS DOWN HERE...
WHAT THE HEY--?!
Y'KNOW --
-- I'M JUST WILLING TO BET THAT'S NOT A GOOD SIGN...
SWAASSH
YESS! BWAHAHAH!
...SUCH NOBILITY...
...SUCH PURITY...
...I NEVER IMAGINED...
...SO SWEET A VICTORY...

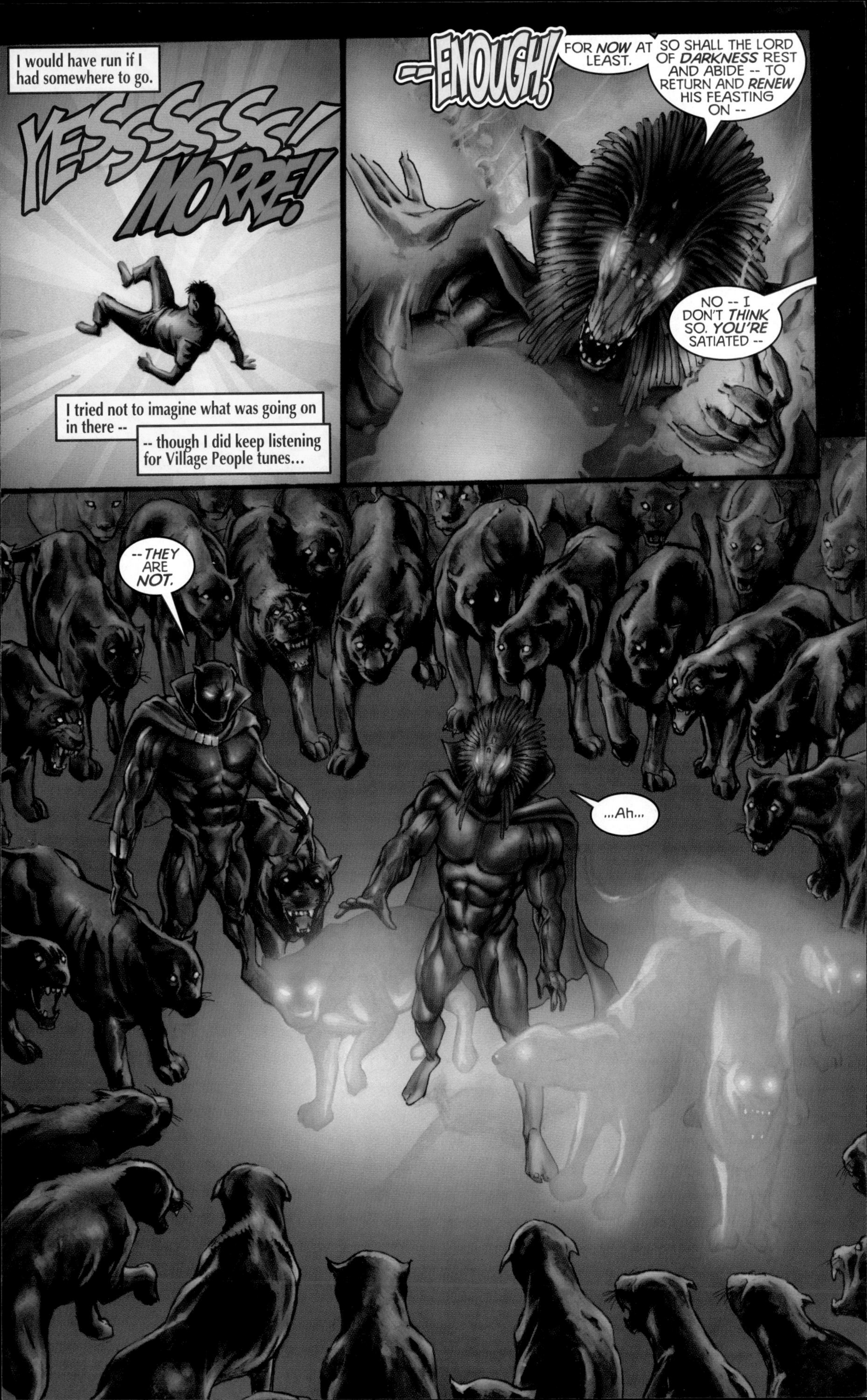

I would have run if I had somewhere to go.
YESSSSSSS! MORRE!
I tried not to imagine what was going on in there --
-- though I did keep listening for Village People tunes...
--ENOUGH!
FOR NOW AT LEAST.
SO SHALL THE LORD OF DARKNESS REST AND ABIDE -- TO RETURN AND RENEW HIS FEASTING ON --
NO -- I DON'T THINK SO. YOU'RE SATIATED --
--THEY ARE NOT.
...Ah...

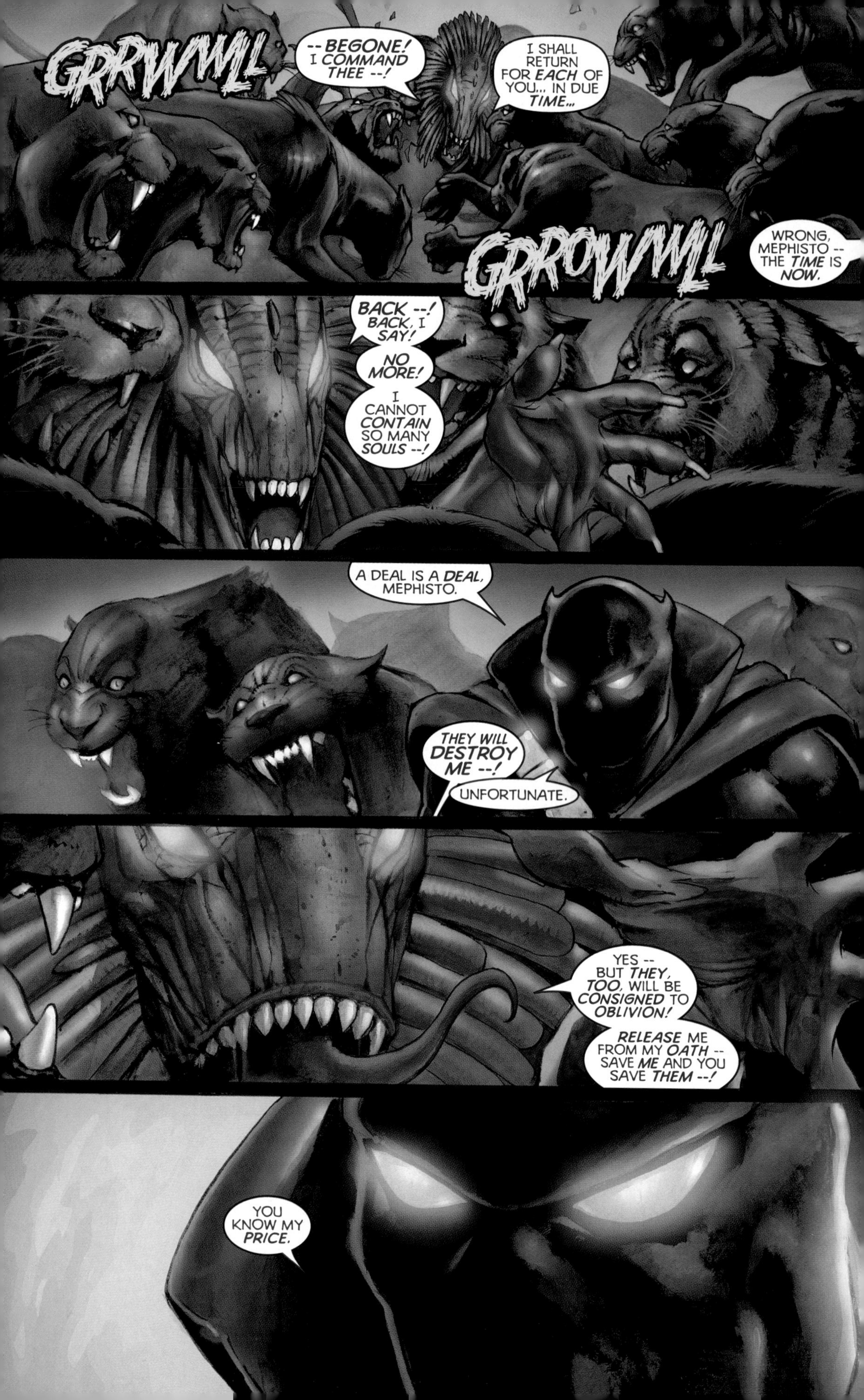
GRRWWL
-- BEGONE! I COMMAND THEE --!
I SHALL RETURN FOR EACH OF YOU... IN DUE TIME...
GRROWWL
WRONG, MEPHISTO -- THE TIME IS NOW.
BACK --! BACK, I SAY!
NO MORE!
I CANNOT CONTAIN SO MANY SOULS --!
A DEAL IS A DEAL, MEPHISTO.
THEY WILL DESTROY ME --!
UNFORTUNATE.
YES -- BUT THEY, TOO, WILL BE CONSIGNED TO OBLIVION!
RELEASE ME FROM MY OATH -- SAVE ME AND YOU SAVE THEM --!
YOU KNOW MY PRICE.

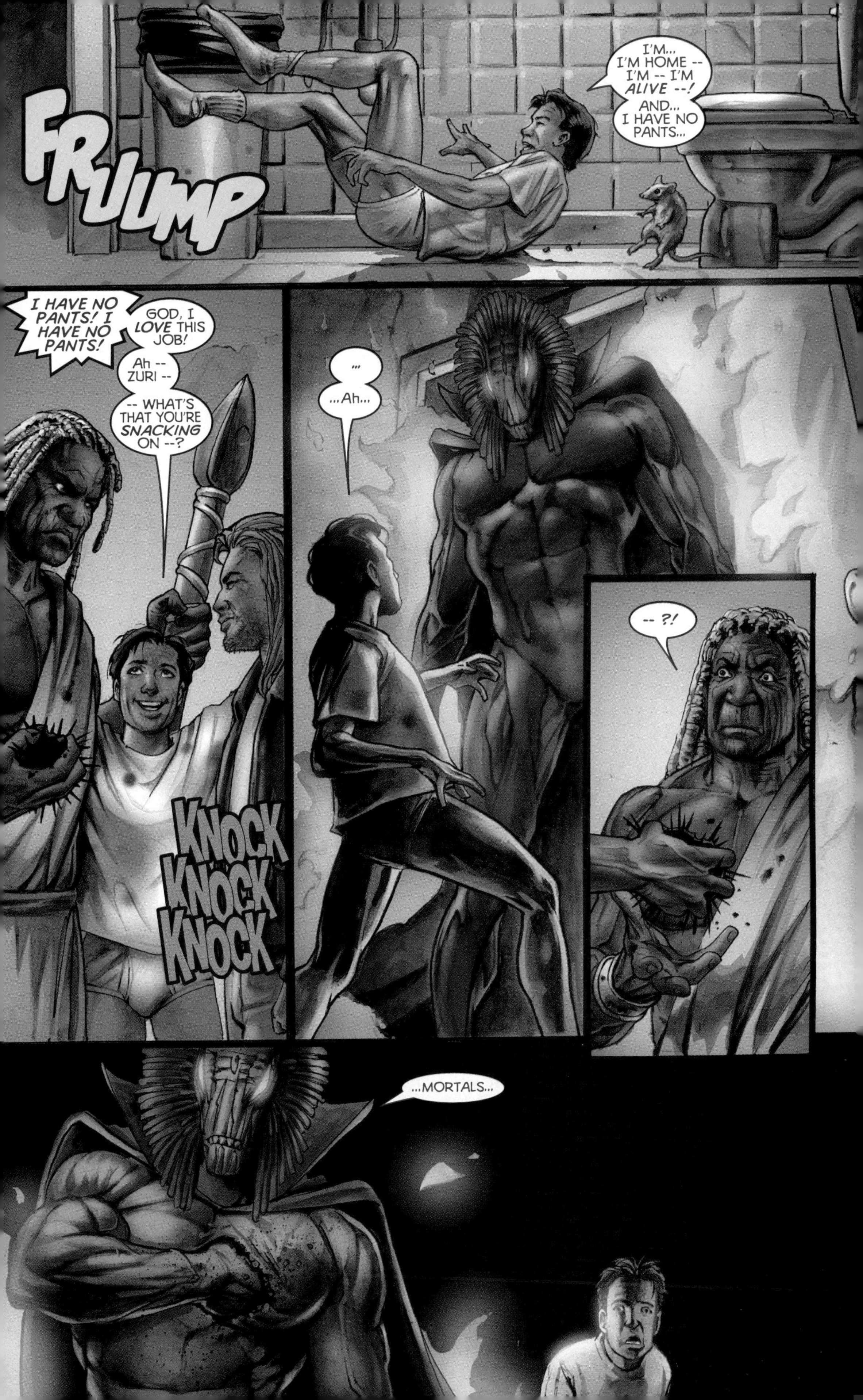
FRUUMP
I'M... I'M HOME -- I'M -- I'M ALIVE --!
AND... I HAVE NO PANTS...
I HAVE NO PANTS! I HAVE NO PANTS!
GOD, I LOVE THIS JOB!
Ah -- ZURI --
-- WHAT'S THAT YOU'RE SNACKING ON --?
KNOCK KNOCK KNOCK
...
...Ah...
-- ?!
...MORTALS...

ART OF THE DEAL

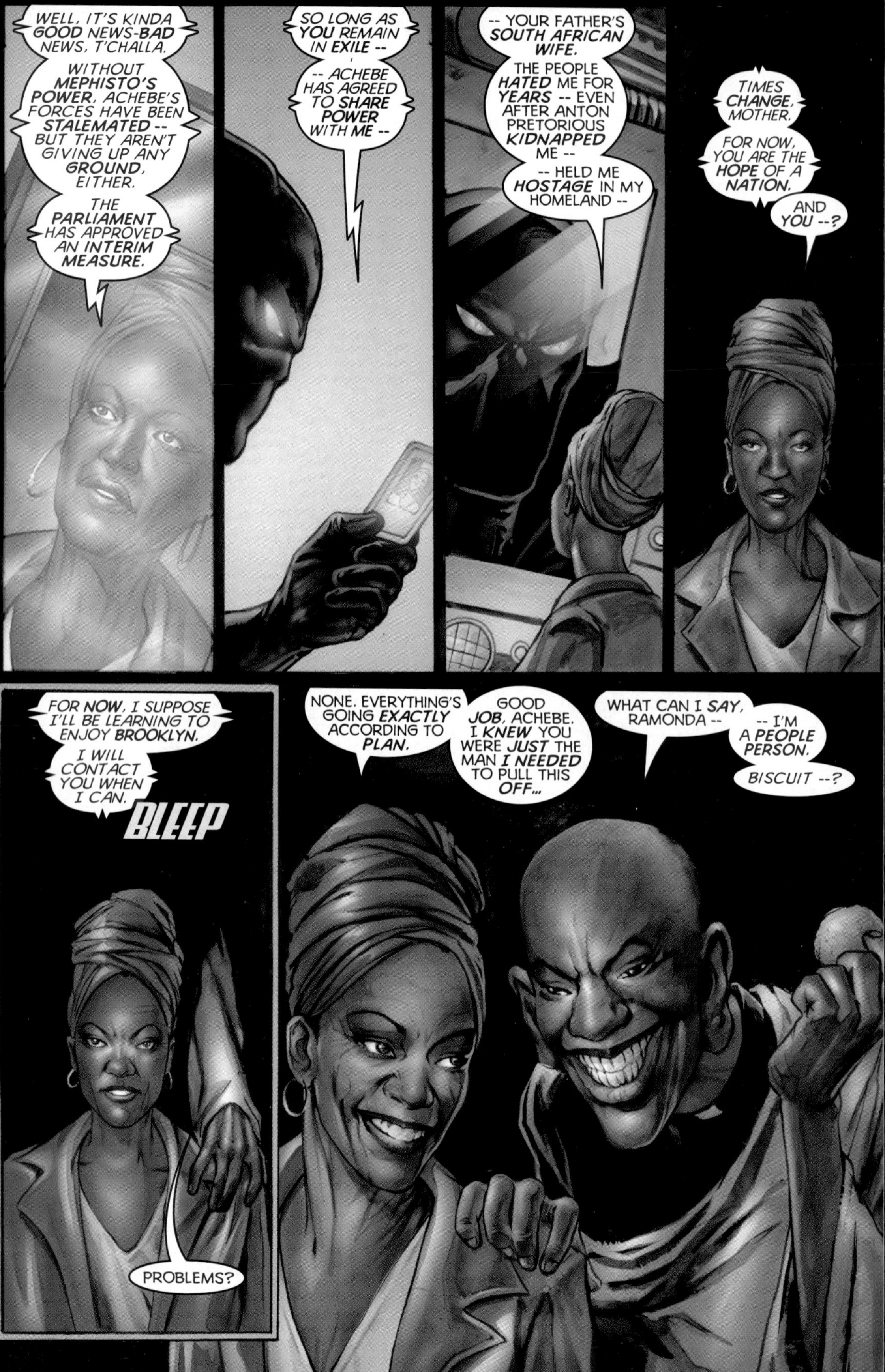
WELL, IT'S KINDA GOOD NEWS-BAD NEWS, T'CHALLA.
WITHOUT MEPHISTO'S POWER, ACHEBE'S FORCES HAVE BEEN STALEMATED -- BUT THEY AREN'T GIVING UP ANY GROUND, EITHER.
THE PARLIAMENT HAS APPROVED AN INTERIM MEASURE.
SO LONG AS YOU REMAIN IN EXILE --
-- ACHEBE HAS AGREED TO SHARE POWER WITH ME --
-- YOUR FATHER'S SOUTH AFRICAN WIFE.
THE PEOPLE HATED ME FOR YEARS -- EVEN AFTER ANTON PRETORIOUS KIDNAPPED ME --
-- HELD ME HOSTAGE IN MY HOMELAND --
TIMES CHANGE, MOTHER.
FOR NOW, YOU ARE THE HOPE OF A NATION.
AND YOU --?
FOR NOW, I SUPPOSE I'LL BE LEARNING TO ENJOY BROOKLYN.
I WILL CONTACT YOU WHEN I CAN.
BLEEP
PROBLEMS?
NONE. EVERYTHING'S GOING EXACTLY ACCORDING TO PLAN.
GOOD JOB, ACHEBE. I KNEW YOU WERE JUST THE MAN I NEEDED TO PULL THIS OFF...
WHAT CAN I SAY, RAMONDA --
-- I'M A PEOPLE PERSON.
BISCUIT --?

SKETCHBOOK

As an added bonus, these pages will provide you with a glimpse of the creative minds of Mark Texeira and Vince Evans. You will get to see their layout pages placed against the finished pieces to see how good they really are.

B.P.3:
19:
JAMIE 1:
JAMIE 2:
JAMIE 3:
NIKI 7:
NK 8:
JAMIE 4:
THING 9:
TCALA 11:
MRF. 12:
H. TORCH 13

B.P.3:
18:
TCALA 4:
TCALA 6:
TCALA 7:
TCALA 8:
TCALA 9:
KLAW 10:
JAMIE 11:
JAMIE 12:
TCLA. 13:
JAMIE 14:
JAMIE 15:
J.R. SMILE EVIL.

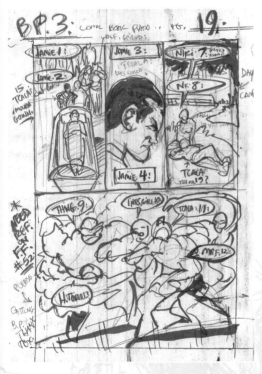

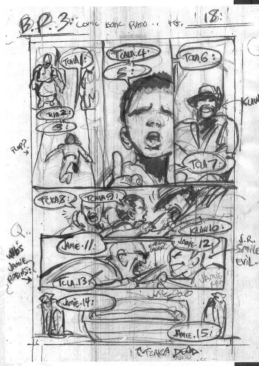

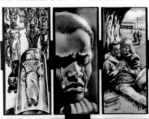

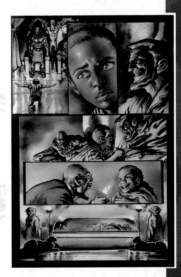

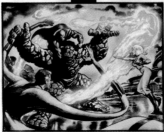

THESE ARE THE LAYOUTS FOR PAGES 18 AND 19 OF ISSUE #3 BY MARK TEXEIRA.

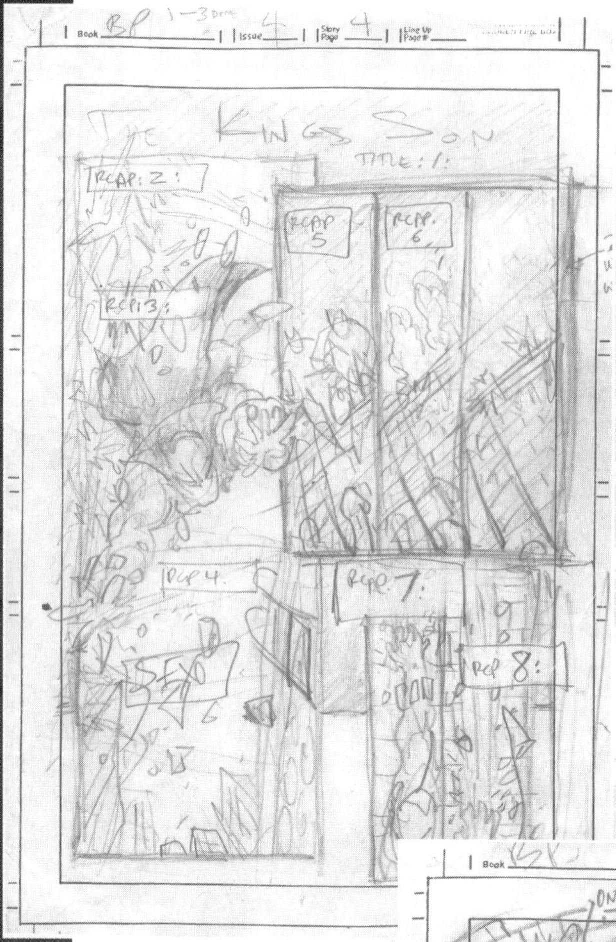
Book BP
Issue 4
Story Page 4
Line Up Page #
The Kings Son
TITLE: 1:
RECAP: 2:
RECAP 5
RECAP 6
RECAP 3:
RECAP 4.
RECAP 7
RECAP 8:

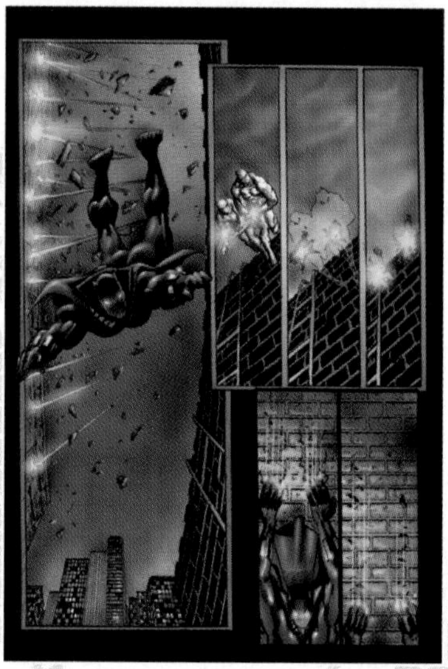

MARK'S LAYOUT FOR PAGE 4 OF ISSUE #4 WHERE T'CHALLA FIGHTS THE WAKANDAN DOGS OF WAR.

THIS IS MARK'S LAYOUT FOR PAGE 5, CONTINUING THE FIGHT AGAINST THE WAKANDAN DOGS OF WAR.

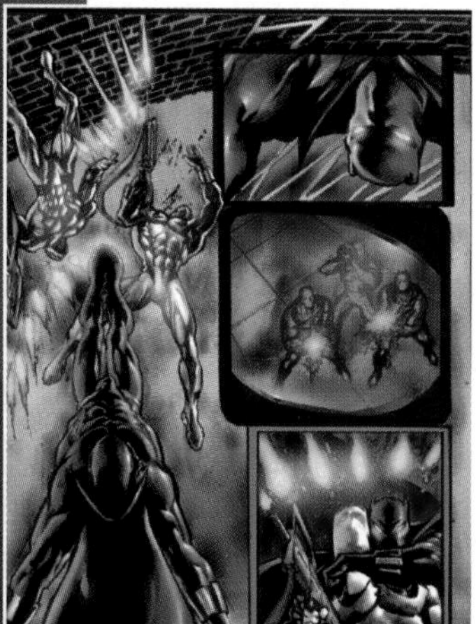

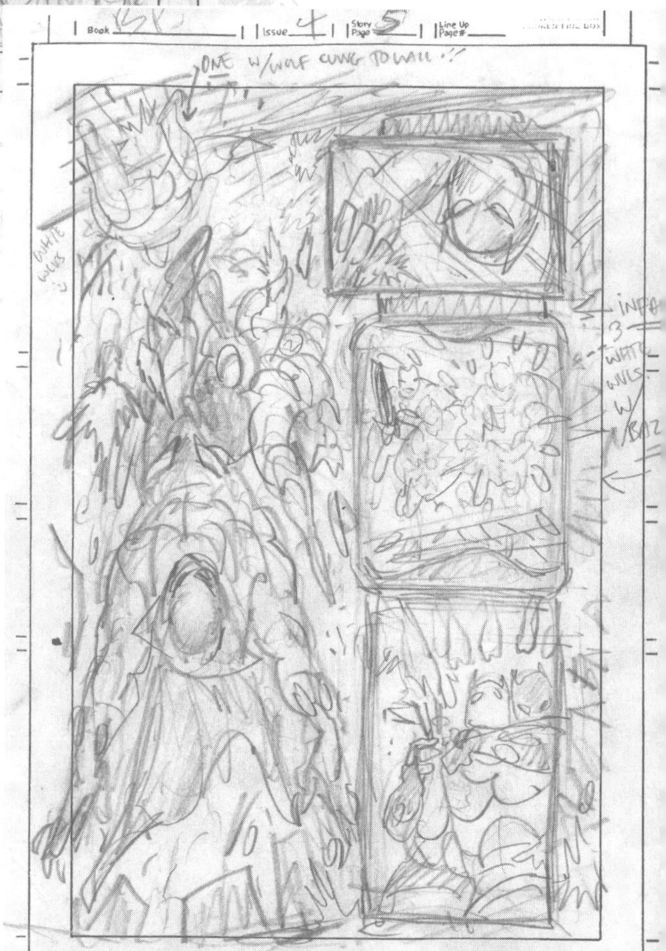
Book BP
Issue 4
Story Page 5
Line Up Page #
ONE W/WOLF CLING TO WALL!!

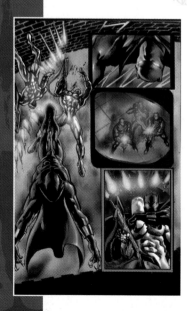

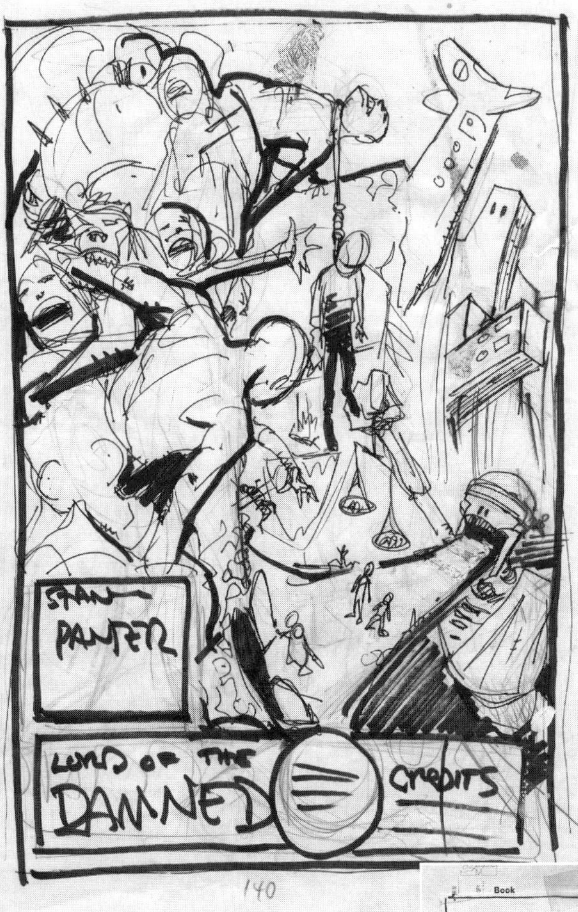
STAN PANTER
LORD OF THE DAMNED
CREDITS
140

THIS IS VINCE'S ORIGINAL IDEA FOR THE GATES OF HELL.

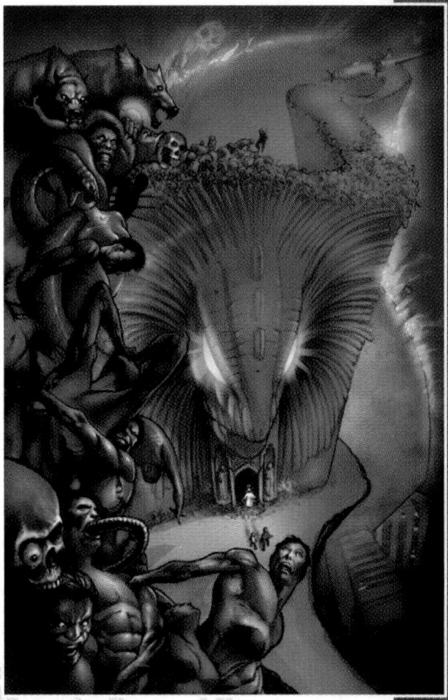

VINCE EVAN'S LAYOUT FOR PAGE 13 OF ISSUE #5.

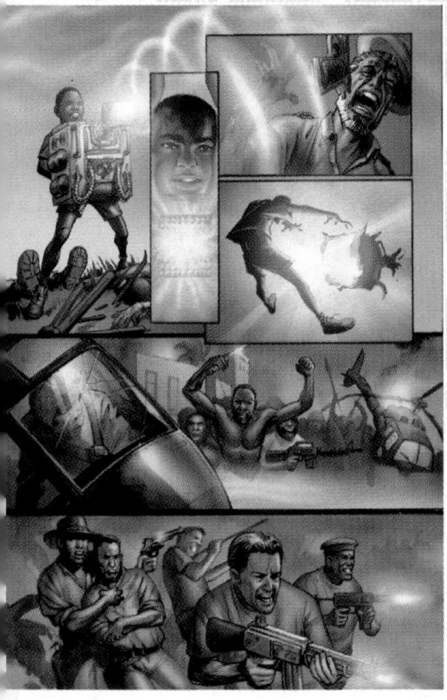

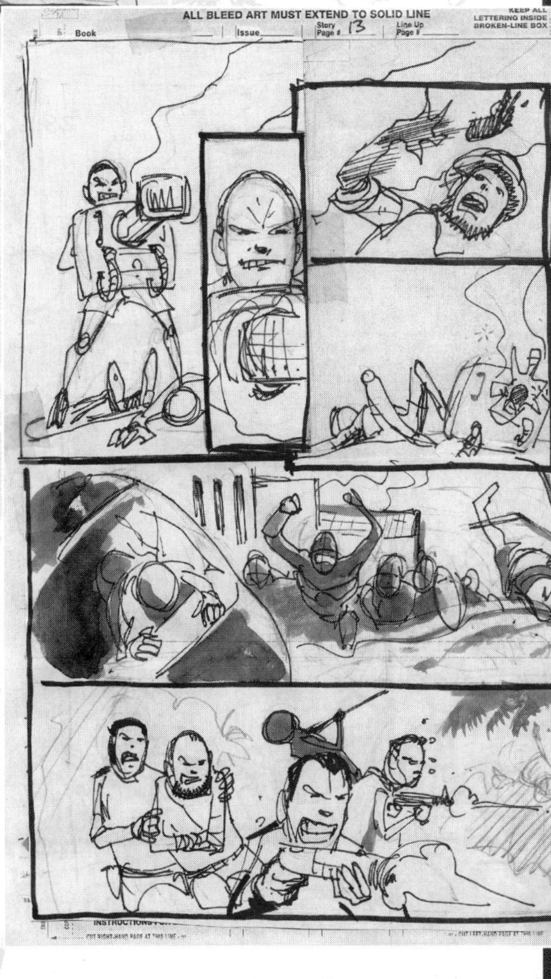
ALL BLEED ART MUST EXTEND TO SOLID LINE
KEEP ALL LETTERING INSIDE BROKEN-LINE BOX
Book
Issue
Story Page # 13
Line Up Page #

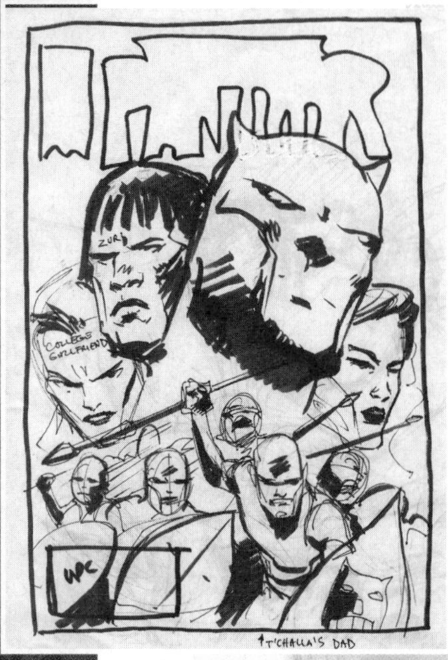
ZURI
T'CHALLA'S DAD

COVER CONCEPT FOR
BLACK PANTHER #5
BY VINCE EVANS

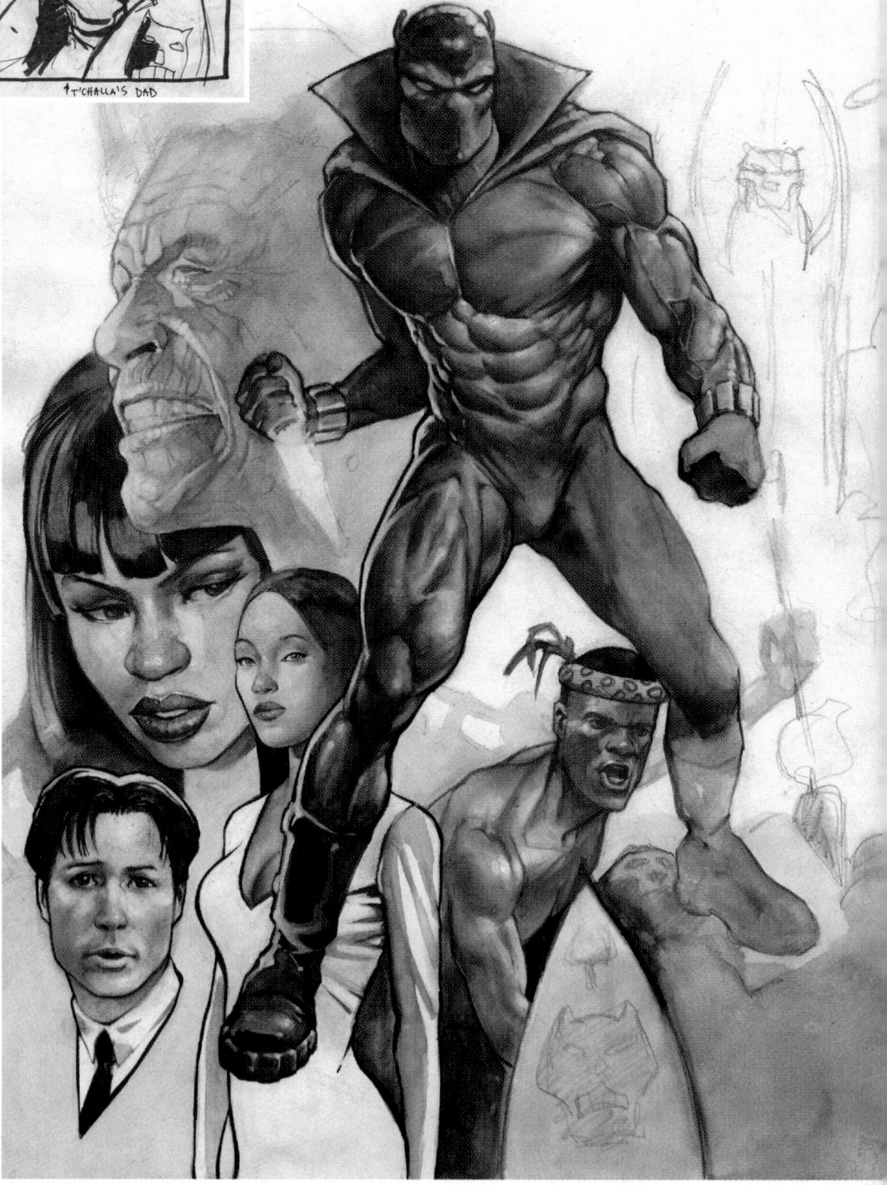

UNFINISHED COVER FOR BLACK PANTHER #5

BY VINCE EVANS